Galileo in Rome

Galileo in Rome

The Rise and Fall of a Troublesome Genius

William R. Shea and Mariano Artigas

OXFORD
UNIVERSITY PRESS

OXFORD
UNIVERSITY PRESS

Oxford New York
Auckland Bangkok Buenos Aires Cape Town Chennai
Dar es Salaam Delhi Hong Kong Istanbul Karachi Kolkata
Kuala Lumpur Madrid Melbourne Mexico City Mumbai Nairobi
São Paulo Shanghai Taipei Tokyo Toronto

First published by Oxford University Press, Inc., 2003
198 Madison Avenue, New York, New York 10016
www.oup.com

Issued as an Oxford University Press paperback, 2004
ISBN 0-19-517758-4 (pbk)

The Library of Congress has catalogued the cloth edition as follows:
Artigas, Mariano.
  Galileo in Rome : the rise and fall of a troublesome genius / Mariano
Artigas and William R. Shea.
      p. cm.
Includes bibliographical references and index.
ISBN 0-19-516598-5
1. Galilei, Galileo, 1564-1642—Journeys—Italy—Rome.
2. Religion and science—History—16th century.
3. Astronomers—Italy—Biography.
I. Shea, William R.
II. Title.
QB36.G2 A69 2003
520'.92—dc21   2003004247

Book design by planettheo.com

9 8 7 6 5 4 3 2 1
Printed in the United States of America on acid-free paper

CONTENTS

ACKNOWLEDGEMENTS

We wish to thank most warmly the Templeton Foundation for provid-ing us with a grant to coordinate our work and carry out research in the archives in Rome and Florence. We are also grateful to Paolo Galluzzi and his staff at the Institute and Museum of the History of Science in Florence, to Monsignor Alejandro Cifres, who has made the Archives of the Holy Office in the Vatican a friendly place to work, and to the officials of the Vatican Library, the Biblioteca di Archeologia e Storia dell'Arte and the Biblioteca Vallinceliana in Rome. We owe special thanks to Lucia Caravale of the Società Dante Alighieri in Rome for making available documents regarding the Palazzo Firenze, where Galileo spent a great part of his time in Rome, and to several others whom we are pleased to mention here: Corrado Calisi of the Biblioteca della Camera dei Deputati, who introduced us to the Galileo Rooms that were formerly part of the convent of Santa Maria sopra Minerva, where Galileo was tried; Irene Trevor of the American Academy in Rome, who graciously allowed us to visit the Casa Rustica, where Cesi's dinner in honour of Galileo took place in 1611; Cosimo di Fazio, who provided information on the Florentine residences of Galileo and en-abled us to visit the Convent of San Mateo in Arcetri; Mario Sirignano, of the Accademia dei Lincei who taught us to walk in Galileo's footsteps in Rome; the librarians of the Biblioteca Nazionale and of the Archivio di Stato in Florence; Rafael Martinez of the Pontifical University of the Holy Cross in Rome, who undertook a detailed study of a manuscript on Galileo that contains novel and exciting material that one of us (Mariano) came across in the Archives of the Congregation for the Doctrine of the Faith in the Vatican (formerly the Holy Office). Special thanks to Eugenio Calimani, the Dean of the Faculty of Science of the University of Padua, for providing a friendly and stimulating environment in which to complete our book.

INTRODUCTION

Galileo is the father of modern science and a major figure in the history of mankind. He belongs to the small group of thinkers who transformed Western culture, and his clash with ecclesiastical authorities is one of the most dramatic incidents in the long history of the relations between science and religion.

In 1633 the Roman Inquisition condemned Galileo for teaching that the earth moves. The trial was the outcome of a series of events that are described in this book and are usually referred to as the Galileo Affair. It extended over a period of several years, during which different popes, cardinals, and civil personalities entered the scene and made their exit. We can even speak of two Galileo trials, one in 1616 and the other in 1633, although only the second was a trial in the legal sense. The new science, which today pervades our entire life, was just emerging, and very few were able to realize what was happening at the time. Most people were not ready to abandon cherished traditional ideas for daring hypotheses that had yet to be proved.

Galileo made six long visits to Rome, totaling over five hundred days, during which he met the pope, high-ranking members of the Church and the nobility, as well as leading figures of the literary and scientific establishment. His career can be seen in a novel and fascinating way when studied from the vantage point of the city where he was most anxious to be known and approved. This is what our work does for the first time. Each chapter corresponds to one trip, thereby providing a clear framework for the main events of Galileo's life and allowing a fresh insight into the nature of the problems that he faced.

Galileo was deeply influenced by his close contacts with members of the ecclesiastical and the scientific community in Rome and, as time went on, he changed his agenda to fit new circumstances. He sometimes met with success, but he ultimately overplayed his hand and the outcome was dramatic. On the short term, his strategy was a failure; on the long term, he clearly emerged the winner.

The six trips occurred over a period of 46 years. The first took place in 1587, when Galileo, then 23 years old, went to Rome to meet scientists who might help him obtain a university appointment. With the assistance of Christopher Clavius, a Roman Jesuit professor, he got his first job at the University of Pisa in 1589 and, in 1592, he moved to the University of Padua, where he spent the next 18 years. After the publication of his astronomical discoveries had transformed him into a celebrity, Galileo returned to Florence, where he became the mathematician and philosopher of the grand duke of Tuscany. The next year, in 1611, he undertook a second and triumphal trip to Rome. He was made welcome by top-level members of the Church and the teaching profession. Unfortunately, his celebrity also gave rise to jealousy and opposition, especially when he began defending in public the Copernican view that the Earth is in motion and revolves around the Sun. This went against the commonsensical view that the Earth (and therefore humanity) is at the center of the universe, a belief that current scientific shared with tradition and Christian doctrine.

The opposition first arose among Aristotelian professors, but they soon managed to involve clerics who did not relish having to reinterpret Scripture in the light of new ideas. Galileo found out that he had been denounced to the Holy Office, and he traveled to Rome for the third time in December 1615 in order defend himself and avoid the condemnation of the heliocentric theory. He was brilliant in discussion, but to no avail. Copernicus's book on the motion of the Earth was banned in 1616, and Galileo was admonished not to teach it. He returned to Florence and was silent on the matter until his friend and admirer Maffeo Barberini was elected pope in 1623, taking the name of Urban VIII. A year later Galileo made his fourth trip to Rome, where he was received six times by the pope. This trip was another triumph, and Galileo felt he could now publish his ideas as long as they were presented as conjectures. This is how his celebrated *Dialogue on the Two Chief World Systems* came to be written, and in 1630 Galileo made a fifth trip to Rome to request permission to print the book. A number of complications arose, and the work only appeared in Florence in 1632. A loud outcry was raised and Galileo was summoned to Rome, where he was put on trial in 1633. His book was censored, and he was condemned to prison, a sentence that was immediately commuted to house arrest.

The Galileo Affair remains as fascinating as ever, and it has much to teach us that is relevant to our own day. We believe it is the first step in a proper assessment of the relations between science and religion, and we hope that our account will help readers come to grips with the issue and enable them to answer for themselves questions that often arise concerning the affair. We have avoided technicalities, but the book is based on first-hand research and the reader will find the sources of our quotations at the end of the book. We have carefully checked out the slightest details and have been able to correct inaccuracies that are found in the best books on the subject. We have combined our respective knowledge of science and religion (one of us teaches history of science, and the other is a philosopher who is also a physicist and a Roman Catholic priest). The priest often saw Galileo's point before the historian; the historian frequently reminded the priest that the Church had sound arguments.

Job Hunting and the Path to Rome

FIRST TRIP • 1587

In the autumn of 1587, a young man of 23 arrived from Florence on his first trip to the Eternal City. His name was Galileo Galilei, and, in accordance with an Italian custom of calling great men by their first name, we shall continue to refer to him as Galileo. In an age when class consciousness was on the rise in Italy, Galileo was proud of the fact that he descended from a noble family. Originally called Bonaiuti, they had exchanged that name for Galilei in the fourteenth century, although they kept their coat of arms unchanged, a red stepladder on a gold shield, forming a pictograph of the word *buonaiuti,* which literally means *good help.* The first Galileo Galilei, the older brother of the young Galileo's great-grandfather, was a successful doctor and an influential professor at the University of Florence. He also held high office in the Republic and was elected *gonfaloniere* or chief magistrate in 1445. He died around 1450 and was buried with public honors in the church of Santa Croce in

Florence, where visitors to this day can admire his full-length marble figure in the floor of the nave, near the main entrance door. The second Galileo Galilei, the scientist who is the hero of our story, could not know in 1587 that he would one day become even more famous, and that his tomb would be erected in the same church, just a few meters away from the effigy of his ancestor.

Vincenzio, the father of our Galileo, lived in reduced circumstances but enjoyed a distinguished reputation as a lute player and a musical theorist. By his wife, Giulia Ammannati, Vincenzio had three sons, Galileo, Michelangelo, and Benedetto (who died in infancy), and four daughters of whom only two, Virginia and Livia, survived. The children were all given a musical training, and Galileo became a good organist as well as an outstanding lute player. He continued to play throughout his life, and he derived great solace from the instrument in later years, especially when blindness was added to his other afflictions. His younger brother, Michelangelo, became a music teacher and spent most of his professional career at the court of the Duke of Bavaria in Munich.

Galileo's father supplemented his meager income as a musicologist by dealing in cloth and textile fabrics in the maritime city of Pisa, which was part of Tuscany. It is in this city that his eldest son, Galileo, was born on 15 February 1564, just three days before his celebrated countryman, the great artist and sculptor Michelangelo Buonarroti, closed his eyes in Rome.

Galileo received his early education in Pisa, but the family returned to Florence when he was ten years old. He was then sent to the Benedictine school of Vallombrosa, near Florence, but had to be removed because of an inflammation of his eyes, a problem that recurred later in life. He enrolled in the Faculty of Arts at the University of Pisa in September 1581 but left after three and a half years without taking a degree. This practice was not uncommon at the time, and it was not held against him when he later applied for a university post. Publications and good references were more useful than a piece of paper that said "Master" or "Doctor."

The pages of the grand duke were given courses in mathematics by Ostilio Ricci and Galileo was allowed to attend them. He soon discovered that his real interest was not medicine, as he had thought, but mathematics, which was enjoying a great revival with the publication of the original writings of Euclid and Archimedes. This does not mean that Galileo neglected literature and the arts altogether, for around this time he drafted essays on some of the great Italian writers such as Dante, Ariosto, and Tasso. He also showed considerable skill in drawing and, had circumstances permitted him to choose his own career, he would have elected to become a painter. His talent as a draftsman and colorist later won him the admiration of some of the most famous artists of his day. Ludovico Cigoli, perhaps the best-known painter working in Rome at the beginning of the seventeenth century, used to say that Galileo had been his teacher in the art of perspective and that whatever reputation he enjoyed as an artist was due to his advice and encouragement.

EMPLOYMENT BECKONS

When he left the university in the summer of 1585, however, a career as a painter was out of the question. With his growing family and small means, Vincenzio expected his oldest son to get a job. Galileo agreed, and he began to give private lessons in mathematics to students in Florence and the neighboring city of Siena. However, he realized that this would not get him far. What he needed was a permanent job and, in mathematics, this meant a position in a university. Galileo decided to apply for the next vacancy that occurred, and in the meantime he knew what he had to do. First, he had to produce an original piece of work and, second, he needed good references. The first was a condition for the second, and while Galileo was casting about for a suitable topic he heard, perhaps from the lips of Ostilio Ricci, the famous story about Archimedes and the goldsmith who had been given a certain amount of gold to fashion a crown for Hiero, the ruler of Syracuse. When the work was finished, Hiero suspected that the goldsmith had swindled him by mixing the gold with some baser metal, and he applied to Archimedes in the hope of detecting the imposture.

The goldsmith had made sure that the crown weighed as much as the quantity of gold that had been supplied, but since silver, weight for weight, is of greater bulk than gold, if silver had been added, the crown would be bulkier. So much was certain, but the problem was to measure the bulk (and therefore test the purity of the metal) without destroying the work of art by melting the crown into a regular figure. Archimedes was almost driven to distraction by this conundrum, and he decided to take a break and go to the public baths. As he stepped into the pool, which was full to the rim, he realized that a quantity of water of the same bulk as his body must overflow before he could immerse himself completely. In a flash, he saw the solution to his problem and rushed out of the public bath, stark naked, calling out in Greek, "Eureka! Eureka!" (I have found it! I have found it!). Having calmed down somewhat, he returned to his house, procured two masses of metal, one of silver and the other of gold, each of equal weight as the crown. He filled a vessel with water right to the top and placed it in a larger container. He then plunged the mass of silver into the vessel and carefully collected the water that overflowed. He repeated the same procedure with the mass of gold and found that a smaller quantity of water had overflowed. Next he plunged the crown into the vessel and observed that it displaced more of the fluid than the gold had done but less than the silver. The crown was clearly neither pure gold nor pure silver but a mixture of both! This experiment made Galileo think as furiously as Archimedes himself. He realized that a more massive body such as gold is more closely compacted than a less massive one such as silver and, hence, weighs more per volume. He felt that Archimedes's method, though correct in principle, was not rigorous enough, and he built an ingenious precision balance, what we now call a hydrostatical balance, to measure the respective weights of the metals more accurately.

The chair of mathematics at the University of Bologna was vacant and Galileo decided to try his chance. But practical skills, however important, were not enough to secure a position in a university. Original mathematical work was required, and Galileo decided to investigate geometrical problems related to the center of gravity of solids. The result was a paper that was not published in a journal because there was as yet no mathematical review, but it was put in circulation and sent to several eminent mathematicians including Giuseppe Moletti, the professor of mathematics at the University of Padua, and the Marquis Guidobaldo del Monte, the author of influential works on mathematics and mechanics. Both replied very graciously and congratulated the young man.

THE LEADING JESUIT MATHEMATICIAN

In Italy of the Counter Reformation, ecclesiastical support was not something to be neglected, and Galileo took steps to secure it by submitting his work to the Jesuits, who were considered the most learned and up-to-date order in the Catholic Church. Their main institution of higher learning was the Roman College, founded in 1551, and the professor of mathematics, Christopher Clavius, was celebrated all over Europe. A letter of recommendation by him would be worth its weight in gold.

The Society of Jesus was founded by Ignatius Loyola and approved by Pope Paul III in 1540. By 1581 there were over 5,000 members, and, in 1612, when a census was taken, they numbered 13,112 members. They excelled in teaching and by 1580 had opened 140 colleges, a number that rose to 245 at the beginning of the following century. They specialized in theology and philosophy, but they did not neglect mathematics and the natural sciences. Several Jesuits made important contributions to the advancement of learning, but the most successful was Christopher Clavius, who had left his native Bamberg in Germany to join the Society in Rome in 1555 when he was only 17. The years 1555 to 1557 were particularly difficult for the Jesuits because the election of Pope Paul IV created hostility between the papacy and Spain. The young Society, almost destitute, could not afford to maintain all their recruits in Rome, and for this reason many were dispersed to other Jesuit colleges. Thus Clavius was sent to study in Portugal in 1556 and returned to Rome four years later. He was ordained to the priesthood in 1564, the year of Galileo's birth. Shortly thereafter he was appointed professor of mathematics at the Roman College, a post he was to occupy until his death in 1612.

CALENDAR REFORM

One of the highlights of Clavius's career was the role he played in reforming the calendar as part of a commission that was instituted by Pope Gregory XIII in the mid-1570s. The Church saw this as a pressing matter because Easter, the main Christian feast, does not fall on a fixed date like Christmas but is celebrated by Western Christians on the first Sunday after the full moon that occurs upon or just after the vernal equinox. In practice this means between 22 March and 25 April. The Julian calendar, introduced under Julius Caesar in 46 B.C., was sorely out of step with the seasons and the equinoxes. This calendar, which assumed that the year contains exactly 365 days and a quarter, added an extra day every fourth year. Since the length of the year is actually a little less than 365 days and a quarter, this led to an error of about 3 days in every 400 years. The commission of Gregory XIII set matters right by omitting three leap years in every four centuries. Under the old scheme, any year was a leap year if its number was divisible by four. Under the new one, years whose numbers are divisible by 100 but not by 400 are not leap years. Hence 1800 and 1900 were not leap years, but 2000 was and 2400 will be. This reduces the error to about 1 day in 4,000 years. The Gregorian reform that was introduced in 1582 caught up with the real year by omitting ten days. Thus the day following 4 October 1582 was 15 October, 1582. Saint Theresa of Avila, the great Spanish mystic, died on the night of 4–15 October 1582.

The reform may seem straightforward or even trivial to us but it gave rise to acrimonious debates. Workers feared that they would lose paydays, and riots erupted in many cities. Clavius had to spend a considerable amount of time explaining the bases and applications of the new calendar, with very limited success outside Catholic countries. The Gregorian calendar was not adopted in England until 1752 and in Russia only in 1918.

THE LEADING JESUIT THEOLOGIAN

Clavius may have been the leading mathematician at the Roman College, but the most prestigious professor was the theologian and future cardinal Robert Bellarmine, who came from a noble Tuscan family. His uncle had been elected pope with the name Marcel II in 1555 but had died shortly thereafter. In 1560, when he was 18, Bellarmine went to Rome to join the Jesuits. He became a member of the staff of the University of Louvain in 1569, and in 1576 he was appointed professor of theology at the Roman College. A generous and saintly person, he was also a man of discipline and order who disliked the doctrinal confusion that followed in the wake of the Reformation. It appeared to him that the task of theology was chiefly to systematize and clarify the faith, conceived as a body of coherent intellectual propositions, in such a way as to maximize its certainty and finality.

Bellarmine articulated Catholic doctrines into systems so that they might be directed, in their most unequivocal and effective form, against doubt and heresy. Indeed, to make confrontation easier he even systematized the views of his opponents. His best-known works are the four volumes of *Controversies*, which had run through 30 editions by the end of the seventeenth century. They were so popular that when the second volume was published in 1588, all the copies at the Frankfurt Book Fair were sold immediately. They included Bellarmine's lectures at the Roman College and consisted of a clarification of Catholic doctrine by contrasting it with Protestant theology. This is not to say that Bellarmine and his Protestant adversaries were totally at odds, as is shown by the fact that one of Bellarmine's devotional works, *The Art of Dying Well*, was translated into English by an Anglican priest and went into at least two editions.

Galileo may have met Bellarmine in 1587 but they would have had little in common at the time. Bellarmine, who was 45, was a major representative of Catholic thought, Galileo a mere unemployed mathematician trying to attract attention to his first paper. Bellarmine became rector of the Roman College in 1592 but his administrative skills were soon needed elsewhere, and he was sent to Naples to head the Jesuit Province in 1595. The pope then decided that his services were even more urgently required in Rome, summoned him back, and appointed him cardinal. Bellarmine's name was mentioned at the two conclaves he attended, but he did not wish to be considered a candidate for the papacy. In 1606, when Cardinal Camilo Borghese became Pope Paul V, Bellarmine agreed to handle the controversial issues that arose with Venice (1606), the Anglican Church (1607–1609), and the French Gallicans (1610–1612). Bellarmine had examined the dossier of the Italian thinker Giordano Bruno, a one-time Dominican friar who ended up being burnt at the stake in Rome in 1600. Bruno was condemned for his unorthodox views in theology, but he had also embraced the Copernican system, which may have made the motion of the earth suspect. In 1587, Galileo was not committed to the new theory, but he was probably aware of its existence and may have already begun toying with its possibilities.

THE COUNCIL OF TRENT

To understand Bellarmine's role we have to say something about the Council of Trent and the Catholic Counter Reformation, of which he was one of the most prominent spokesmen. The Church had held general or ecumenical councils at various times since antiquity. The Council of Trent, named after the city in northern Italy where it was held, was convened in 1545 in the hope of reuniting Protestants and Catholics. The Protestants were skeptical of Roman intentions and refused to come, with the result that the Council of Trent was mainly attended by Italian bishops. Of 270 bishops present at one time or another between 1545 and 1563, 187 were Italian, 31 Spanish, 26 French, and 2 German. The growing Italian influence can also be seen at the level of the Sacred College of Cardinals, which, at the beginning of the sixteenth century, numbered 35 of whom 21 (68 percent) were Italian. By 1598, when the number had risen to 57, 46 (more than 80 percent) were from Italy.

Of the many doctrinal issues that were discussed at Trent, two were to become important for Galileo, namely the interpretation of Scripture and the doctrine of the Eucharist. At the Fourth Session of the council, on 8 April 1546, the following declaration concerning Holy Scripture was approved:

> Furthermore, to check unbridled spirits, the council decrees that, in matters of faith and morals pertaining to the edification of Christian doctrine, no one, relying on his own judgement, shall distort the Holy Scriptures in accordance with his own conceptions, and presume to interpret them contrary to that sense which holy mother Church, to whom it belongs to judge of their true sense and interpretation, has held and holds, or even contrary to the unanimous teaching of the Fathers, even though such interpretations should never at any time have been published. Those who act contrary to this shall be made known by the ordinaries [i.e., bishops] and punished in accordance with the penalties prescribed by the law.

The Catholic Church wished to stress the importance of tradition and the magisterium against the Protestants who downplayed their relevance. The key words in the decree that we have just quoted are "in matters of faith and morals." The council operated in this theological context, and no one at the time seems to have thought that science in general, and much less the specific hypothesis that the Earth moves, recently put forward by Copernicus, could be a religious issue.

If scriptural exegesis was a sore point between Catholics and Protestants, the doctrine of the Eucharist was equally controversial. The crux of the matter was the interpretation of Christ's words at the Last Supper: "This is my body; this is my blood." Some Protestants favored a purely spiritual or symbolic interpretation while Catholics and other Protestants insisted on a *real* presence of Christ in the consecrated bread and wine. This latter position was upheld by the Council of Trent and, to emphasize that the bread and the wine were changed into the body and blood of the

Savior, they used the technical term "transubstantiation," which became a bone of contention with the Protestants. The decree was also to cause problems for scientists, like Galileo, who favored atomism. Some theologians claimed that the atomic theory was incompatible with the teaching of the Council of Trent because it did away with the distinction between substance and accidental properties. These theologians believed that the distinction was required to render intelligible the doctrine whereby the substance of the consecrated host becomes Christ's body while the appearances remain those of bread. We will see how this issue became serious when we consider Galileo's fourth trip to Rome in 1624.

The Papal Bull with which Pope Pius IV approved the decrees of the Council of Trent was signed on 26 January 1564, a few days before Galileo's birth. These decrees provided the *doctrinal background* against which the relations between science and religion would henceforth be discussed in Catholic countries. The *administrative background* was shaped by the development of the pontifical government, or the Roman Curia, as it was usually called. Two new Congregations (what we would today call ministries) of the Curia are of special significance. One is the Holy Office, the other the Congregation of the Index.

The Holy Office was the third, modernized version of two earlier Tribunals of the Inquisition. The first was the medieval Inquisition created in the twelfth century to combat heretical and social movements such as the Albigenses in the south of France and northern Italy. The second was the Spanish Inquisition, which operated independently but had been recognized by the pope and lasted until the nineteenth century. The third, the Holy Office, was established by Pope Paul III in 1542 as a bulwark against the spread of Protestantism and was later raised to the rank of the first of the Congregations and installed, in 1566, next to St. Peter's in a building with which Galileo was later to become only too well acquainted.

The Congregation of the Index, whose job was to censor books, was created after the Holy Office. An index of proscribed books existed since the Fourth Lateran Council of 1515, but it had been administered locally by bishops or universities. Paul IV thought it should be handled from

Rome, and in 1559 he issued the first official Index of Prohibited Books, a list that included all the works of Erasmus, the complete productions of sixty-one printers, and all the translations of the Bible into vernacular languages. It was so harsh that it was actually mitigated by the Council of Trent in 1562. Shortly thereafter, Pius V (1566–1572) changed the nature of the index, intending it no longer as a fixed list of condemned writings but as a continuous action of vigilance and censorship. In order to oversee this enterprise he set up the Congregation of the Index in 1572.

THE NEW ROME OF THE COUNTER REFORMATION

When Galileo arrived in Rome in 1587 he could not have failed to be impressed by the urban renewal that had unexpectedly been set in motion a couple of years earlier when a mild-mannered and soft-spoken Franciscan became Pope Sixtus V. At 64, and with a reputation for indifferent health, Sixtus V had been seen as a "transitional" pontiff who would not live long and would not upset anyone. Events were to show otherwise. During the five years of his pontificate, Sixtus was more active than any pope within living memory. He was convinced that a shabby Rome was a disgrace and that Christendom needed a symbol of victory over paganism and heresy. He was also indignant at the fact that Rome's 140,000 inhabitants lived huddled close to the Tiber, which often flooded and caused severe hardship and disease. Sixtus asked the simple question, Why should they not live on higher ground? The Roman hills of the Quirinal, the Esquiline, and the Viminal had been settled in ancient times, and Sixtus V made this possible again, laying out new streets and constructing a major aqueduct to solve the city's recurrent shortage of drinking water. He also rendered the streets of Rome safer than they had been for decades. He remodelled the Lateran and the Vatican palaces, and, two weeks before his death on 27 August 1590, he was able to admire the completed dome of St. Peter's from his residence on the Quirinal, which is now the residence of the president of the Italian republic. Indeed, he turned Rome into an open-air museum.

Sixtus carried his reforms to the heart of the pontifical administration. In 1588 he enlarged the Curia to 15 permanent Congregations, composed of several cardinals, and he confirmed the priority of the Holy Office. To remind everyone of the triumph of Christianity he had the ancient columns of Trajan and Marcus Aurelius crowned with the statues of Saint Peter and Saint Paul. He also fitted with crosses four huge obelisks that had been brought to Rome under the Romans. He had one erected on the Piazza del Popolo, and the others in front of the Lateran, Santa Maria Maggiore, and St. Peter's. The most spectacular of these engineering feats consisted in moving the very heavy obelisk that had stood in the Circus of Caligula and Nero. Renaissance popes had considered moving the 25-meter-high column, but Michelangelo and Sangallo had dissuaded them. Sixtus V persuaded his architect, Domenico Fontana, that it was feasible. After six months of preparation, the obelisk was carried on a specially designed oak carriage to the center of St. Peter's Square, and, on 10 September 1586, it was raised by 800 workers and 140 horses. The crowd had been asked to remain silent but suddenly a loud yell of, "Water! Water!" was heard. A worker had noticed that the dry ropes were getting too warm and might burst in flame, and he had the courage to disobey orders and sound the alarm. The foreman grasped the urgency of the situation, and the ropes were immediately drenched with water. The day was saved and the worker was handsomely rewarded by the pope.

Galileo, like any visitor at the time, was struck by the dynamism of the papacy. Rome was important, and Galileo took this lesson to heart. He never forgot that the approval of the Church was crucial, and he was to return to the Eternal City on five more occasions with this in mind: in 1611, to have his telescopic discoveries approved; in 1615–1616, to try to vindicate Copernicanism; in 1624, to find out whether he could write about the motion of the Earth; in 1630, to secure permission to publish his *Dialogue*; and in 1633, to face the wrath of the Roman authorities. But, in 1587, all these trips were unforeseeable. What struck people that year was not unpredictable in itself, but it took everyone by surprise: on 19

October 1587 the grand duke of Tuscany, Francesco I, died at the untimely age of 42.

A CARDINAL BECOMES GRAND DUKE

The grand duke was childless, and the succession passed to his younger brother, Ferdinando, who had not envisaged this outcome and had become a cardinal as many members of his family had done before him. The Medici had even had two popes. Some of the most dramatic events of the Reformation had occurred under their pontificates: Luther nailed his theses on the door of the cathedral of Wittenberg under Leo X (Giovanni Medici, 1513–1521), and Henry VIII severed ties with Rome under Clement VII (Giulio Medici, 1523–1534). These two popes also intervened in local Tuscan politics. After Rome was sacked by the mercenaries of Emperor Charles V in 1527, Clement VII agreed to support his rule and crowned him emperor in Bologna. In exchange, Charles marched against the Republic of Florence to reinstate the Medici.

Some years later Cosimo I de Medici, who came to power in 1537, persuaded the pope to crown him grand duke of Tuscany. When his successor, Francesco I, became grand duke in 1574, he had already followed the family tradition of marrying out of political interest and had wed Joan of Austria, the sister of the future emperor Maximilian. When she died, Francesco married his Venetian mistress, Bianca Capello. The only son from his first marriage died in 1582, and, because he had no child from Bianca, his brother Ferdinando was next in line of succession. But Ferdinando had been destined for a very different career. His powerful father had convinced the pope to make him a cardinal when he was only 13 years old. Ferdinando went to Rome to receive his red hat in 1565 and the next year, at the age of 16, he took part in the conclave that elected Pope Pius VI. From 1569 onward Ferdinando lived in Rome, close to the Pantheon, in the Palazzo Firenze, which is now the headquarters of the Dante Alighieri Society. It should be noted that a cardinal in those days was not required to be ordained, and Ferdinando never intended to take holy orders. His role was largely political and diplomatic, and he behaved like a prince, not a priest. With a personal staff of 130 persons, his aim was to impress visitors with the wealth and power of Florence. He even convinced his father, Cosimo I, to increase his annual stipend from 28,500 to 36,000 scudi, and, after his father's death in 1574, this rose to 80,000 scudi. In order to have an idea of what this amount represented, we can mention that at the height of his career Galileo was paid 1,000 scudi, a huge salary for a professor. Ferdinando received eighty times as much, but it must be said that out of his allowance he was expected to pay the wages of his staff and maintain a huge building that was in constant need of repairs.

When Galileo arrived in Rome in 1587, Ferdinando had probably already left for Tuscany to see his brother, Francesco I. Relations between the brothers had cooled after Francesco's marriage to Bianca Capello. Their meeting took place in the Medici villa of Poggio a Caiano some fifteen kilometers to the northeast of Florence in a lovely wooded area where the grand duke was fond of hunting. This was his way to escape from the pressure of work and pains in the stomach from which he increasingly suffered. Upon returning from hunting on October 8, he felt worse than usual and took some medication of his own devising. His condition quickly deteriorated and he passed away on October 19, to be followed by Bianca Capello on the very next day. The untimely and coincidental deaths of the granducal pair made tongues wag. To preclude any suspicion of wrongdoing, Ferdinando ordered an autopsy. The physician found that Francesco I had died of cirrhosis of the liver and Bianca of a tumor. In all likelihood Francesco, who dabbled in alchemy, hastened his own demise with one of his exotic potions. Nonetheless, the circumstances were hardly pleasant for Ferdinando, although he was never accused of having a hand in the deaths of his brother and his sister-in-law.

The Florentines again made a show of respecting republican forms and duly "elected" Ferdinando grand duke. He was by then 38 years old. He resigned his cardinalate and asked the pope to allow him to marry. Spain and Austria declared themselves willing to provide the bride, but

Ferdinando preferred Christina of Lorraine, who was reputed to be a devout Catholic. She was also the niece of Catherine de Medici, the queen of France, who was fond of her and had seen to her education. This strengthened ties with France and paved the way for a second wedding, that of Maria de Medici, the daughter of Francesco I, to Henri IV.

The wedding of Ferdinando and Christina was celebrated with great festivities in Florence. The new grand duchess was known not to have arrived empty handed but with a dowry of 60,000 crowns and the duchy of Urbino to boot. Christina was to play a crucial role in Galileo's career by inviting him to come from Padua to give private lessons in the summer to the young Prince Cosimo, the heir to the grand duchy. Years later, Christina was also responsible for stimulating Galileo's interest in the relations between science and religion, and his most important utterance on the topic will take the form of a letter to her in 1615.

THE MEETING WITH CLAVIUS

When Galileo called on Clavius at the Roman College in the autumn of 1587, he brought with him an essay on the centers of gravity of solids that was both original and ingenious. Clavius was impressed but raised a number of questions, and the two mathematicians carried on a friendly correspondence after Galileo returned to Florence. Early in 1588, Clavius even promised to send him a copy of his new book on the reform of the calendar as soon as it appeared.

Galileo now had the Jesuits on his side. They were not the only allies he had cultivated in Rome. He had also managed to win the approval of Cardinal Enrico Caetani, who had recently been papal legate to Bologna and was about to become the pope's envoy to Paris. The cardinal sent a warm letter of recommendation to the University of Bologna in which he said that he would view it as a personal favour if Galileo was awarded the chair of mathematics.

Did Galileo discuss Copernicanism with Clavius, Caetani, or other scholars? There is nothing to indicate this in the correspondence, but we know that Galileo had composed in 1586–1587 a manuscript, *Treatise on the Sphere, or Cosmography,* that he used for his private teaching in Florence and Siena. It is a conventional discussion of climatic geography and spherical astronomy following the thirteenth-century *Sphere* of Sacrobosco (John Holywood) that had been a standard undergraduate textbook for over three centuries. It contained no discussion of planetary astronomy, but it did outline arguments to show that the Earth was at rest at the center of the universe. So it may be assumed that in 1587 Galileo took the geocentric system for granted. After all, the Earth does not seem to move, and we *see* the Sun rise in the morning and set in the evening. The Ancients had devised two main astronomical models to account for celestial observations. These went under the names of Aristotle and Ptolemy, and we must say a few words about them.

TRADITIONAL ASTRONOMY

The great majority of stars do not appear to change position in relation to one another but form an unchanging pattern in the sky. The Babylonians gave names to the more conspicuous groups of fixed stars, called constellations, which appear to rotate in circles about a point called the pole of the heavens. Those near the pole can be seen to perform a complete circle, and those farther from it dip below the horizon. The time they take to make one complete turn is called a sidereal day. The pole is closely marked by the bright star Polaris, easily found from its relation to the conspicuous constellation Ursa Major.

There are, however, seven celestial bodies visible to the naked eye whose positions vary in relation to the fixed stars. These are the Sun, the Moon, Mercury, Venus, Mars, Jupiter, and Saturn. The movement of the Moon among the stars is so rapid that it can be noticed in a few hours. That of the planets can be detected if they are observed on successive nights, but the path they follow is not straight, nor is it always covered at the same speed. For instance, the planet Mars can be seen approaching from the west in April, slowing down in June, and then moving backward against the background of fixed stars until mid-August, when it resumes its eastward progression. The apparent stops are called *stations,* and the backward motions *retrogradations.* The retrogradations of Mars are always of this general form and duration, but they do not always occur at the same time or in the same part of the sky.

In the fourth century B.C. in ancient Greece, an astronomer named Eudoxus invented a system to explain how the planets move. Each planet is attached to a sphere whose axis is connected to the inside of another sphere, whose own axis is attached to a third, and so on. The system of Eudoxus gave a rough approximation to the position of the planets, but it suffered from an inherent weakness: It did not allow the distance of the planets to vary, which meant that they could neither approach the Earth nor recede from it. How, then, does one explain the variations in their brightness and apparent size, as well as the fact that solar eclipses are sometimes total and sometimes partial?

Without departing from the assumption that the Earth was at rest and the Sun in motion, the second-century Alexandrian astronomer Claudius Ptolemy found a better way to explain the apparent path of the planets by placing each planet on a circle, called an *epicycle,* attached to another circle called the *deferent* or "carrying" circle. Thus the Ptolemaic system is often described as based on epicycle and deferent. The result is that the planet traces out a curve with a series of loops or cusps. It is clear that this curve, which results from the combination of epicycle and deferent, sometimes brings the planet nearer the center than at other times. Furthermore, when the planet is on the inside of each loop, an observer can see it move with retrograde motion. It is only necessary to choose the relative size of the epicycle and the deferent, and the relative speed of rotation of the two circles in order to make the motion of the planet conform with observation.

Ptolemy's systems gave results that are surprisingly good, but he went about his work in what is for us a curious way. He tackled each construction piecemeal; that is, he took up each problem one by one, and dealt with it as though other aspects of the planet's motion were irrelevant to what he was doing. This raises the question of what Ptolemy was trying to achieve. He was certainly not attempting to devise a unified cosmology. Rather he seems to have assumed that his job as an astronomer was "to save the appearances," as the phrase went, namely, "to account for the way heavenly bodies appeared," not to offer a *physical explanation* of their motion. If a planet showed an irregularity in speed, and another in size, some astronomers took the liberty of explaining the first by an epicycle and the second by two epicycles or vice versa! The question of the reality of these constructions was never raised by Ptolemy.

Copernicus was dissatisfied with this arbitrary way of doing astronomy and he proposed a radically different system by moving the Sun to the center and locating the Earth among the planets. Galileo had probably heard of this innovation before 1587, but it is only after his first trip to Rome that he will start asking himself whether it really made sense.

CHAPTER TWO

The Door of Fame
Springs Open

SECOND TRIP • 29 MARCH–4 JUNE 1611

When he first went to Rome in 1587, Galileo was an impecunious 23-year-old mathematical student looking for a job. When he returned for the second time in 1611, he was, at 47, a famous professor. The support of Clavius and other mathematicians had enabled him to get a teaching position first at the University of Pisa (1589–1592), and then at the University of Padua (1592–1610). His recent telescopic discoveries had captured the imagination of everyone in Europe, and the grand duke of Tuscany had just made him his official mathematician and philosopher. He had been freed from the drudgery of administrative work and the constraints of teaching, but he now depended entirely on the goodwill of his young patron, Cosimo II. Galileo had taught him mathematics, and Cosimo II was to remain grateful throughout his life to his former tutor, but the radical distinction between monarch and subject was never questioned nor was it in any way ambiguous. Galileo would not have been able to go to Rome in 1611 without the grand duke's formal acquiescence. In practice this meant that Galileo had to write to the secretary of state, Belisario Vinta, whose position may be compared to that of a prime minister in our modern states. Vinta opened the letters addressed to the Grand Duke, advised him on the appropriate answer, and conveyed his reply to correspondents.

Galileo suffered from some form of chronic rheumatism, and Florence would have been unbearable for him in the winter were it not for Filippo Salviati, who invited him frequently to his villa a few kilometers outside the city, where the air was more pleasant and the rooms better heated. In the winter of 1610-1611, Galileo was in particularly poor health. If this was the case, why his desire to rush to Rome? He did not much enjoy travelling, and he never left Italy or journeyed beyond a radius of 300 kilometers from his native Tuscany. In order to understand why he felt it was so important to go to Rome we must step back a little and consider the events of 1609–1610 that had completely transformed his position in the academic world.

In the summer of 1609 Galileo was still a professor at the University of Padua, where he was only moderately satisfied with his teaching load and less than happy with a salary that was one-quarter of that of Cesare Cremonini, the professor of philosophy. His study of astronomy had led him to believe that the Earth moved around the Sun, and as early as 1597 he had written to the German astronomer Johann Kepler to say that he was also a Copernican. But he did not teach the new system in his public lectures, and the motion of the Earth might have remained a conjecture for him had not something new occurred. The novelty did not descend from the ethereal regions of speculation. It was the mundane outcome of people playing around with convex lenses, in Italy around 1590, in the Netherlands in 1604, and in the whole of Europe by the summer of 1609. The result was a primitive telescope that was sold at fairs. Children and adults alike amused themselves by looking at objects that were bigger but rather hazy. Galileo heard about the device when he made a trip to Venice in July 1609. He did not actually see one of these playthings, but he realized that he could improve upon it by combining a concave lens with a convex one. The result was the opera-glass, which shows objects the right way up and not upside down. Galileo convinced worthy senators in Venice to climb to the top of a tower, whence they were able to see boats coming to port a good two hours before they could be spotted by the naked eye. The strategic advantage of the new instrument was not lost on a maritime power, and Galileo's salary was increased from 520 to 1,000 florins per year. Unfortunately, after the first flush of enthusiasm, the senators heard the sobering news that the telescope was already widespread throughout Europe, and when the official document was drawn up it stipulated that Galileo would only get his raise at the expiration of his existing contract a year later and that he would be barred, for life, from any increase of salary.

This incident understandably made Galileo sour. He had not claimed to be the inventor of the telescope, and if the senators had compared his instrument with those made by others they would have found that his own was far superior. Let the Venetian Republic keep the telescope! He would make a better one and offer it to a more enlightened patron. Better still, he would show that much more could be revealed not only on land and sea but beyond the reaches of human navigation. He pointed the telescope to the heavens in November 1609, and, for the first time in history, the human eye had a close-up view of the Moon.

CELESTIAL NOVELTIES

Galileo's reason for examining the Moon was probably to confirm a conjecture already made in antiquity by Plutarch that the light and dark features of the lunar surface are evidence that there are mountains on the Moon. Galileo focused his fifteen-power telescope on the terminator that separates the illuminated portion of the crescent Moon from the dark one, and he noticed that bright points appeared in the dark part close to the terminator. He correctly interpreted these spots as mountain peaks that are struck by the light of the rising Sun, just as happens on Earth. Galileo then turned his telescope on to the stars and found that they popped out from everywhere. In one small corner of the sky, he discovered more than five hundred stars that had never been observed by the human eye. Most spectacular still, the Milky Way resolved itself into a swath of densely packed stars.

By January 1610, Galileo had considerably improved his telescope and his means of observation. His device now magnified twenty times, and the lenses were fixed at the ends of a tube in such a way that the one with the eyepiece slid up to allow for proper focusing. The instrument was about a meter long and was mounted on a stable base. On the evening of 7 January, Galileo saw three small but very bright stars in the immediate vicinity of Jupiter. The idea that they might be satellites did not occur to him. What struck him was the fact that they were in the unusual configuration of a short straight line. Looking at Jupiter on the next night, he noticed that whereas two had been to the east and one to the west of Jupiter on the previous evening, they were now all to the west of the planet. Again, he did not suspect that they might be in motion but wondered whether Jupiter might not be moving eastward, although the standard astronomical tables indicated that it was moving westward.

On the ninth, the sky was overcast. On the tenth, he observed two stars to the east of Jupiter. This seemed to dispose of the conjecture that Jupiter might be moving in the wrong direction. On the eleventh, he again saw two stars to the east of Jupiter, but the furthest from the planet was now much brighter. On the twelfth, the third star reappeared to the west of Jupiter. On the thirteenth, a fourth star became visible; three stars were now to the west and one to the east of Jupiter. Why, the stars seemed to behave like satellites of Jupiter! With eagerness, Galileo awaited the evening of the fourteenth to check his hypothesis, but, unfortunately, the sky was again overcast. On the fifteenth, the sky was clear and the four stars reappeared to the west of Jupiter. In Copernican terms, this was the most exciting of Galileo's discoveries, and he tells us why:

> Here we have a powerful and elegant argument to remove the doubts
> of those who accept without difficulty that the planets revolve around

the Sun in the Copernican system, but are so disturbed to see the Moon alone revolve around the Earth while accompanying it in its annual revolution about the Sun, that they believe that this structure of the universe should be rejected as impossible. Now we have not just one planet revolving around another while both make a large circle around the Sun, but our eyes show us four stars that wander around Jupiter, as does the Moon around the Earth, and these stars together with Jupiter describe a large circle around the Sun in a period of twelve years.

To those who objected that the Earth could not orbit around the Sun without losing its Moon, Galileo could now point to the skies and show Jupiter circling around a central body (be it the Earth, as Ptolemy believed, or the Sun, as Copernicus argued) while maintaining not just one but four satellites. If Galileo and Copernicus could not explain why the Earth did not shed its Moon, the followers of Ptolemy were equally at a loss to say why Jupiter held on to its satellites. Formerly the challengers, the geocentrists were becoming the challenged!

THE STARS SPEAK OUT

Knowing that others were also pointing telescopes to the heavens, Galileo rushed into print on March 13, 1610 with a slim booklet of 56 pages entitled *Sidereus Nuncius*, which means *The Sidereal Message*. He named the four satellites of Jupiter Medician Stars in honor of the Medici family and dedicated them to Cosimo II, who had succeeded his father as grand duke of Tuscany a few weeks earlier. In a fulsome letter of dedication to the 20-year old prince, Galileo wrote:

> The Maker of the stars Himself has seemed by clear indications to direct me to assign to these new planets Your Highness's famous name in preference to all others. For just as these stars, like children worthy of their sire, never leave Jupiter's side by much, so—and indeed who does not know this?—clemency, kindness of heart, gentleness of manner,

splendor of royal blood, nobility in public affairs, and excellency of
authority and rule have all fixed their home and habitation in Your
Highness.

When Cosimo was born, Galileo went on, Jupiter occupied the
middle of the heavens to "pour forth all his splendor and majesty" and
confer upon him his "universal influence and power." This lavish tribute
is typical of the sycophantic style that was becoming common, even
necessary, in the baroque age, but the astrological reference should not
be too readily dismissed. Galileo and his contemporaries believed that the
planets exercised a genuine, although not a compelling, influence on
human affairs. The stars did not deprive human beings of their freedom,
but it was wise to study what they had to say about one's chances of
success or risks of failure. Jupiter had enormous significance: Cosimo I,
who became grand duke in 1569, had filled the Palazzo della Signoria,
where he lived and ruled, with frescoes representing Jupiter, the king of
the Pantheon.

Galileo had no doubt that the stars were on his side, and he decided
to use them to fulfil his dream of returning to Florence. On 7 May 1610,
he wrote to Belisario Vinta to suggest that he be recalled to Florence as
court philosopher and mathematician. What is singular about this request
is the title *philosopher* that he added to the more usual one of *mathematician*. Galileo wanted to make it perfectly clear that he saw himself not as
someone who merely toyed with numbers but as a scientist (in those days
a *natural philosopher*) who dealt with the real world.

Vinta immediately took the matter up with the grand duke and by
5 June 1610, he could inform Galileo of the happy outcome. The annual
salary that he was offered, one thousand scudi for life, was comparable to
the one he had in Padua, but he would no longer have to teach and would
be completely free to do research. No sooner had the grand duke signed
his appointment on 10 July 1610 than he got, so to speak, his reward.
Galileo made a new discovery, as he had promised. On 25 July he noticed
that Saturn was composed of three stars. He asked that this be kept a secret

until he had published it. The letter suitably impressed his new employer, but Saturn was to become Galileo's problem child. It seemed to have two close companions that sometimes disappeared, only to reappear in the shape of what he took for handles or ears sticking out on each side of the planet. The puzzle was not solved until 1657, 15 years after Galileo's death, when Christiaan Huygens explained that Saturn is surrounded by a ring that is periodically tilted and looks like a handle when viewed with a telescope whose resolving power is weak.

THE MOTHER OF LOVE

When Galileo arrived in Florence on 12 September 1610, it was not to rest on his laurels but to resume immediately his early observations of the heavens. He was not disappointed for Venus soon spoke out. The "mother of love," as poets called her, went through phases like the Moon. This was important because among the difficulties raised against Copernicus was the objection that Venus should have phases because it lies between the Sun and the Earth. Copernicus had replied that they were too inconspicuous to be seen by the naked eye, and Galileo was anxious to know whether his telescope would enable him to detect them. Venus is usually too close to the Sun to be observed, and it was only in the autumn of 1610 that Galileo was able to confirm that Copernicus had been right: Venus goes through a complete series of phases that vary considerably in size. At its greatest distance from the Earth, it is seen as a perfectly round disk, fully illuminated. As it moves toward the Earth it grows in apparent size until at quadrature (corresponding to the first and third quarter of the Moon) it is half illuminated. At its closest to the Earth, it becomes invisible (like the Moon when it is new). The phases of Venus showed that it did not go round the Earth. But what about the other planets? Even if they also orbited around the Sun, this did not necessarily mean that the Earth behaved likewise. The Danish astronomer, Tycho Brahe, had come up, years before, with a compromise system where the Earth remained at rest but all the planets revolved around the Sun *while* the Sun continued to go around the Earth. Hence the phases of Venus could be used by the followers of Tycho Brahe as well as by those of Copernicus.

On 17 December 1610, Galileo wrote to his former student, Benedetto Castelli, that those who were not convinced of the truth of Copernicanism, *even before the discovery of the phases of Venus*, were bookish philosophers who cared only for the empty applause of the vulgar crowd. This letter reveals a side of Galileo's character that will recur in his private writings and before long in his published works. He was stung by reluctance or, worse, refusal to accept his discoveries, and he was becoming impatient, even arrogant, with people who criticized him. He hit back by exaggerating, as he did in this case by claiming that even before the phases of Venus had been observed there was convincing proof that Copernicus was right. To the end of his life, Galileo held to a simplified version of the Copernican system in which all the planets move in perfect circles. Although he preached open-mindedness, he never lent an ear to Kepler's arguments about elliptical paths.

Well-meaning astronomers who did not have good telescopes experienced serious difficulties. On 22 January 1611 Christopher Grienberger, a Jesuit professor who was always to remain sympathetic to Galileo, wrote him a long letter in which he explained how his extensive experiments with mirrors had initially led him to query whether the lenses did not distort the shape of objects. His doubts were only dispelled when he was provided with a suitable instrument. As the telescopes improved, so did Galileo's reputation, but the sceptics remained numerous, and this is why Galileo wanted to go to Rome.

SEEING AND BELIEVING

The Sidereus Nuncius had opened a lively debate over the reliability of the new instrument of observation. We can see this in the way two ambassadors had reacted. On the very day the booklet appeared, Sir Henry Wotton, the English ambassador to the Republic of Venice, sent a copy home to King James I, calling it "the strangest piece of news" that the king had "ever yet received from any part of the world." He described the sensational news briefly and accurately and promised to send one of the new instruments by the next ship. Before concluding, however, Wotton realized that he might have been too sanguine and covered himself neatly against that risk by adding: "And the author runneth a fortune to be either exceeding famous or exceeding ridiculous." Shortly thereafter, Georg Fugger, the imperial ambassador in Venice, wrote to Kepler, the imperial astronomer at Prague, then the centre of the Holy Roman Empire, that many thought the *Sidereus Nuncius* was just show, and that Galileo had copied a telescope brought by a Dutchman to Venice. Kepler knew better and his response was more than generous. By 19 April 1610, he had written Galileo a letter of endorsement, which he prepared for publication even if he had not yet had the use of a telescope. Giovanni Magini, the professor of mathematics at Bologna, was initially much cooler and told Kepler in May that he thought the discoveries were illusory. A wealthy scientific amateur and friend of the Jesuits, Mark Welser, was still vacillating in January 1611, as we know from a letter he wrote asking Clavius his opinion about Galileo's observations. It was only after Clavius had assured him that they were reliable that he breathed a sigh of relief. If the Jesuits agreed with Galileo that was enough for him.

The Jesuits kept abreast of scientific progress but not every one in Florence was willing to be convinced by an optical tube. A philosopher named Ludovico delle Colombe circulated a manuscript treatise in which he not only ridiculed the motion of the Earth but fired the first theological broadside by claiming that it was at variance with the teaching of Scripture. Delle Colombe piled up scriptural quotations without regard to their context: "You fixed the earth on its foundations" (Psalm 104:5); "God made the orb immobile" (1 Chronicles 16:30); "He suspended the earth above nothingness, that is, above the centre" (Job 26:7); "Before the mountains were constituted with great weight" (Proverbs 8:25); "The heaviness of stone, the weight of sand" (Proverbs 27:3); "Heaven is up, the earth is down" (Proverbs 30:3); "The sun rises, and sets, and returns to its place, from which, reborn, it revolves through the meridian, and is curved toward the North" (Ecclesiastes 1:5); "God made two lights, i.e., a greater light and a smaller light, and the stars, to shine above the earth" (Genesis 1:17), this last quotation being offered as proof that the Moon can in no way be like the Earth.

Delle Colombe considered whether these passages could be interpreted in a non-literal sense: "Definitely not," he decided, "because all theologians, without exception, declare that when Scripture can be understood literally, it ought never be interpreted differently." The literal reading of Scripture and the consensus of the ancient Fathers were unqualified exegetical standards for delle Colombe. Rather than risk a reply, Galileo preferred going to Rome to have his discoveries authenticated. Once the Church had recognized them as real, all would be well!

THE EARLY ROMAN AGENDA

Galileo contacted Belisario Vinta toward the end of 1610 and explained why a trip to Rome was necessary. When he did not receive a formal authorization by 15 January 1611, he reminded Vinta that he was dutifully awaiting instructions from the grand duke and begged leave to say that this was the best time to act and publicize his discoveries. Vinta, who knew that Clavius and Kepler had already sanctioned Galileo's claims, judged that the court risked nothing in allowing him to go. The trip could only heighten the stature of Galileo's patron, the grand duke, whose brother Carlo currently filled the traditional position of resident Medici cardinal in Rome.

Once the trip was approved, Galileo might have been expected to leave forthwith, but he was so indisposed and had such headaches that he postponed his departure for another two months while he recuperated at Salviati's villa. Nonetheless he did not neglect his correspondence and, on 12 February 1611, wrote to his old friend Paolo Sarpi in Venice to say that he was busy replying to his detractors but that the best European mathematicians, including those who had first laughed at him, were now entirely on his side.

At the end of February, the journey seemed imminent, and the grand duke wrote to Giovanni Niccolini, his ambassador in Rome, in terms that leave no doubt that he wanted Galileo to be treated as an official envoy:

> Our beloved Mathematician and Philosopher, Galileo Galilei, is going to Rome, and we have decided that he should stay with you in our palace there. It is our wish that you should make him welcome and take care of his expenses and those of one servant. Make a note of these in order to be reimbursed. You will be glad to see him and you will appreciate his intelligence and pleasantness. He will tell you himself why he is making the trip, and you will help him in every way possible, as he requests and as you see fit, more particularly with the advice of Cardinal del Monte for whom we have given him a letter of recommendation. The business that he will undertake is close to our heart both for its usefulness to the world of learning and the glory of our house. May God keep you and bless you.

But still Galileo did not leave. On 5 March 1611 he informed Clavius that his departure had been delayed because of his poor health and the appalling weather but that he hoped to set out within a week. Meanwhile, tributes to his achievements began to pour in. From Padua, the great humanist and archaeologist Lorenzo Pignoria wrote to say that Galileo's celestial discoveries would eclipse those of Columbus and Vespucci. The duke of Zbaraz informed him that his fame had reached Moscow, adding, for good measure, that his discoveries would ensure that their century would always be remembered.

Summoning all his energy, Galileo decided it was time to make a move and suddenly gave way to impatience. On 19 March he wrote to Belisario Vinta to say that he was eagerly awaiting the horse-drawn litter that would carry him to Rome, where he wanted to arrive by Holy Week "in order to put an end, once and for all, to malignant rumors." He added that he expected a prompt reply "unless the Grand Duke has changed his mind," a qualification that could suggest that he was still of two minds about setting forth. Vinta replied that the court had gone to Livorno, but he had had a word with the grand duchess and a litter was on its way. Galileo did not depart immediately, however, but took a little extra time to obtain a letter of recommendation from Michelangelo Buonarroti (the nephew of the famous artist whose name he carried) for Cardinal Maffeo Barberini, who would become pope as Urban VIII 12 years later and was to preside over the Galileo Affair. The weather finally cleared up and Galileo set out on 23 March. He spent six days on the road in the grand duke's litter, and at night he set up his telescope at every stop along the way—San Casciano, Siena, San Quirico, Acquapendente, Viterbo, and Monterosi—to continue to track the revolutions of Jupiter's moons. This shows how dedicated he was to his work in spite of indifferent health and the cold and dampness of March evenings.

ROMAN HOLIDAY

Galileo was the honored guest of the grand duke in Rome. But where? The Medici owned several palaces in Rome. From the letter of Cosimo II it seems that the residence of the Tuscan ambassador was intended, and this has frequently been assumed to be the Villa Medici on the Pincio. The embassy, however, was not located there but in the Palazzo Firenze near the Pantheon. This is confirmed by a letter from Galileo to Belisario Vinta at the time when the ambassador, Giovanni Niccolini, was about to retire later in May. In order not to inconvenience the new ambassador, Piero Guicciardini, Galileo offered to leave the embassy and take up residence in the Villa Medici. Guicciardini declined and Galileo remained as his house guest in the Palazzo Firenze.

Giovanni Niccolini, who was nearing the end of a distinguished 23-year career as Tuscan ambassador, welcomed Galileo when he arrived on 29 March, which was Holy Tuesday that year. On the very next day he reported to the grand duke that Galileo had arrived safely with two

servants (instead of one as authorized) and that lodgings had been provided for all of them.

Galileo lost no time and sprung into action on the very day he arrived
by calling on Cardinal del Monte. Three days later, on Good Friday, he
commented on the warmth of the Roman welcome:

> I arrived in good health on Holy Tuesday and I handed over the letter
> of the Grand Duke to the Ambassador, who welcomed me very courte-
> ously and with whom I am staying. On the very same day, I called on
> Cardinal del Monte to whom I gave the other letter from the Grand
> Duke, and I told him briefly about the purpose of my trip. The Cardinal
> received me very courteously and listened attentively to what I had to
> say before expressing the firm hope that I would not leave without
> having been able to give a full and satisfactory account of the complete
> truth of what I have discovered, observed and written.

The next day, 30 March, Galileo went to the Roman College to meet
Clavius and his younger colleagues, Christopher Grienberger and Odo
Maelcote, who who carried out telescopic observations for Clavius, who
was now well into his seventies. "I found that these Fathers," wrote
Galileo to Vinta,

> have finally recognized the genuineness of the Medicean planets, and
> continue the regular observations that they began two months ago. We
> compared them with my own and they agree entirely. They also are
> working hard to find their periods of revolution but they agree with the
> Mathematician of the Emperor [Kepler] that it will be very difficult and
> almost impossible. I hope, however, to discover and determine them,
> and I trust that God Almighty, who made me the grace of discovering
> so many new marvels from his hand, will grant me to find the exact
> period of their revolutions. Perhaps, by the time I return, I shall have
> achieved this and be in a position to determine the places and positions
> that these new planets will have at any time in the future or that they

occupied in the past, provided I have the strength to continue my observations late into the night, as I have done until now.

Galileo may not have been a conventionally devout Catholic, but he was deeply convinced that God had singled him out to make not only *some* but *all* the new celestial discoveries. He treated the contributions of other astronomers as inferior to his own. This was deplorable, and it led a malicious but perceptive critic to accuse him, when he returned to Florence, of trying to add a terrestrial empire to the one he had already claimed in the heavens. Galileo may have had an excessive conceit of himself, but he was head and shoulders above his rivals. The grand duke could rightly be proud of his scientific envoy.

On 2 April, the eve of Easter, Galileo went to Cardinal Maffeo Barberini's residence to present the letter of recommendation from Michelangelo Buonarroti, as well as another written by Antonio de' Medici. No sooner had Galileo left than the Cardinal wrote to both Buonarroti and Antonio de' Medici to say that he would be delighted to help Galileo in any way in his power. The Rome sojourn could not have begun under better auspices: High-ranking prelates lionized him and famous professors treated him as the leading authority in his field.

The Counter Reformation did not curtail the Roman passion for public and private festivities. Gatherings where artists showed their work and writers read their latest poems were frequent and well attended. Particularly successful was the informal academy of Giovanni Battista Deti, the nephew of Pope Clement III, who had appointed him cardinal in 1599, when he was only 17 years old. In the week of Easter, Galileo was invited to one of Deti's meetings, where he met four cardinals, as well as numerous prelates and other dignitaries. Galileo informed a Florentine correspondent that he had enjoyed the learned talk given by Giovanni Battista Strozzi but that he did not join in the discussion for fear of appearing too pushy since this was the first time he had been invited. He assured his correspondent that he would not be deterred by such considerations in the future. The topic was pride.

STARGAZERS

In less than a week, Galileo had called on cardinals Barberini and Del Monte, greeted several other prelates at the Academy of Deti, and spoken to the Jesuits. He had also paid a courtesy call on Cardinal Ottavio Bandini, who belonged to a prominent Florentine family and to whom Galileo had been recommended. Bandini had a house next to the residence of the pope on the Quirinal, and he asked Galileo to organize telescopic observations in his garden for members of the Roman high society.

Galileo also displayed his instrument elsewhere, often in the setting of an evening meal and to the accompaniment of music. One such banquet, at which he was the guest of honor, was to have lasting consequences for his work. It was organized by an idealistic young nobleman, Federico Cesi, Marquis of Monticelli. In 1603, at the age of 18, Cesi had founded with three friends the Accademia dei Lincei (Academy of the Lynxes or Lyncean Academy), which had the notable feature that its members were not to confine themselves to literature or the arts but were to give pride of place to the study of nature and mathematics. The choice of the sharp-eyed lynx as an emblem stressed the importance Cesi attached to faithful observation of nature, and at official ceremonies he often wore a lynx pendant on a gold chain. Until 1610, when he became financially independent, Cesi had been able to do little, but he was now eager to pool his wealth, curiosity, and foresight into a cooperative endeavor, free from traditional academic constraints. He had a keen sense that Galileo had opened a new field of investigation. At the dinner party that Cesi arranged on Thursday 14 April to honor Galileo, the telescope was used in broad daylight before the meal to look at buildings in the city, and after the meal, when it became dark, at the night sky.

A first-rate *metteur en scène*, Cesi had not neglected to inform the press, and a couple of days later Romans could read in the *Avvisi* (a forerunner of the gossip columns of our daily newspapers) that the mathematician Galileo Galilei, "whom the Grand Duke had appointed professor at Pisa with a salary of one thousand scudi," had arrived in

Rome. Then, as now, the press assumed that a high salary indicated scientific excellence. Informed about Galileo's high status, the reader was well disposed to accept that he had found four satellites around Jupiter. The account added that he had recently discussed this discovery with Clavius, a clever way of conveying the impression that the Jesuits backed his claims.

The dinner was held in the vineyard of Monsignor Malvasia on the summit of the Janiculum, the highest of the Roman hills. The lodge where it took place was demolished in the nineteenth century and replaced by a small villa whose view is now obstructed by the main building of the American Academy in Rome. In the seventeenth century the view from the vineyard was unimpeded. The Villa Medici could be seen on the Pincio to the left, and straight across the Tiber was the basilica of St. John Lateran, some three miles away. Galileo trained his telescope on the loggia above the side entrance of the church to allow the guests to read for themselves the chiselled inscription that had been placed there by Sixtus V in 1585, the first year of his pontificate: *Sixtus/Pontifex Maximus/anno primo.* The participants who enjoyed this close-up view were an international group: Johann Faber and Johann Schreck hailed from Germany, Jan Eck from Holland, and Joannes Demisiani from Greece. The Italian contingent consisted of five persons and included Galileo, Cesi, and Giulio Cesare La Galla, a professor of philosophy at the University of Rome.

Faber was a medical doctor who taught at the University of Rome, and acted as Cesi's closest collaborator. It was Faber who informed Mark Welser about the banquet and mentioned that they had observed the satellites of Jupiter and read the inscription on the loggia of the basilica. This is confirmed by La Galla, who adds that they were also able to count the windows, even the smallest ones, on the facade of the residence of the duke of Altemps on a hill in the countryside some 25 kilometers away. It was also on this occasion that the new instrument, which Galileo had called in Latin *perspicillum* (lens) and in Italian *occhiale* (spyglass), was given the name under which it is now known, *telescope,* by the Greek scholar Giovanni Demisiani or by Cesi himself.

A CARDINAL ENQUIRES

We mentioned that Robert Bellarmine was the most distinguished professor at the Roman College when Galileo visited the prestigious institution in 1587. By 1611 Bellarmine was even more famous. He had been appointed cardinal 13 years earlier and, at 68, he was still an active member of important Roman Congregations, including the Holy Office. He generally kept abreast of scientific developments and after looking through a telescope, he dropped a note on 19 April to his fellow Jesuits at the Roman College to ask their opinion about Galileo's discoveries. The four professors of mathematics and natural philosophy, Christopher Clavius, Christopher Grienberger, Odo Maelcote and Giovanni Paolo Lembo, replied on 24 April with a cautious but perfectly adequate endorsement of the *Sidereus Nuncius*. The telescope had certainly shown stars hitherto invisible, but it was doubtful whether the Milky Way was composed entirely of stars. Saturn looked egg shaped and oblong, unlike Jupiter and Mars, but the two starlets to the left and right were not sufficiently detached to affirm that they were really stars. Venus had phases like the Moon. The surface of the Moon seemed uneven, but Clavius thought it more probable that it was really smooth, while the other Jesuits considered it uneven, although they would not say that the matter was beyond doubt. On the crucial question of Jupiter's satellites, they all agreed that they were real.

Was Bellarmine merely indulging his interest as an amateur astronomer or was he wondering whether the discoveries everyone was talking about might raise theological difficulties? It seems reasonable to assume that Bellarmine was glad to have his colleagues confirm the validity of Galileo's claims, but he must have sensed that they were potentially troublesome for the Aristotelian natural philosophy that was taught in the Jesuit schools. The mountainous and irregular surface of the Moon was at variance with the traditional notion that the heavens were perfect and unchangeable; the four satellites of Jupiter showed that not all heavenly bodies revolved around the Earth; the phases of Venus established that at least one planet went around the Sun; finally, the countless number of stars altered the picture of the universe. All this was not easy to fit into the grooves of traditional natural philosophy, but Bellarmine's main concern was with the problems posed by the interpretation of Scripture. The Bible speaks of the Sun rising and setting, and, although it might be possible to interpret such passages as ordinary language and not as a statement of scientific fact, it was surely premature to undertake such a delicate task. Bellarmine may also have been reminded of Bruno's wild speculations about innumerable worlds and the general belief that this subverted the importance of the incarnation of Christ.

A few days later, on 17 May, Bellarmine attended a meeting of the Inquisition that minuted, "See whether Galileo, professor of philosophy and mathematics is mentioned in the case of Doctor Cesare Cremonini." Cremonini had been Galileo's colleague and friend in Padua, and as early as 1604 both had been denounced to the local Inquisition: Cremonini for dubious orthodoxy in the way he interpreted the immortality of the soul according to Aristotle, and Galileo for believing that the stars determine human behavior. The charges had been quietly dropped, and we can only guess why someone at the Holy Office now wanted to check whether Galileo's name was associated with that of Cremonini, who continued to be denounced for his views on the immortality of the soul. Galileo's large circle of acquaintances included several priests but also some notorious bon vivants and controversial figures like Cremonini. Such relationships might have seemed suspect to Bellarmine, but he was a conscientious person and anxious to be fair. A check on anyone spreading novel ideas was in any case a routine matter in Rome during the Counter Reformation, and Galileo probably never heard that his name had cropped up at a meeting of the cardinal inquisitors.

We must also bear in mind that the pattern of studies for all Jesuit colleges had been laid down in the *Ratio Studiorum,* a collection of guidelines in which teachers were enjoined to follow St. Thomas Aquinas in theology and Aristotle in philosophy. The prime concern of the Jesuit authorities was orthodoxy and the promotion of a reasonable amount of uniformity in their educational institutions. Lecturers were not to introduce new opinions without consulting their superiors, and those who were prone to novelties or of too free a mind were to be assigned other tasks and removed from teaching. These stringent provisions were confirmed while Galileo was in Rome. On 24 May 1611, the Jesuit general, Claudio Aquaviva, addressed a letter to the society in which he insisted on the implementation of the *Ratio*. The caution that the Jesuits displayed in accepting Galileo's discoveries was just what might be expected, but once they were convinced he was right they showed their appreciation handsomely, as we shall soon see.

PAPAL SALUTE

While the professors of the Roman College were preparing their report for Cardinal Bellarmine, the Tuscan ambassador had requested an audience with the pope, Paul V, the name Cardinal Camillo Borghese had chosen when elected in 1605. He was the scion of a wealthy and powerful family. Their former seat, the Villa Borghese, is still one of the most admired and frequently visited of the great Roman houses. The famous art collection that it now stores is an extension of the splendid works of art that the Borghese had acquired from the fifteenth century onward. Not unlike Sixtus V, Paul V was a man of considerable energy and determination. He enforced the decrees of the Council of Trent that called for bishops to reside in their own dioceses simply by expelling from Rome those who were there without urgent business. He was not particularly gifted in diplomacy and easily took, and provoked, umbrage. His pontificate was marked by a bitter jurisdictional quarrel with Venice in which Cardinals Baronio and Bellarmine acted for the Holy See while Paolo Sarpi, a friend of Galileo, defended the interests of the maritime republic.

The pope, who was a canon lawyer by training, could not brook any behavior that seemed to challenge the legal power of the Church, and he excommunicated the Doge, the Senate, and the whole government of Venice. When this did not produce results, Paul V placed the Republic under interdict; in other words, he forbade priests to administer sacraments. Most of the clergy in Venice, both regular and secular, sided with the Venetian authorities, but the Jesuits and two other religious congregations obeyed the pope and were promptly expelled from the territory of Venice. In 1607, after one year of wrangling, an agreement was worked out and the pope withdrew his interdict and lifted the excommunication. But no sooner was peace restored in Italy than another conflict arose with England, where James I imposed in 1605 an Oath of Allegiance that ordered his subjects to rejects as "impious and heretical" any papal interference with religious or political affairs in the United Kingdom. Bellarmine was entrusted with making the case for Rome, and this is how he became something of a bogeyman in England and was often portrayed as the archetype of Jesuit cunning.

At home, Paul V embarked on the immense task of completing St. Peter's. The plans that Bramante had drawn in 1506 and those that Michelangelo made some 40 years later were never given the green light. The magnificent church that we admire today is the result of a lengthy and often messy story of architectural changes, and it might not have been finished without Paul V, who, in 1607, made the difficult decision to tear down the old ruinous Constantine basilica and extend the new church by a vast nave with an imposing facade by Carlo Maderna. This was nearing completion when Galileo arrived in Rome, but the huge inscription that runs across the facade, PAULUS V BORGHESIUS ROMANUS, was something he was only to see on his next trip in 1615.

In the summer the pope resided on the Quirinal, but in April, when Galileo and the ambassador paid their courtesy visit, he was still at the Vatican. The *Avvisi*, which we have mentioned earlier, allows us to follow the pope as he went about Rome in a litter, on horseback, and on foot to inspect public works, preside at religious ceremonies, and promote artistic and cultural activities. This is how we know that the pope had visited the vineyard of Monsignor Malvasia a week before Federico Cesi gave a banquet there in honor of Galileo. To be received by the pope was quite an honor for Galileo, and after the audience he immediately wrote to his friend, Filippo Salviati, knowing full well that

Salviati would not only talk about his friend's Roman success but would pass the letter around:

> I do not have time to write personal letters to all my friends and patrons, and in writing to you I shall imagine that I am writing to all. I have been received and fêted by many illustrious cardinals, prelates and princes who wanted to see the things I have observed and were much pleased, as I was too, on my part, in viewing the marvels of their statuary, paintings, frescoed rooms, palaces, gardens, and so on.
>
> This morning I went to pay my respects to his Holiness, and I was introduced by His Excellency our illustrious Ambassador, who told me that I had been treated with exceptional favor because his Holiness would not let me say a word kneeling but immediately commanded me to stand up.

Galileo went on to mention that the Jesuits were all on his side but that not everyone understood what he was about, and he regretted that some (unspecified) people should have written from Florence that the grand duke was ill pleased when he left for Rome. The friendly way with which the pope had received him and the approval of the Jesuits enabled Galileo to dismiss his critics as laughable, but events would show that they were not entirely a joking matter.

THE NEW LYNCEAN

Three days after the papal audience, Galileo was solemnly received by Federico Cesi in his palace, which can be admired to this day in the Via della Maschera d'Oro in the heart of Rome. The purpose of the visit was to make Galileo a member of the Lyncean Academy, a privilege that had only been conferred on four persons since 1603. Galileo's formal acceptance, in Latin, can still be read in the membership book: "I, Galileo Galilei Lyncean, son of Vincenzio, Florentine, age forty-eight years, in Rome. Written in my own hand on 25 April of the year of grace 1611." In the same year four other members were added, including two who had attended the banquet on the Janiculum, the Roman hill next to the Vatican: Johann Schreck (alias Terentius), who was 35, and Johann Faber, who was 37. All in all, 32 scholars and scientists were admitted before Cesi's death in 1630, when the activities of the academy ceased.

The Lyncean Academy was a loose association based on personal ties with Cesi (Prince Cesi after 1613, when this title was conferred on him by the pope), who concentrated all power and control in his own, admittedly generous, hands. He was a patron rather than a scientist, but he had the good sense to recognize Galileo's greatness and to publish at his own expense Galileo's *Letters on the Sunspots* in 1613 and his *Assayer* in 1623. He fully intended to publish Galileo's masterpiece, the *Dialogue on the Two Chief World Systems,* but he died before the work had run the gauntlet of censorship and was licensed for print. Had Cesi been alive in 1632 when the book finally appeared it might have sailed past the shoals of the Inquisition.

Galileo was always proud to be a member of the Lyncean Academy, and he prominently displayed this title on the cover of his books. But in Rome in 1611 he knew that he had to be active on more than one front, and he did not neglect astronomical observation. Kepler had thought that it would be impossible to determine the periods of Jupiter's satellites, but Galileo was able to work them out to a very good approximation while in Rome. He also trained his telescope on the Sun, and, by April, he was showing notable people a most unexpected spectacle: The Sun was covered with spots. It was natural for Galileo and for others to wish to examine the Sun as well as the planets, but no one could look at the flaming ball for more than a fleeting instant without being blinded. The solution initially was to place a neutral blue or green lens over the objective of the telescope, or to cover the lens with soot. However, a better method was found by Galileo's former student, Benedetto Castelli, who let the image of the Sun fall on a screen placed behind the telescope. Galileo was therefore able to see clearly that the surface of the Sun was covered with spots. This was a momentous discovery, since the Aristotelians maintained that nothing changed in the heavens, and the spots were a clear indication that the Sun itself was not made of an imperishable and incorruptible substance.

A Jesuit professor in Germany, Christopher Scheiner, also saw the sunspots, but he conjectured that they were small satellites like those that Galileo had seen around Jupiter. If they were some kind of clouds, this would indicate that the Sun is not perfect and immutable. In order to avoid this, Scheiner conjectured that they were real bodies orbiting at some distance from the Sun. Galileo rejected this hypothesis and took great care to show that they were on or very close to the surface and that their motion indicated that the Sun rotates on its axis.

Among Galileo's Florentine friends in Rome was Monsignor Piero Dini, a nephew of Cardinal Bandini who held high office at the Vatican. Dini was a skillful diplomat, and the advice that he would later give Galileo was among the best he ever received. He was a shrewd observer of the Roman scene, and his letters to friends are a useful source of information. On 7 May 1611 he reported to Cosimo Sassetti in Perugia: "every day Galileo converts some of the heretics who did not believe him, although there are still a few who, in order to escape knowing the truth about the stars around Jupiter, do not even want to look at them." The reluctance to look through the telescope on the part of people who had made the attempt and seen little or nothing is understandable. The telescope was not only difficult to focus, but the field of vision was extremely small and, unless it was held very firmly, it was no easy matter to point it at an object as large as the Moon, let alone the small satellites of Jupiter. The answer was to mount the telescope on a stand, but even then impatient or short-sighted philosophers often saw a blurred image that confirmed their prejudices. On 14 May Sassetti replied to Dini, who passed the letter on to Galileo, as we know from a copy that Galileo made himself and is still extant. It embodied the qualms of some professors of the University of Perugia. Since Galileo went to the trouble of copying this letter and then replying to it, the reader will want to see it for himself:

Loud voices are raised against Galileo. I spoke to two of the main protesters, who would not be converted by Ptolemy himself were he converted! I should be grateful for an answer to an objection that I heard and that seems very reasonable: the spyglass makes us see things that are not really there, or if they exist then they are so small that they exert no influence. It seems to me that they are saying that there is no shortage of such small objects in the heavens. This objection is buttressed by a large number of arguments and proofs, starting with the creation of Adam, etc, as your Reverence knows better than I do.

GALILEO FACES OBJECTIONS

Dini suggested to Galileo that it would be politic to reply to the objections raised by professors of the University of Perugia, and in spite of his hectic activities Galileo took the time to pen a lengthy reply, which he addressed to Dini. The people in Perugia, who could not catch sight of the Jovian satellites and therefore questioned their very existence, just had inferior instruments. Better lenses would show them that these satellites were not optical illusions! Indeed they had been observed all over Europe, and Galileo declared himself ready to pay 10,000 scudi (ten times his annual salary) to anyone who could construct an optical instrument that would place fictitious satellites around one planet but not around all the others.

Galileo then discussed at some length the objection that the celestial bodies disclosed by the telescope were so small that they could not exert any influence on earth. This difficulty was raised by those who cast horoscopes, a task that astronomers then considered part of their job. Galileo made it clear that he never intended to affirm or to deny that the newly discovered stars exert some influence, but that "if he had to say something, he would, speaking personally, be very cautious in pronouncing that the Medicean stars lack influence when other stars do. It would seem bold, not to say reckless, to want to limit the knowledge and the working of nature to what I can understand of it." As we can see, the question had a philosophical edge. It also had a political one: The satellites that bore the name of the Medici had become a matter of state, and Galileo could hardly allow them to be dismissed as lacking influence.

Potentially more ticklish was the ambiguous reference to Adam and the implied theological stricture. In the penultimate paragraph of his letter, Galileo sidestepped the whole issue by declaring that Dini was better qualified to deal with this matter. What did the professors of the University of Perugia have in mind by bringing in Adam? In the light of subsequent events, it would seem that they were uncomfortable with the notion that the Earth was no longer at the center of the world. This had seemed not only physically natural but theologically suitable since the most important cosmic event of history, the incarnation of Jesus Christ, occurred on Earth. The incarnation was never defined as happening at the physical center of the world, but tradition associated the centrality of Christ's redeeming mission with the hub of the universe. Although geocentrism was never a Christian dogma, it was to take time before biblical statements about the Sun rising or setting were interpreted as commonsensical utterances without any scientific implications. The world has not only to be understood, it must also be imagined.

A ROMAN CELEBRATION

But these were mere clouds on the horizon. In Rome, on Friday 13 May, the Jesuits had just given Galileo the equivalent of a modern honorary doctorate in a lavish ceremony at the Roman College. The Dutch Jesuit Odo Maelcote read an address in Latin about *The Sidereal Message* in the presence of the entire Roman College, several cardinals, and notabilities, including Cesi. The Jesuit scientist first discussed the newly invented telescope and the geometrical proofs of the magnification it provided. Next he offered a brief description of Galileo's observations of the lunar body, the moons of Jupiter, the fixed stars, the phases of Venus, and the curious shape of Saturn. The address, entitled "The Sidereal Message of the Roman College" was not published, but excerpts were prepared by Grienberger, presumably for distribution in the order.

Father Maelcote offered a picturesque description of the potted surface of the Moon:

> We can observe at the tips of the Moon's horns certain brilliant peaks, or rather, I might say, small globules like the shining beads of a Rosary, some scattered among themselves, others strung together as if by a thread. So, too, can many bubble-like spots be seen especially around the lower horn: that part of the lunar surface is adorned and painted by them as if by the eyes of a peacock's tail.

Maelcote did not go as far as to confirm the existence of peaks and mountains on the Moon, and, in deference to the objections expressed earlier by Christopher Clavius, he recalled that he was himself only a celestial messenger and that his audience was free to attribute the spots on the Moon to "the uneven density and rarity of the lunar body" or "to something else," as they chose.

Prior to Galileo the Moon was generally compared to a crystal ball, and its apparent spots were dismissed as optical illusions caused by atmospheric conditions. Clavius's personal reluctance to accept that the Moon was rough and covered with deep depressions rested on two reasons, one scientific, the other symbolic. The first was that the illuminated edges of the Moon in all its phases show themselves perfectly round, without those indentations that one would expect from the inequalities of its surface. The second reason is that there was a popular religious representation of the Virgin Mary with her feet resting on the surface of a perfectly spherical Moon. Clavius would not have wished to make a doctrinal point out of an icon, but we can understand his regard for the Marian convention and his reluctance to admit too readily the bumps and dents that would render a traditional image inappropriate.

The destruction of the pure and perfect Moon was a lengthier process than Galileo had anticipated. When Ludovico delle Colombe heard about Clavius's scepticism about mountains on the Moon, he wrote to say that he shared his doubts. A copy of the letter was passed on to

Galileo by Gallanzone Gallanzoni the secretary of Cardinal Joyeuse, who wanted to know how he would reply. Galileo, at his wittiest, complied:

> If anyone is allowed to imagine whatever he pleases, then someone could say that the Moon is surrounded by a crystalline substance that is transparent and invisible. I will grant this provided that, with equal courtesy, I be allowed to say that the crystal has on its outer surface a large number of huge mountains, that are thirty times as high as the terrestrial ones, and invisible because they are diaphanous.

One might just as well, Galileo adds, define *Earth* to include the atmosphere at the top of the highest mountain and declare that "the Earth is perfectly spherical." We witness here how Galileo's sarcasm could be amusing but also dangerous. He laughed delle Colombe off the stage, but what was really required was a scientific answer and, in this instance, Galileo might have replied that the full Moon appears perfectly circular because the mountains on its surface are close together, so that at the distance of the Earth the intervening depressions are not discernible.

TRIUMPHAL RETURN

When Galileo left Rome on Saturday, 4 June 1611, he could be happy with the result of his trip and look forward to a hero's welcome in Florence when he handed the grand duke the glowing report that Cardinal Francesco Maria del Monte had prepared for him:

> Galileo has, during his stay in Rome, given great satisfaction, and I think he received as much, for he had the opportunity of showing his discoveries so well, that the learned and notable in this city all found them no less true and well-founded than astonishing. Were we still living under the ancient republic of Rome, I am certain that a statue would have been erected in his honor on the Capitol.

If we bear in mind that the equestrian statue on the Capitol is that of the emperor Marcus Aurelius, we can see how highly Galileo was being praised. Cardinal del Monte was not the only prelate to sing his praise. Cardinal Farnese gave a banquet for him prior to his departure and even accompanied him as far as Caprarola, the country seat of the Farnese family.

Cardinal Maffeo Barberini had become Galileo's admirer, and this was made clear at a dinner given by the grand duke in Florence on 2 October 1611. Galileo and Flaminio Papazzone, an Aristotelian professor of philosophy, had been invited to publicly discuss whether the shape of bodies has something to do with their ability to float. Galileo argued that shape is irrelevant; Papazzone replied that, on the contrary, it is often decisive. Cardinal Ferdinando Gonzaga, who was also present, sided with Papazzone, while Cardinal Barberini upheld Galileo's position. Shortly thereafter, Galileo fell ill and was unable to bid farewell to Cardinal Barberini, who was going on to Bologna. The Cardinal's friendly concern is evident from the letter he wrote to Galileo from that city on 11 October 1611:

> I am very sorry that you were unable to see me before I left the city. It is not that I consider a sign of your friendship as necessary, for it is well known to me, but because you were ill. May God keep you not only because outstanding persons, such as yourself, deserve a long life of public service, but because of the particular affection that I have and always will have for you. I am happy to be able to say this, and to thank you for the time that you spent with me.
>
> Your affectionate brother,
Cardinal Barberini

This warm letter is particularly remarkable for the last sentence and the final greeting in which Cardinal Barberini describes himself as an affectionate brother. Even if we make allowances for the baroque penchant for flowery language, there is no doubt that the cardinal genuinely admired Galileo and was anxious to help him. Friendship spurned, or perceived as such, and, worse still, friendship betrayed often give rise to deep resentment. It is sad that this will be the fate of the relations between Galileo and Barberini that were so cordial in 1611.

MISGIVINGS

We have seen that the Holy Office checked on Galileo's possible involvement with Cremonini. Although nothing came of this enquiry, it shows how easily the waters could become choppy. The endorsement of his celestial discoveries by the Jesuits had allowed Galileo to take the further step of arguing in favor of the motion of the Earth on the numerous occasions when he was asked to say a few words about the significance of his telescopic observations. Eyebrows had been raised, however, and when Galileo planned a third trip to Rome four years later, the Roman ambassador, Piero Guicciardini, was the first to express concern. Guicciardini had been Galileo's host after replacing ambassador Niccolini in April 1611, so he had personally experienced some of tensions around Galileo's discoveries. In a note of 5 December 1615 to Curzio Picchena, the secretary of state of the grand duke, he did not mince his words:

> I hear that *Galileo is coming here*. Annibale Primi informs me that, on orders from the Grand Duke received from you, he is to expect him at the Garden [the Villa Medici]. I met him here when I first arrived and he spent a few days with me [in 1611]. His teaching, and something else, was not to the taste of the Advisors *and the Cardinals of the Holy Office*. Among others, *Bellarmine* told me that, however great their respect for the Grand Duke, if Galileo had stayed here too long, they could not have avoided looking into the matter. I gave Galileo a hint or a warning since he was staying here, but I fear that it did not give him great pleasure.

Guicciardini and Galileo had not hit it off, but the ambassador was a man of the world and a well-informed diplomat. The matter was more delicate than Galileo surmised, as we can infer from the fact that the italicized words of the letter are in cipher. Upon receipt in Florence, they were decoded and written just above. Clearly the ambassador did not want the information of Galileo's arrival or the references to Bellarmine and the Holy Office to fall into the wrong hands. The roads that led from Rome were not always paved with good intentions.

CHAPTER THREE

Roman Clouds

THIRD TRIP • 10 DECEMBER 1615–4 JUNE 1616

Four years after his second trip, Galileo decided that it was time to return to Rome. In the meanwhile, he had published a *Discourse on Floating Bodies*, and *Letters on the Sunspots*, in which he argued that sunspots were some kind of clouds near the surface of the Sun. This was a blow to Aristotelianism and an argument in favor of a new cosmology. But Galileo did not want to travel to Rome merely to discuss astronomy. He had come to realize that what he had to do was defend himself against the accusation that what he taught went against Scripture.

Galileo had become aware of the sensitivities of the ecclesiastical authorities when he had submitted his *Letters on the Sunspots* to obtain the license to print it. The cavils of the censors forced successive revisions, and brought Galileo into contact with the day-to-day running of the Counter Reformation. The book was to have opened with a letter from Mark Welser in which he quoted from Matthew 11:12, "The kingdom of heavens suffers violence, and men of violence take it by force." The censors objected to the quotation because it might give the impression that astronomers wanted to conquer a domain that belonged to theologians. To allay these fears, the passage was para- phrased to read: "Already the minds of men assail the heavens, and the more valiant conquer them." Although there was no significant change in content, the biblical passage had disappeared! In a second passage Galileo had written that "divine goodness" had directed him to openly describe the Copernican system. The censors had him substitute "favor- able winds."

Elsewhere Galileo had called the immutability of the heavens "not only false, but erroneous and repugnant to the indubitable truth of Scripture," and he had attributed the new astronomy to divine inspiration. When the censors demurred, he produced a new draft in which he called his own theory "most agreeable to the indubitable truths of Holy Writ" and praised his predecessors for their subtlety in finding ways of reconcil- ing biblical passages on the mutability of the heavens with the apparent evidence in favor of their immutability. The tacit implication was that, since theologians had long interpreted the texts to show their agreement with Aristotelian doctrine, there already existed in the church a nonliteral way of reading biblical passages on astronomy. The censors deemed the revision inadequate and demanded a third version, in which Galileo reluctantly excised all mention of Scripture.

The attitudes of both the censors and Galileo are instructive. On the one hand, the censors adamantly refused a layman the right to meddle with Scripture. On the other, Galileo was inclined to describe his point of view as "divinely inspired" and to brand that of his opponents as "contrary to Scripture." The popular conception of Galileo as a martyr for freedom of thought is an oversimplification. That his views were different from those of the majority of the academic establishment did not make him a liberal. He cherished the hope that the Church would endorse his opinions and, with many of his contemporaries, looked to an enlightened papacy as an effective instrument of scientific progress. But what Galileo does not seem to have understood is that the Catholic Church, attacked by Protes- tants for neglecting the Bible, found itself compelled, in self-defense, to harden its position. Whatever appeared to contradict Holy Writ had to be treated with the utmost caution.

THE PIGEON LEAGUE

We have already seen that a conservative Aristotelian by the name of Ludovico delle Colombe had criticized the idea of the motion of the Earth. Galileo had never dignified him with a formal reply. Delle Colombe now proceeded to attack Galileo's *Discourse on Floating Bodies*, declaring himself "an anti-Galilean, out of respect for Aristotle, the great leader of academies, the head of so many schools, the subject of so many poems, the labor of so many historians, and the man who read more books than there were days in his life, and wrote more than he counted years." Colombe's description of himself as an anti-Galilean inspired Galileo's supporters to call themselves *Galileists*, and to refer to their opponents as *pigeons*, or members of the *Pigeon League*, a pun on the word *colombo*, which means *pigeon* in Italian. They were to prove very troublesome birds. On 16 December 1611, the painter Cigoli wrote to Galileo from Rome:

> I have been told by a friend of mine, a priest who is very fond of you, that a gang of ill-disposed men, who are envious of your virtue and merits, met at the residence of the Archbishop of Florence, and put their heads together in a mad quest for some means by which they could damage you, either with regard to the motion of the Earth or otherwise. One of them asked a preacher to state from the pulpit that you were asserting outlandish things. The priest, seeing the animosity against you, replied as a good Christian and a member of a religious order ought to do. I write this that your eyes may be open to the envy and malice of these evildoers.

If Cigoli was well informed, this was disquieting. The archbishop of Florence, Alessandro Marzimedici, was not ill disposed toward Galileo and may have been his student in Padua, but Galileo's adversaries were high enough in rank to be allowed to hold meetings in the episcopal palace.

MORE TROUBLES

The next sign of trouble came several months later from a member of the Dominicans, one of the main religious orders in Florence. Named after their founder, St. Dominic, they saw themselves as the bulwark of orthodoxy and were often named inquisitors by the Holy Office. Punning on their name *Dominicanes* (the plural of Dominicans also means *dogs of the Lord* in Latin), they had themselves represented in paintings as white and black sheep dogs defending their flock from wolves. They were also known to bark at the slightest scent of heresy. When Galileo was told that on 2 November 1612, All Souls' Day, a Dominican named Niccolò Lorini had attacked his views at a meeting in Florence, he asked for an explanation. The friar immediately complied with the following answer:

> The suspicion that I entered into a discussion of philosophical matters against anyone on All Souls' Day is completely false and without foundation . . . I did, however, not in order to argue but merely to avoid appearing a blockhead when the discussion was started by others, say a few words just to show I was alive. I said, as I still say, that this opinion of Ipernicus—or whatever his name is—would appear to be hostile to divine Scripture. But it is of little consequence to me, for I have other things to do; for me it is enough that no occasion should be given to anyone for believing that we are what we are not. For I am confident that all our nobility is steadfastly Catholic.

Lorini, then 67 years of age, was himself a member of the nobility, and he enjoyed some distinction in his order. He had served as prior of his convent of Santa Maria Novella, and he taught Church history in Florence. In 1585 he had even been invited to preach in the Sistine Chapel at the Vatican. He was much appreciated by the grand duke but especially by his devout mother, the Grand Duchess Christina, and his equally religious wife, the Archduchess Maria Maddalena. Lorini's ignorance of the correct spelling of Copernicus's name makes it unlikely that he made astronomy the subject of his leisure hours.

Galileo accepted Lorini's account of what had happened, and he joked about the incident a few weeks later in a letter to Cesi:

> Here also they do not rest from scheming, and the more because their enemy is close at hand. But since they are numerically few and belong to that league (for thus they refer to themselves in private) which may be recognized by Your Excellency in their writings, I laugh at them. Here in Florence there is a clumsy speaker who has decided to detest the mobility of the earth, but this good fellow is so unfamiliar with the author of that doctrine that he calls him "Ipernicus." Behold whence and by whom poor philosophy is subjected to extortion!

But Galileo knew that theology was a serious issue even before the Lorini incident, and he had written a letter to Cardinal Carlo Conti in Rome to ask him whether he believed that the Bible favored Aristotelian astronomy. The cardinal replied by distinguishing between the incorrupt-ibility of the heavens and the immobility of the Earth. As far as the first was concerned, Scripture rather went against the Aristotelian claim that no change could occur in the heavens, but whether recent telescopic discoveries actually proved that change does occur "requires much study," wrote the cardinal. He gave three reasons for this caution. First, celestial bodies are very far and can only be known after a long period of observation; second, we cannot simply affirm that they are subject to change, we have to explain how; and, third, in the specific case of sunspots, they could be immutable starlets and not cloudlike objects that really change in shape.

On the more radical idea of the motion of the Earth, the Cardinal considered daily rotation as acceptable since this would not remove the

Earth from the center of the world. The annual motion around the Sun he found, "less in agreement with Scripture," because we would have to interpret passages where the Sun and the planets are said to move as popular ways of speaking. This is something "that should not be admitted without great necessity," he warned. Such an interpretation was attempted by the Spanish theologian Diego Zuñiga in his *Commentary on Job* but practically no one followed him.

Clearly what was required was proof that the Earth really moves, and it is one of the ironies of history that a few days after receiving Cardinal Conti's letter, Galileo got another one that could have helped him do just that. It is dated 21 July 1612 and also came from Rome, where it was penned by Federico Cesi, who tells Galileo about Kepler's discovery that the orbits of the planets are elliptical:

> I believe with Kepler that to compel the planets to follow perfect circles is to confine them to a path from which they often escape. I realize, like you, that many orbits are not concentric to the Sun or the Earth but that some are concentric to the Earth and others to the Sun, and perhaps all to the Sun if their trajectories are elliptical as Kepler says.

The crucial sentence is the last one: Unless the orbits of the planets are elliptical they cannot have the Sun as their center or, more precisely, at one of the two focuses of the ellipse, as Kepler also said. Unfortunately, Galileo seems never to have taken this idea seriously. He may have been deterred by Kepler's mystical asides, but the main reason was that he was deeply convinced that natural and unending motion (in the absence of retarding forces such as air) can only be perfectly circular.

Galileo's *Letters on the Sunspots* finally appeared in March 1613. The censors had made a fuss about references to the Bible, but they had allowed Galileo to openly adopt the Copernican system and link the proof with his own discoveries. From this time on, until the Holy Office clamped down on him in 1616, Galileo would defend it on all occasions. His name became so closely associated with the motion of the Earth in the popular mind that he was sometimes regarded as the one who had originated the idea, which caused him no little amusement.

LUNCH WITH THE PATRONS

Galileo engineered an appointment at the University of Pisa for his favorite disciple, Benedetto Castelli. No sooner had Castelli arrived in November 1613 than the overseer of the university, Arturo d'Elci, called him in to say that he must under no circumstances discuss the motion of the Earth in his lectures. Castelli assured him that he had no such intention, wisely adding that his own teacher, Galileo, had never done so in 24 years of teaching. Castelli was true to his word, but less than a month later the forbidden topic was raised under circumstances that compelled him to argue the case for Copernicanism. It was an event that turned out to be of crucial importance for Galileo.

The Tuscan court had arrived in Pisa for their annual winter visit, and their serene highnesses invited to their table the learned and notable of the city. Their highnesses were actually three: the Grand Duke Cosimo II, his mother Christina, who had retained her title of grand duchess after the death of Ferdinando I in 1609, and Cosimo's wife, Maria Maddalena, who had to be content with the title of archduchess that she had brought with her from her native Austria. Castelli and a colleague, Cosimo Boscaglia, who taught philosophy, were favored with an invitation. Here is the account of the luncheon that Castelli sent Galileo on Saturday 14 December 1613:

> Thursday morning I was at table with our Patrons and when asked by the Grand Duke about the university, I gave him a detailed account of everything, with which he showed himself much pleased. He asked me if I had a telescope. I said yes, and I began to tell about an observation of the Medicean planets I had made just the night before. Madama Christina wanted to know their position, whereupon the talk turned to the necessity of their being real objects and not illusions of the telescope.

Professor Boscaglia agreed that they were indeed real, and Castelli proceeded to tell them about Galileo's determination of the orbits of Jupiter's satellites. The meal ended pleasantly, and Castelli took his leave, but "hardly had I come out of the palace," the letter continues,

> when I was overtaken by the porter of Madama Christina, who called me back. But before I tell you what followed, you must first know that while we were at table Doctor Boscaglia had had Madama's ear for a while, and while conceding as real all the things you have discovered in the sky, he said that only the motion of the Earth was somehow incredible, and could not take place especially because Holy Scripture was obviously contrary to that view.

Madama Christina was known at court as a devout Catholic who listened to her confessor and was devoted to the pope even when His Holiness's interests might be at variance with those of the Tuscan government. She also knew her Bible and could refer to the Book of Josuah where the Sun is ordered to stand still. If the earth moved, Josuah would have ordered it and not the Sun to stop!

Upon re-entering the Pisan Palace Castelli found that some of the guests were still there including Professor Boscaglia, Paolo Giordano Orsini, a cousin of the Grand Duke, and Antonio de' Medici, an adopted son of the Duke's grandfather, Cosimo I. The grand duchess, Castelli went on,

> began to argue Holy Scripture against me. Thereupon, after having made suitable disclaimers, I commenced to play the theologian with such assurance and dignity that it would have done you good to hear me. Don Antonio assisted me, giving me such heart that instead of being dismayed by the majesty of Their Highnesses I carried things off like a paladin. I quite won over the Grand Duke and his Archduchess, while Don Paolo came to my assistance with a very apt quotation from

Scripture. Only Madama Christina remained against me, but from her manner I judged that she did this only to hear my replies. Professor Boscaglia never said a word.

Castelli mentioned that Niccolò Arrighetti, a mutual friend, would presently call on Galileo to tell him more. This he did within a few days and confirmed that the grand duchess had quizzed Castelli about the compatibility of Copernicanism with Scripture. Although she was not displeased with Castelli's answers, her mind was not completely at rest.

AN ASTRONOMER'S LETTER

Galileo saw that he must intervene, and within a week he put his own reflections on paper in the form of a *Letter to Castelli*, which could be shown to friends. This was to be his first but not his last incursion into theology. Personally, he saw no conflict between science and religion, and he was anxious that no line of battle should be drawn between the two. "Scripture cannot err," wrote Galileo, "but its interpreters can,"

> especially when they would always base themselves on the literal meaning of the words. For in this way not only many contradictions would be apparent, but even grave heresies and blasphemies, since then it would be necessary to give God hands and feet and eyes, and human and bodily emotions such as anger, regret, hatred and sometimes forgetfulness of things past, and ignorance of the future.

Galileo stressed that this way of speaking had been introduced into the Bible for the sake of the masses, and only to aid them in matters concerning salvation. "Sacred Scripture and nature," he declared, "both derive from the Divine Word, the former as dictated by the Holy Spirit and the latter as the faithful executrix of God's commands." No truth discovered in nature can contradict the Bible. Indeed Copernican astronomy even makes the miracle of Josuah arresting the Sun more easy to understand, according to Galileo, because if the Sun stood still the Earth would stop spinning and the day would be automatically prolonged! This explanation of the miracle of Joshua, however ingenious, was highly speculative, and it cast Galileo in the dangerous role of telling theologians how to interpret the Bible.

It might be naive to read every passage of the Bible literally, but was it not sheer arrogance to impose upon it a purely speculative theory? After all, where was the proof that Copernicus, or Galileo for that matter, offered for the motion of the Earth? Galileo declared that because "two truths can never contradict each other, it is the task of wise expositors to try to find the true meanings of sacred passages in accordance with natural conclusions that have been previously rendered certain and secure by sense experience or necessary demonstration." The problem that Galileo faced was that we see the Sun rise in the morning and set in the evening. Only if he could show that this is an optical illusion, could he argue that sensory experience cannot always be relied upon.

Galileo did not shirk the task of giving such a demonstration, but he was frequently ill during the next year and progress was slow. He had the pleasure of learning that Father Grienberger, who had succeeded Father Clavius at the Roman College, had accepted his conclusions concerning sunspots after at first supporting the views of his fellow Jesuit, Christopher Scheiner. When the Genovese patrician and amateur scientist Giovanni Battista Baliani asked Galileo about his astronomical views, Galileo replied on 12 March 1614: "*As far as the opinion of Copernicus is concerned, I really hold it to be certain,* not only on account of the appearance of Venus, the sunspots, and the Medicean stars, but for other reasons, as well as for many more that I have found and that seem to me decisive." Galileo felt that the Church would make a serious error if it rejected Copernicanism, but he was too sanguine about the cogency of his demonstration. This was to prove his Achilles heel.

THUNDER FROM THE PULPIT

In Rome, the general of the Jesuits, Claudio Aquaviva, was bent on keeping the members of his society out of the perilous waters of controversy. On 14 December 1613, the very day Castelli had given Galileo an account of his luncheon at the Tuscan court, Aquaviva had written a letter in which he insisted that Aristotelian natural philosophy be taught in Jesuit schools. This made the astronomers of the Roman College extra cautious. In June 1614, Giovanni Bardi, a Roman friend, wrote to Galileo to say that Father Grienberger had told him that he now had to follow Aristotle in his teaching although he would gladly have spoken out in favor of Galileo. It was unfortunate that the Jesuits should be made to uphold traditional views just at the time when Galileo was claiming that the sunspots sounded the death knell of the Aristotelian position. The Dominicans also followed Aristotle and one of their members, a young firebrand named Tommaso Caccini, carried out what someone had suggested at a meeting of the Pigeon League in the home of the archbishop of Pisa. On the fourth Sunday of Advent, which fell that year on 21 December 1614, Caccini attacked Galileo from the pulpit of Santa Maria Novella, one of the main churches of Florence.

Caccini seems to have chosen as his text the passage in the first chapter of the Acts of the Apostles, in which two men clad in white said to the disciples after Jesus' ascension into heaven: "Men of Galilee, why do you stand here looking at the sky?" In the Latin version, which Caccini quoted, "Men of Galilee" is *"Viri Galilei,"* which can be rendered as "Men of [Galileo] Galilei." The pun startled the congregation, but there was more to come. Caccini launched into a denunciation of Galileo, the Copernican system, and all mathematicians, whom he branded as enemies of Church and State. He was dead serious. He was also bigoted and given to slander, and he let the Dominicans in Rome know that he had ferreted out a new heresy. One of his correspondents, a preacher-general of the order named Luigi Maraffi, thought Caccini had flown off the handle and wrote to Galileo to express his regret that such stupidities should have been uttered by a member of his religious order. Galileo had himself written to Federico Cesi, asking how he could obtain redress. The advice that he received from the religious, yet worldly wise, prince could have taught him much about the Roman milieu he was so sorely to misjudge:

> Concerning the opinion of Copernicus, Bellarmine himself, who is one
> of the heads of the Congregation that deals with these matters, told me
> that he considers it heretical, and that the motion of the earth is undoubt-
> edly against Scripture; so you can see for yourself. I have always feared
> that if Copernicus were discussed in the Congregation of the Index, they
> would proscribe him.

THE DENUNCIATION

Cesi urged Galileo to avoid discussing Copernicus for the time being and to bear in mind "that it is very easy to proscribe a book or suspend it, and that this is done *even in case of doubt*." Cesi did not fear that Copernicanism would be officially declared heretical but that it might be condemned in a milder, but nonetheless embarrassing, way by being put on the Index, as was often done. Why, Bellarmine himself had had one of his books placed on the Index in 1590 by Sixtus V on the grounds that he was not hard enough on those who criticized the temporal power of the papacy! Fortunately for Bellarmine, Sixtus V died before the new edition of the Index could be published, and his successor, Urban VII, who was only on the throne of St. Peter for 12 days (15–27 September 1590), removed the book before the proscribed list went to press.

Niccolò Lorini, the Dominican who had criticized what's-his-name Ipernicus, met Castelli in Pisa at the end of 1614 and said how sad he was that Caccini had let himself get so far out of hand. Castelli thought Lorini had had a change of heart, but his optimism was premature. Lorini may have felt that Caccini had gone too far, but while he was in Pisa someone gave him a copy of Galileo's *Letter to Castelli,* written a year before. Upon his return to Florence, he discussed it with his fellow priests and they reached the conclusion that it was most objectionable. Filled with holy zeal, the aged and influential Dominican decided to forward the letter to Cardinal Sfondrati, the prefect of the Congregation of the Index. Lorini carefully avoided mentioning Galileo in the covering letter, but he called for an investigation of the views expressed by the "Galileists," all good Christians, admittedly, but a bit too clever and obstinate in their opinion. Lorini described them as spreading all sorts of impertinence, such as the view that Scripture takes the last place in disputes about natural effects and that astronomical arguments count far more than biblical statements.

Lorini's letter and Galileo's *Letter to Castelli* were examined by the Holy Office at its meeting on Wednesday, 25 February 1615, which was held at the residence of Cardinal Bellarmine in the presence of six other cardinals, the commissioner of the Holy Office, the assessor, and the notary. Since the only solid evidence that Lorini submitted was a copy of the *Letter to Castelli,* the Holy Office decided to request the archbishop of Florence to obtain and submit the original. Cardinal Garcia Millini wrote personally to the archbishop of Pisa, where Castelli resided, in the hope of expediting matters. Lorini's copy of the *Letter to Castelli* was inaccurate in places, but Galileo's views were not studiously distorted. Lorini had skillfully shielded himself from personal interrogation by requesting that his cover letter be treated not as a judicial deposition but as an informal letter written out of sense of service toward his patron, Cardinal Sfondrati.

The next move was made by Caccini, who had come to Rome in quest of preferment. He took the unusual step of asking to appear before the Inquisition. At a meeting of the Holy Office on Thursday, 19 March 1615, the pope decided that Caccini should be heard. The next day, Caccini called on Commissioner Seghizzi. He recounted how he had, in his sermon on the fourth Sunday of Advent, modestly reproved Copernicanism as contrary to Scripture, the interpretation of the Fathers, and the Councils of Lateran and Trent. It was public knowledge that Galileo held two propositions that were at variance with the Faith: one, that the Earth moves, and second that the Sun stands still. Caccini went on to tarnish Galileo's reputation by accusing him of having undesirable relations. Lorini, Caccini said, suspected Galileo's orthodoxy because he corresponded with Paolo Sarpi in Venice, and belonged to an academy that was in touch with Germans (meaning heretics). The summary identification of Germans with heresy gives us a clue to Caccini's lack of discrimination, but the charge of corresponding with Germans was to be included years later in the preamble to Galileo's condemnation. The Holy Office was more interested in specific charges, however, and asked Caccini for other witnesses. He provided the names of two: Ferdinando Ximenes, a Dominican, and Gianozzo Attavanti, a young Florentine nobleman.

On Thursday, 2 April 1615, at a meeting of the Holy Office attended by seven cardinals, the pope decided to forward Caccini's deposition to the Florentine inquisitor with instructions to interrogate the two witnesses. No undue haste was displayed by the Florentine inquisitor, and Ximenes and Attavanti were only heard on 13 and 14 November 1615. When Attavanti was asked what he thought of Galileo's orthodoxy he replied that he considered him a very good Catholic, for how else could he be in the employ of the grand duke! This is another side of the affair: as the court's official philosopher and mathematician, Galileo could not be criticized without implying that his patron had somehow been remiss. The depositions of Ximenes and Attavanti were sent to Rome and, at the meeting of the Holy Office held at the home of Cardinal Sfondrati on Wednesday, 25 November, Ximenes's deposition was read out loud. It was decided to have Galileo's *Letters on the Sunspots* examined since this work was mentioned by both Caccini and Attavanti.

THE FIRST TRIAL

Can we speak of a "first trial" of Galileo? The sessions of 19 March, 2 April, and 25 November 1615 were regular meetings of the Tribunal of the Inquisition, and were usually presided over by the pope when they were held on a Thursday. But the proceedings never went beyond gathering evidence in the wake of the denunciations of Lorini and Caccini, and Galileo was never formally charged, nor even informed. Years later, matters would take a very different turn.

The deliberations of the Holy Office were secret, but Galileo had got wind of something and feared that his *Letter to Castelli* might have been forwarded to Rome in an altered form. He promptly asked Castelli to return the original, and when he received it he made a copy (perhaps with a few changes) and sent it to Monsignor Piero Dini in Rome, asking that it be shown to his "very great friend" Father Grienberger and, if possible, to Cardinal Bellarmine. In his cover letter, dated 16 February 1615, Galileo explained that he had written to Castelli in haste and that he was busy revising and expanding the letter. He devoted most of his energies to this task and enlisted the help of Castelli, who in turn asked a Barnabite priest to supply passages from St. Augustine and other doctors of the Church in support of Galileo's interpretation of the Bible.

Meanwhile, as we have seen, the Holy Office had received Lorini's denunciation and the archbishop of Pisa had been requested to tactfully obtain the original of Galileo's letter. How the archbishop acquitted himself of this task is known from Castelli's account to Galileo on 12 March 1615:

> He took me to his office, seated me, and began to ask after your health. I had scarcely finished answering when he began to exhort me to give up certain extravagant opinions, and particularly that of the Earth's motion. He said that this was for my own good and that he meant me no harm because these opinions, in addition to being silly, were dangerous, scandalous, and rash, being directly contrary to Scripture. Overcome by such benevolence, I could do no other than reply that I was eager to comply with his suggestions, and that it only remained for me to accommodate my mind to the reasons that I might hope from his profound wisdom and sound learning. He took for me but a single reason from his stock, omitting all others, and the substance of it was that since all created things are made for the service of man, it clearly

follows as a necessary consequence that the Earth cannot move like the stars. Had I been able to see the necessary connection, I might have changed opinion, but His Excellency had to repeat that these opinions were folly and madness, that they had been your ruin, that he had been given wholesome notice of it, and that you had been refuted. He even went on to say (getting really hot under the collar) that it was soon to be made known to you and to His Serene Highness and to everyone that these ideas are all silly and deserve condemnation. Then he asked me if I would kindly show him that letter that you had written to me. When I said I had no copy of it, he asked me to ask you for one, which I hereby do. Please put the finishing touches to your composition, which we shall copy here immediately if you wish. Perhaps, this will be enough for his Excellency. *I say perhaps, not more.*

The last sentence, in italics in the original, is the first sign that the battle was to be fraught with uncertainty for all concerned.

ROMAN DIPLOMACY

While Castelli was shadowboxing with the archbishop, Galileo's Roman friends Piero Dini and Giovanni Ciampoli were busy undoing the damage that might have been caused by Lorini. On 27 February 1615, Ciampoli saw Cardinal Maffeo Barberini and reported to Galileo the next day as follows:

Cardinal Barberini, who, as you know from experience, has always admired your worth, told me only yesterday evening that with respect to these opinions he would like greater caution in not going beyond the arguments used by Ptolemy and Copernicus and, finally, in not exceeding the limitations of physics and mathematics. For theologians claim that the explanation of Scripture is their field, and if new things are brought in, even by an admirable mind, not everyone is dispassionate enough to take them as they are said. One person amplifies, the next one alters, so that what came from the author's own mouth becomes so transformed in spreading that he can no longer recognize it as his own. And I know what he means. Your opinion regarding the phenomena of light and shadow in the bright and dark parts of the moon draws an analogy between the lunar globe and the Earth. Somebody then enlarges on this, and says that you place human inhabitants on the Moon. The next fellow starts to dispute how these can be descended from Adam, or how they can have come off Noah's ark, and many other extravagances you never dreamed of. Hence to declare frequently that one places oneself under the authority of those who have jurisdiction over the minds of people in the interpretation of Scripture is to remove this pretext for malice. Perhaps you think I go too far in playing the sage with you, but please forgive me, and recognize the infinite esteem that makes me speak thus.

A week later it was Dini's turn to report. He had given copies of the *Letter to Castelli* to Father Grienberger and Cardinal Bellarmine and had had a long conversation with the cardinal, who told him that the issue had not been raised since he had spoken to Galileo in 1611. "Concerning Copernicus," Dini adds,

> Bellarmine says there is no question of his book being prohibited; the worst that might happen, according to him, would be the addition of some material in the margins of that book to the effect that Copernicus had introduced his theory in order to save the appearances, or some such thing—just as others introduced epicycles without believing in their existence. Using the same care you may deal at any time with these matters.

The greatest scriptural hurdle to Copernicanism, according to Bellarmine, was a verse in Psalm 19 about the Sun going forth as a giant, which all interpreters treated as attributing motion to the Sun. When Dini said that this could be considered a common form of speech, the cardinal replied that a reinterpretation of Scripture should not be hastily adopted, but then neither should it be hastily ruled out, and he would be happy to see what Galileo had to say. He added that he would consult Father Grienberger, and Dini called on the Jesuit mathematician the very next morning to know what he would tell the cardinal. Grienberger said that he would have preferred Galileo to provide proofs for the motion of the Earth before talking about Scripture, and that it seemed to him that his arguments were more plausible than decisive.

Although Dini's letter to Galileo is dated 7 March 1615, his conversation with Bellarmine probably took place before 25 February, the day on which Lorini's denunciation of Galileo was discussed at the Holy Office in Bellarmine's presence. It is of course possible that the conversation was held later and that Bellarmine, who was sworn to secrecy about what was discussed at the Holy Office, was referring only to what he had heard outside the Tribunal of the Inquisition.

One thing is clear: Bellarmine's friendly advice, transmitted by Dini, was that Galileo should not go outside mathematics and physics and should avoid provoking theologians by teaching them how to read the Bible. This was easier said than done. Galileo would have been happy to stick to his own subject, but what was he to do when others used Scripture to reject what he was saying?

On 14 March 1615 Dini wrote to say that he had just seen Cardinal Maffeo Barberini, who confirmed what he had already said to Galileo, namely that he should be careful and speak "as a professor of mathematics." The Cardinal also assured Dini that he had never heard about the problem that worried Galileo, "although such matters are generally first broached in our Congregation or in that of Bellarmine." This statement is important in order to understand subsequent developments of the Galileo Affair. Cardinal Barberini was a member of the Congregation of the Index, which was charged with censuring books. He was not a member, like Bellarmine, of the Congregation of the Holy Office (the Tribunal of the Inquisition), and he was not informed of their deliberations unless publications were concerned. The relations between the all-powerful Holy Office and the Congregation of the Index can be compared to those between the office of the prime minister and one of the ministries in our modern states. The ministries are not told about everything that is discussed in the prime minister's office but only about what is relevant to their work. Clearly Barberini was not apprised of Lorini's denunciation. Indeed, until several years after his election as pope, he will not even suspect that Galileo's name had been mentioned at the time, let alone that he had been denounced by Lorini and Caccini.

A THEOLOGICAL BOMBSHELL

Matters were brought to a head by the arrival in Rome at the beginning of 1615 of a Carmelite priest, Paolo Antonio Foscarini, who had just published in Naples a letter on the *Opinion of the Pythagoreans and Copernicus Regarding the Motion of the Earth*. Foscarini made a forceful but serene plea for the compatibility of the Copernican hypothesis with Scripture. He did not assert that the new theory was true but argued that the Bible was written to be understood by everyone and hence employed popular rather than scientific language. God chose to reveal only what could not be discovered by the light of reason; the rest he left to human disputation. In forwarding the book to Galileo on 7 March 1615, Cesi wrote: "It could not have come out at a better time, unless it does some damage by increasing the fury of the opponents, but I do not think that this will be the case . . . He is now preaching in Rome." Foscarini was not only preaching there but also offering to meet all comers in debate on the matter, and he had sent a copy of his book to Cardinal Bellarmine for his opinion.

Galileo was understandably worried since he doubted whether Foscarini was qualified to defend the legitimate autonomy of physics. He asked Ciampoli for details of what was going on in Rome, and on 21 March his friend tried to reassure him:

> I confirm once again what I wrote a few days ago: these "great rumors" have made a lot of noise in the ears of four or five people and no more.

Monsignor Dini and I have done our best to discover whether there is a great move afoot, and we have found absolutely nothing, nor is anything known to have been said about one. I imagine that the authors of this rumor believe themselves to make up a good part of Rome since they called notorious something that no one can be found to have discussed. Hence you may relax about this particular, for you do not lack affectionate friends who admire more than ever the eminence of your merits.

But after these comforting words, Ciampoli went on to show himself less optimistic than Cesi about the fate of Foscarini's book, "which," he thought, "runs the risk of being suspended at the next meeting of the Holy Office because it deals with Scripture." The message was clear: Lie low and keep out of the sacristy!

Galileo, however, felt that he had been dragged into the sacristy, and on 23 March, 1615 he sent Dini a long letter in which he offered a spirited defense of his views. He feared that the authorities were in danger of being misled into believing that Copernicus had proposed heliocentrism only hypothetically and would feel free to condemn it. Only someone who had not read Copernicus could claim that he did not put it forward as true. There was no doubt that he believed that the Earth moved and the Sun stood still. There was no room for compromise: Copernicanism had to be either condemned or accepted outright.

Galileo wanted his letter to be widely circulated in Rome, and Dini initially agreed to show it to Bellarmine but soon thought better of it. Ciampoli also felt that it would be unwise to try to test the strength of the enemy's fortifications when no war had been declared. Bellarmine and Barberini had called for restraint, but instead of playing the dove Galileo declared himself a hawk. He would have done well to heed his friends' words of caution, but he was not a man to avoid a fight, especially when he believed he could win. In April 1615, he sent Castelli the long-delayed revised version of his letter as the archbishop had requested. Castelli read it to the archbishop and some canons, as he reported on 9 April 1615:

The Archbishop praised the letter in a stiff and formal way, I mean with a few dry words. The others liked the style, the elegance, the subtlety, and above all the modesty and reverence with which you deal with the Bible. I believe that the Archbishop, when he saw that a friar [Foscarini], who is also a theologian, published a defence of this opinion with a solemn display of crucifixes and saints was more impressed by this than by the arguments. He would not have believed it possible. But enough, he no longer declares that these things are foolish, and he begins to say that Copernicus was truly a great man and a brilliant mind.

CARDINAL BELLARMINE'S VIEWPOINT

The "crucifixes and saints" that Castelli mentions were displayed on the title page of Foscarini's book. They may have swayed the archbishop of Pisa but they left Cardinal Bellarmine unmoved. Instead of admiring the artwork he read the text carefully. What is even more impressive, he took time off from a very busy schedule to write, in his own hand, a thoughtful and considerate reply. His letter of 12 April 1615 to Foscarini is one of the most important documents in the debate over Copernicanism and Scripture, and it shows that Bellarmine was fully apprised of the difficulties. He begins, courteously, by saying that Foscarini and Galileo "are prudent to content themselves with speaking only hypothetically, as I have always believed Copernicus did." Bellarmine thought that Copernicus had put forward his system as a calculating device to determine more accurately the position of the planets. That was fine; what he objected to was a real-life scenario for which there was no proof. The Council of Trent, Bellarmine took pains to point out, objected to an interpretation of Scripture that was contrary to the consensus of the Fathers, all of whom took the passage about the Sun's motion literally:

> The words, *the Sun also rises and the Sun goes down and hastens to his place where he arose, etc,* were those of Salomon, who not only spoke by divine inspiration but was a man wise above all others and most learned in the

human sciences and in the knowledge of all created things. His wisdom was from God, and it is not likely that he would affirm something that went against some truth that was already demonstrated, or likely to be. Now if you tell me that Solomon spoke only according to appearances, and that it seems to us that the Sun goes around when actually it is the Earth that moves, as it seems to one on a ship that the shore moves away from the ship, I shall answer that though it may appear to a voyager as if the shore were receding from the vessel on which he stands rather than the vessel from the shore, yet he knows this to be an illusion and is able to correct it because he sees clearly that it is the ship and not the shore that is in movement. But as to the Sun and the Earth, a wise man has no need to correct his judgement, for his experience tells him plainly that the Earth is standing still and that his eyes are not deceived when they report that the Sun, the Moon and the stars are in motion.

\

Bellarmine did not consider whether the statements about the motion of the Sun were just an unexamined assumption but immediately expressed his own theological conviction that there can be no errors in the Bible. For him it is no answer to say that the motion of the Earth is not a matter of faith because what is at stake is not the subject matter but the veracity of its source, namely the Holy spirit. It is just as heretical to deny that Abraham had 2 sons and Jacob 12 as to say that Christ was not born of a virgin. Furthermore, Bellarmine stressed the logical point that although Copernicanism might work as an astronomical system, this did not mean that it was physically true. In case of doubt it would not be reasonable to ask the Church to dismiss the common interpretation of Scripture. If a proof of the motion of the Earth were available, then we would want to carefully examine the scriptural passages that seem contrary and "admit that we do not understand them rather than say that something that has been proved is false." But he had, as yet, seen no such proof.

Lest we misunderstand the historical situation, we must bear in mind that the Galileo whom we celebrate as the father of the scientific revolution was not the man his contemporaries knew. He had not published the works on mechanics for which he later became famous, and he was nearing fifty without having written the *System of the World* that he had advertised as early as 1610. His reputation rested on his telescopic discoveries, admittedly brilliant but due in large part to the availability of good lenses in the Venetian Republic. He had seen new things sooner and perhaps a little better than others, but this was due to an optical tube rather than his mastery of optics, about which he knew little. He was undoubtedly a versatile writer and an entertaining speaker, but professionals considered him a gifted amateur when it came to philosophy. There was no indication that he was a particularly good teacher, and he never lectured at the University of Pisa, where his colleagues complained that he was overpaid.

Galileo was considered clever at the court of the grand duke and he had friends in high places, but not everyone recognized him as a superstar. Furthermore, he had no training whatsoever in theology. He had been asked, very politely, to prove that the Earth really moved before expecting everyone to reinterpret the Scriptures. Instead of making a gesture to comply, he had become increasingly annoyed at what seemed to him the pig-headedness of the academic world. Galileo was getting restive and felt that he had to hit back, though his health was worse than ever. In May 1615 he confided to Dini:

> As far as I am concerned, any discussion of Sacred Scripture might have lain dormant forever; no astronomer or scientist who remained within proper bounds has ever got into such things. Yet while I follow the teachings of a book [Copernicus's] accepted by the Church, there come out against me philosophers quite ignorant of such matters who tell me that they contain propositions contrary to the Faith. So far as possible, I should like to show them that they are mistaken, but my mouth is shut and I am ordered not to go into the Scriptures. This amounts to saying that Copernicus' book, accepted by the Church, contains heresies and may be preached against by anyone who pleases, while it is forbidden

for anyone to get into the controversy and show that it is not contrary
to Scripture.

Galileo describes the philosophers he is supposed to convince as too
stupid to understand what astronomy is all about, but he says that he
would not despair if he could use his tongue instead of his pen. This is
why he has to go to Rome. In his mind this was the only honorable
course, and he genuinely believed that it was also in the best interest of
the Church. Bellarmine and Maffeo Barberini believed that Copernicus
had proposed his theory as pure speculation. But they were wrong, as
Galileo knew. To defend Copernicus on such grounds would be a paltry
evasion.

THE CORRECT INTERPRETATION OF SCRIPTURE

Galileo completed his revision of the *Letter to Castelli,* which became
known to posterity as the *Letter to the Grand Duchess Christina of Lorraine,*
his most brilliant treatise on how scriptural texts should be used in matters
of science. In that work, he considers what the Council of Trent said about
the consensus of the Fathers, but he does not see this as an obstacle. A
proposition that was understood in the same way by all the Fathers is not
binding unless it was actually examined and discussed. In others words,
unexamined ideas, however common, have no doctrinal status. The
motion of the Earth is a case in point. It was never discussed adequately
and, in any case, the Council of Trent was concerned with matters of faith
and morals, not natural science.

Galileo agreed with the theologians that everything in the Bible is
inspired. He also held that two truths cannot contradict each other: There
can be no fudging the issue by claiming that something can be true in
philosophy but false in theology. But here is the rub: Bellarmine and
Maffeo Barberini considered that the question of truth did not arise in the
case of astronomical models because they thought they were just tools
for calculation. Theologians expected astronomers to remain within the

confines of this *instrumentalist* interpretation of scientific knowledge, which Galileo refused to do. He believed that the Earth *really* moved.

The fact that the Bible contains metaphorical language gave Galileo his entry: Descriptions of God as walking, talking, and using his hands were used by the sacred writers in order to be understood by simple and unlettered common people. Scripture clearly accommodates itself to human limitations and speaks a language that ordinary folk can grasp. This is why it refers to astronomical events in everyday terms and avoids technical discussion.

Galileo could have rested his case here, but he wanted more. He was convinced of his ability to persuade any open-minded person that Copernicanism was a solid theory "of which we have," he wrote, "or firmly believe we could have, undoubted certainty, through experience, long observations and conclusive demonstrations." Were it merely a conjecture that contained something contrary to Scripture, then it should "be reckoned undoubtedly false and shown to be so by every possible means." Had Galileo been able to demonstrate the truth of Copernicanism, all would have been well, but he did not have and was never to have such proof.

What Galileo proposed was not only damaging to his own position but seriously misconceived. Science progresses by conjectures that are refuted but even more so by conjectures that are confirmed, and theologians were right to be cautious about ideas that lay outside their domain of expertise. The sensible thing to do is often to "Wait and see," as Cardinals Bellarmine and Barberini preached. We cannot dismiss, however, a legitimate concern that is often overlooked: If science is always to take precedence, might Scripture not be left undefended against wild and subversive ideas put forward in the name of science? The structure of the created universe is something fundamental to the Christian faith in an omnipotent and benevolent creator. If science cannot be derived from Scripture but only from reason and observation, it has nonetheless to be compatible with Scripture rightly understood. If necessary, those passages in Scripture that allude to natural things should be reinterpreted to fit with what is known through science. But the case for a particular scientific theory has to be made and, in the case of Copernicanism, Galileo never had a proof positive that it was true.

A BUSINESS TRIP

Galileo's Roman friends were confident that he would see the point and exercise some restraint, and, on 16 May 1615, Dini suggested that he come to Rome as soon as possible to "be welcomed by everybody because I am told that many Jesuits secretly share your position although they remain silent." In June, Cesi expressed the hope that Foscarini's letter would create a favorable climate, especially when the revised edition, which he expected anytime, came out. Meanwhile, Galileo would do well to speak *hypothetically,* and not say that heliocentrism was physically true.

Galileo completed his *Letter to the Grand Duchess Cristina* and resolved that Rome had to be faced and conquered, and he convinced the secretary of state that the trip was necessary. On 28 November 1615, Grand Duke Cosimo wrote to the Tuscan ambassador in Rome, Piero Guicciardini, to say that Galileo had requested leave to go to Rome "to defend himself against the accusations of his rivals," and that he had gladly given his assent. Galileo was to be provided with two rooms at the Villa Medici because "he needed peace and quiet on account of his poor health," and the ambassador was to help him in every way possible. On the same day, Curzio Picchena, the secretary of state, wrote to Annibale Primi, the administrator of the Villa Medici, spelling out that he was to give Galileo two of his best rooms and provide "full board for himself, a secretary, a valet, and a small mule."

The Tuscan ambassador was less than enthusiastic about Galileo's impending arrival. After acknowledging receipt of the grand duke's instructions, he could not refrain from adding in his letter of 5 December 1615:

> I do not know whether he has changed his theories or his disposition,
> but this I know: certain friars of St. Dominic, who play a major role in

the Holy Office, and others are ill disposed toward him. This is no place to come and argue about the Moon and, especially in these times, arrive with new ideas.

The grand duke wrote letters of recommendation for Galileo to Cardinal Francesco Maria del Monte, and Cardinal Scipione Borghese, the nephew of the pope, and he contacted his two cousins, Paolo Giordano Orsini and his brother Alessandro, who were influential in Rome. Paolo Giordano Orsini had sided with Castelli at the famous luncheon in Pisa when the Grand Duchess Christina has asked about science and Scripture. Alessandro Orsini, who was only 22, was a rising star, and he was created cardinal in December 1615, a few days after Galileo's arrival in Rome.

Galileo was in the dark about what had happened to his *Letter to Castelli*. He was justifiably annoyed at the secret proceedings of the Tribunal of the Inquisition, but there is one aspect that he could appreciate: confidentiality. When a complaint was deposed before the Holy Office, an investigation was initiated but the name of the accused was not publicly divulged. It was only after the matter had been judged serious enough to warrant opening proceedings against the incriminated person that the affair became known. For instance, Cesi, Dini, and Ciampoli were not told how the letter that Foscarini had published was going to be handled. When Foscarini left Rome early in May 1615, Cesi could still write to Galileo that he had not been denounced and had even befriended Cardinal Giovanni Garzia Millini, the vicar general of Rome and a prominent member of the Holy Office. Cesi was too sanguine as events were to show.

REPORTING BACK HOME

Galileo arrived in Rome on 10 December 1615, and, as on his second trip, immediately rushed out to call on the persons for whom he had letters of recommendation. He also made it his duty to keep the Tuscan court informed. Between 12 December 1615 and 20 February 1616, he wrote no less than ten letters to Curzio Picchena, and Picchena sent nine to him. This is practically one a week. In the first letter, written two days after his arrival, Galileo was anxious to let Picchena know that everyone he had seen was delighted at his coming and understood that he wanted to clear his good name against detractors and slanderers. In his correspondence he often mentions his determination to protect his *reputation*. What did he mean by this word? From his letters, it is clear that he was intent on defending himself from the insinuation that he was a masked heretic when he believed himself to be a good Catholic and an obedient son of the Church. This was not merely a political move. It expressed the ideal of a Christian scientist that had matured in his mind and that he saw himself as embodying. He may have been arrogant and naive; he was not being dishonest.

From his next letter, dated 26 December 1615, we learn that Galileo was continuing his long round of visits to cardinals and other dignitaries. He complained that he found this tiring, but he was determined to soldier on even if the task might take months and months. How Galileo was seen by a man about town can be gathered from the frequent letters that Monsignor Antonio Querengo sent to his patron Cardinal Alessandro d'Este in Modena. On 30 December 1615 he reported that Galileo was giving virtuoso displays of his formidable argumentative powers at meetings, usually held in the home of Virginio Cesarini, who was considered one of the brightest young poets in Rome and whose mother was an Orsini. But persuading friends at social gatherings was a far cry from convincing the Holy Office!

Galileo loudly proclaimed that he had come to save his honor. But if he was as white as snow, why bother to travel all the way to Rome? Rumors began to fly. "Perhaps he is not here on his own volition," someone said to Monsignor Querengo. When Cardinal Alessandro d'Este heard this he passed it on to Florence, where Curzio Picchena became worried and wrote to Galileo to say that he was "most anxious to have news" about the outcome of his affairs. On 8 January 1616, Galileo penned a long letter in which he lamented a dreadful rumor alleging that he had fallen into disgrace in the eyes of the grand duke and had been banished to the outskirts of Florence. Fortunately, everyone could now see that he was the honored guest of the grand duke at the Villa Medici. Nonetheless, he had come to realize that he needed at least as many days to justify himself as his enemies had had weeks and months to spread falsehoods about him. The next sentence reveals that Galileo was becoming nervous. Is it true, he asked, that the grand duke is about to order me back to Florence? He beseeched Picchena to assure him that this was not the case because he did not want to leave Rome without having seen his *reputation restored*. By return of post, Picchena hastened to inform him that the rumor was baseless. He had read his letter to their Highnesses, who wanted him to know that he could stay in Rome as long as he wanted.

Greatly comforted, Galileo took up the cudgels as we know from yet another letter of Monsignor Querengo to Cardinal d'Este, dated 20 January 1616:

> You would be delighted to hear Galileo argue, as he often does, in the midst of some fifteen or twenty persons who attack him vigorously, now in one house, now in another. But he is so well buttressed that he laughs them off; and although the novelty of his opinion leaves people unpersuaded, yet he shows that most of the arguments, with which his opponents try to overthrow him, are spurious. Monday in particular, in the house of Federico Ghisilieri, he performed marvellous feats. What I liked most was that, before answering objections, he improved on them and added even better ones, so that, when he demolished them, his opponents looked all the more ridiculous.

Galileo's eloquence and his brilliant repartee made for great sport in the literary circles to which he was repeatedly invited, but the applause that he won had little to do with a genuine understanding of the nature of the argument. Most people enjoyed the liveliness of the discussion but treated the whole matter as a suitable topic for a debating society rather than a serious scientific enquiry. The young Cardinal Alessandro Orsini, who was a genuine admirer of Galileo, recognized the danger and asked Galileo to put his best argument in writing, namely his claim that the tides imply a moving Earth. With remarkable speed, Galileo wrote down in a few days in January his *Discourse on the Tides,* which later became the Fourth Day of the *Dialogue on the Two Chief World Systems.* The water of the oceans, wrote Galileo, are contained inside a moving vessel that turns on its axis once a day and goes around the Sun once a year. The combination of these two motions, which are periodically in the same or in the opposite direction, causes the flow and ebb of the water. The time and magnitude of the tides vary in different locations because of numerous local factors, such as the length and depth of the body of water (this is why small lakes lack tides), and the way it is oriented (the Mediterranean that runs east-west experiences stronger tides that the Red Sea, which is north-south). The theory is ingenious and Galileo argued for it very skilfully, but it happens to be wrong.

The reception that Galileo met with in social gatherings was flattering, but it was difficult for him to reach and speak plainly to the ecclesiastical authorities he wanted so much to convince. On 23 January 1616, he gave Curzio Picchena an account of what he had to cope with:

> My business is far more difficult and takes much longer, owing to outward circumstances, than the nature of it would require, because I cannot speak openly with those persons with whom I have to negotiate, partly to avoid causing a prejudice to any of my friends, partly because they cannot communicate anything to me without running the risk of grave censure. And so I am compelled, with much pain and caution, to seek out third persons who, without even knowing my purpose, may serve as mediators with the principals, so that I can set forth, incidentally as it were, and at their request, the particulars of my case. I have also to set down some points in writing, and to arrange that they should come privately into the hands of those I want to read them, for I find in many quarters that people are more ready to yield to dead writing than to live speech, for the former allows them to agree or dissent without blushing

and, finally, to yield to the arguments since in such discussions we have no witnesses but ourselves. This is not done so easily when we have to change our mind in public.

Galileo must have met with some success for a week later, on 30 January, he was so buoyed up that he wrote to Picchena that "his reputation was growing every day" and that his enemies were in full disarray. Why even Caccini, who had stirred up all the trouble in the first place, had asked if he could come and see him. In the next letter of 6 February, he describes the interview but in guarded language:

> The very person who, from the pulpit over there and then here in some other places, first spoke and plotted against me, stayed with me for over four hours. In the first half-hour, when we were alone, he tried with a great show of submission to make excuses for what had happened over there and offered to make all the amends I could wish.

Galileo did not take Caccini's apologies at face value, but the friar would not have been so abject if he had not been told that Galileo had powerful friends and was in no danger of being personally reprimanded. This left the issue of heliocentrism unresolved, and placed Galileo in something of a quandary. "I have terminated the business as far as my own person is concerned," he wrote in the same letter to Picchena,

> and I could go back home any time, but at issue is a certain doctrine and opinion not unknown to Your Excellency which no longer concerns my person but all those, who in the last eighty years, have approved it in private or public, in sermons, or in published or unpublished works . . . I owe it to my conscience as a devout Catholic, to provide what help I can from the knowledge I derive from the science that I profess.

Galileo pinned his hope on the young Cardinal Alessandro Orsini, who was willing to become his spokesman and even speak to the pope.

The grand duke was asked to signify his approval with a letter that was promptly despatched and reached Orsini on 20 February. By the twenty-fourth he had had a word with the pope, but, as we shall see, it was too little, too late.

THE AXE FALLS

The next thing Galileo heard was that he was being summoned to see Cardinal Bellarmine on the twenty-sixth. When he presented himself, he was ordered not to argue in favor of Copernicanism. This was a bolt out of the blue for Galileo, but it was the logical outcome of a quick succession of events that we must now consider.

The grand duke had told Cardinal Orsini to consider Galileo's affairs as his very own, but it was neither the cardinal nor Galileo who notified him about the melancholy outcome of Galileo's campaign in favor of Copernicanism. The bad news arrived in the form of a letter from the Tuscan ambassador, written on March 4:

> Galileo has relied more on his own counsel than on that of his friends. Cardinal del Monte and myself, and also several Cardinals from the Holy Office, tried to persuade him to be quiet and not to go on irritating the issue. If he wanted to hold this Copernican opinion, he was told, let him hold it quietly and not spend so much effort in trying to have others share it. Everyone feared that his coming here might be prejudicial and dangerous and that, instead of justifying himself and triumphing over his enemies, he could end up with an affront. As he felt people were not very warm about what he intended, he pestered and wearied several cardinals, then threw himself on the favor of Cardinal Orsini and extracted to that purpose a warm recommendation from Your Highness. Last Wednesday in Consistory, the Cardinal, I do not know with what circumspection and prudence, spoke to the Pope on behalf of Galileo. The Pope told him it would be well if he persuaded him to give up that opinion. When Orsini replied, and insisted, the Pope cut him

short and told him he would refer the business to the Cardinals of the Holy Office. As soon as Orsini had left, His Holiness summoned Bellarmine and, after brief discussion, they decided that Galileo's opinion was erroneous and heretical. The day before yesterday, as I hear, they had a Congregation on the matter to have it declared such. Copernicus, and the other authors who wrote on this, will be amended and corrected, or prohibited. I believe that Galileo is not going to suffer personally because, being prudent, he will feel and desire as Holy Church does.

The ambassador went on to lament that Galileo was too passionately involved in what he said and unable to see that the pope was not interested in intellectual fireworks. Paul V was a practical man and was said to prefer new jobs for workmen to new ideas from scholars. The ambassador got it almost—but not quite—right, as we now know from documents that can be consulted in the archives of the Holy Office, and from which we will draw.

On Thursday, 19 February, the Holy Office decided to submit to a panel of 11 experts the following propositions: "The Sun is the center of the world and hence immovable of local motion. The Earth is not the center of the world, nor immovable but moves according to the whole of itself, also with a diurnal motion."

The awkward English reflects the original Italian that was derived from Caccini's delation. When the consultants met on Wednesday, 24 February they divided the proposition into two separate Latin ones: the first for the Sun and the second for the Earth. They unanimously agreed that they deserved the following "qualifications" or censure notes. The first proposition, which had been slightly altered to read, "The Sun is the center of the world and completely immovable of local motion," was declared "foolish and absurd in philosophy, and formally heretical, inasmuch as it expressly contradicts the doctrine of the Holy Scripture in many passages, both in their literal meaning and according to the general interpretation of the Fathers and Doctors." The second proposition, which affirmed that the Earth moves, was declared "to receive the same censure in philosophy and, as regards theological truth, to be at least erroneous in faith."

The experts could only advise, but all decisions rested with the pope and the cardinal inquisitors or with just the pope. The very next day, on Thursday, 25 February Cardinal Millini notified the commissioner and the assessor of the Holy Office that the recommendation of the experts had been communicated to the pope, who decided on the following course of action: Bellarmine was to summon Galileo and admonish him to abandon Copernicanism. If he refused, the commissioner of the Holy Office was to formally order him, in the presence of a notary, not to teach, defend, or even discuss it. Should he refuse, he was to be incarcerated. It is interesting to note that recommendation of censure was minuted but *never published.* This had important legal consequences since Canon law explicitly states that an unpublished decision does not have a binding character. In other words, the censure never acquired juridical status.

The pope had foreseen three possible scenarios. First, Galileo assents without demurring, and that is the end of the procedure. Second, he tries to vindicate himself or defend Copernicanism; there is a change of scene, and Commissioner Seghizzi enters with witnesses and formally forbids Galileo to maintain heliocentrism. Third, Galileo persists in his refusal, and the curtain falls as he is led offstage. What was to happen if he were to go to prison is not stated, but we can assume that he would have been sent to trial. Fortunately, things did not go that far.

FURTHER EVIDENCE

There is a short document in the archives of the Holy Office that summarizes what actually took place: "On the 26th His Excellency Cardinal Bellarmine warned Galileo of the error of the aforesaid opinion etc. and afterwards the precept was enjoined on him by the Father Commissioner as above, etc." The use of *etc* is common in internal documents that refer to customary procedures and has no special significance. Here *etc.* means something like "as was ordered" in the first instance, and "as is usually done" in the second. It would seem, therefore, that the first two scenarios were enacted, although the document does not say that Galileo refused to comply.

A second document in the archives states that at a meeting of the Holy Office on Thursday, 3 March 1616, which was attended by the pope and seven cardinals, Cardinal Bellarmine reported that, as instructed by the Holy Office, he admonished Galileo to abandon the opinion, which he had held until then, that the Sun is at rest and the Earth in motion, and Galileo accepted. This document does not provide new information, but there exists a third document that is more detailed and is more frequently cited because it surfaced at Galileo's trial in 1633. It is now considered authentic, but some nineteenth-century historians thought it was a forgery because it is neither notarized nor signed, as is normally the case. According to this document, Galileo was admonished by Bellarmine in the cardinal's residence in the presence of Commissioner Shegizzi, some members of his staff, and two guests, who had come to see the cardinal. Galileo was told by Cardinal Bellarmine to abandon the error of Copernicanism,

> and immediately thereafter, before me and before witnesses, the Cardinal being still present, the said Galileo was by the said Commissioner commanded and enjoined, in the name of His Holiness the Pope and the whole Congregation of the Holy Office, to relinquish altogether the said opinion that the Sun is the center of the world and at rest and that the Earth moves; nor henceforth to hold, teach, or defend it in any way verbally or in writing. Otherwise proceedings would be taken against him by the Holy Office. The said Galileo acquiesced in this ruling and promised to obey.

This minute was probably penned by some zealous official (who speaks in the first person) who wanted to record that the Commissioner had actually stepped in to give Galileo a strict injunction to relinquish Copernicanism altogether. Bellarmine may have felt that his own admonition had been sufficient, and the minute was left unsigned in the dossier. When it was found in 1633, it put Galileo in the uncomfortable position of having apparently acquiesced, in the wording of the minute, not to hold, teach, or defend Copernicanism *in any way, verbally or in writing.* To break such a promise would be a much more serious offence than would a contravention of the warning not to go beyond using Copernicanism "as a convenient hypothesis" to facilitate computations. This is how Galileo later remembered having been instructed.

COPERNICUS ON THE INDEX

We now move from the Holy Office to the Congregation of the Index, where five Cardinals, including Maffeo Barberini, met in Bellarmine's office on Tuesday, 1 March 1616. After discussion, they recommended that the works they had been asked to judge be censured, but not exactly in the terms that had been proposed by the experts. Someone must have objected to the qualification *heretical,* which was dropped. Two days later at the meeting of the Holy Office, the new resolution was conveyed to the pope, as procedure required, and the pope ordered that it be published. This was done in a decree released by the Congregation of the Index on Saturday, 5 March. The document began by banning five books on topics unrelated to astronomy and went on as follows:

> It has also come to the knowledge of the said Congregation that the Pythagorean doctrine of the motion of the Earth and the immobility of the Sun, which is false and altogether opposed to Holy Scripture is also taught by Nicolaus Copernicus in his *De Revolutionibus Orbium Coelestium,* and Diego de Zuñiga in his *Commentary on Job,* and is now being spread abroad and accepted by many. This can be seen from a certain letter of a Carmelite Father, entitled *Letter of Father Paolo Foscarini, Carmelite, on the Opinion of the Pythagoreans and of Copernicus Regarding the Motion of the Earth, and the Stability of the Sun, and on the New Pythagorean System of the World.* Naples: Printed by Lazzaro Scorrigio, 1615. In this

letter the said Father tries to show that the aforesaid doctrine of the immobility of the Sun in the center of the world and of the Earth's motion is true and not opposed to Holy Scripture. Therefore, in order that this opinion may not insinuate itself any further to the prejudice of Catholic truth, it has been decided that the said Nicolaus Copernicus' *De Revolutionibus Orbium*, and Diego de Zuñiga, *On Job*, be suspended until corrected. The book of the Carmelite Father, Paolo Antonio Foscarini, is altogether prohibited and condemned, and all other works in which the same is taught are likewise prohibited, and the present Decree prohibits, condemns, and suspends them all respectively.

This decree is remarkable in a number of ways. First, it is the only document to have been published, and hence to have legal status. Second, Galileo is not mentioned. Third, Copernicus's *De Revolutionibus* is not banned outright but taken out of circulation until corrections are made. Fourth, although the panel of experts had called the immobility of the Sun "formally heretical," the decree merely states that the doctrine is "false and contrary to Holy Scripture." This point is significant. The Congregation of the Index could have been expected to endorse the censure as it had been approved by the Holy Office. The fact that it did not means that someone objected at the meeting of 3 March 1616. Indeed, not one but two cardinals did, as we know from three sources. The first is an entry in the diary of Giovanfrancesco Buonamici, who happened to be in Rome many years later when Galileo was tried in 1633. He made enquiries about the background of the affair and, on 2 May 1633, wrote as follows: "In the time of Paul V this opinion was opposed as erroneous and contrary to many passages of Sacred Scripture; therefore, Paul V was of the opinion to declare it contrary to the Faith; but on account of the opposition of the Cardinals Bonifazio Caetano and Maffeo Barberini, now Urban VIII, the Pope was stopped right at the beginning."

The second source is a letter of Castelli to Galileo of 16 March 1630 in which he says that he heard from Prince Cesi that Tommaso Campanella recently informed Urban VIII that he had been on the verge of converting some German Protestants but that they backed away because of the decree banning Copernicus. The pope winced, and reportedly answered, "This was never our intention, and if it had been left to us, that Decree would not have been made." The third source is a conversation that Galileo had with Cardinal Frederick Zollern when he went on his fourth trip to Rome in 1624:

> Zollern left yesterday for Germany, and he told me that he had spoken with His Holiness about Copernicus, and mentioned that the heretics are all of this opinion and hold it as most certain, and that we should therefore proceed very circumspectly in coming to any determination. His Holiness replied that the Holy Church had not condemned it and was not about to condemn it as heretical, but only as temerarious, but that it was not to be feared that it would ever be demonstrated as necessarily true.

Cardinal Bonifazio Caetani, who was mentioned by Buonamici along with Cardinal Maffeo Barberini, was a member of the Congregation of the Index but not of the Holy Office. He was interested in astronomy and astrology and, even before Copernicus's *De Revolutionibus* was discussed by his congregation, he had written to Tommaso Campanella in Naples to ask him what he thought about Copernicus and Galileo. Campanella was never to become a Copernican, but he wanted to preserve the intellectual freedom of Catholic scientists, and he sent the cardinal a lengthy reply at the end of February or early in March. We do not know whether Cardinal Caetani received this letter before the Decree of 1616, but the fact that he wanted to be informed speaks in favor of his honesty. Campanella's letter was published in Germany in 1622 as the *Apologia pro Galileo* and was promptly added to the list of proscribed books by the Congregation of the Index. Caetani did not live to see this happen but, before his death in June 1617, he had agreed to make the revisions that were required before Copernicus's *De Revolutionibus* could be reissued. This task was carried out by his assistant, Francesco Ingoli, who presented a list of corrections at a meeting of the Congregation of the Index on 2 April 1618. To play it safe, the Cardinals submitted the corrections to the Jesuit mathematicians of the Roman College. They agreed with them, and Ingoli's proposals were approved by the Congregation of the Index on 3 July. Nonetheless, matters dragged on for another two years, and it was only on 1 May 1620 that the Congregation of the Index decided that the *De Revolutionibus*, described as a work "in which many useful things are found," could be printed with Ingoli's corrections. These amounted to very little beyond crossing out or amending the rare passages where the motion of the Earth was clearly acknowledged. But no publisher seemed interested, and a revised edition never appeared. Libraries with copies of the original work were expected to pen in the corrections. This was done for about half the copies in Italy. Elsewhere in Europe, virtually no one bothered.

GALILEO'S DOUBLE GAME

Transparency is a great virtue. Things that are done in the open are less likely to be distorted or used in ways that were not intended. But privacy is also an important aspect of social life, and the most liberal citizen will value confidentiality when his purse or his life is at stake. Galileo had not been asked to defend himself before the Tribunal of the Inquisition, and the admonition that he received from Cardinal Bellarmine took him by complete surprise. Yet once the warning had been administered he could rely on the discretion of those who had ordered or communicated it. If he did not tell anyone, it would never be bruited. He chose, wisely, to keep mum. On 6 March, he wrote to Curzio Picchena, the secretary of state, to say that he had not written the week before *because nothing had happened.* As we know, one of the most important events in his life had taken place: He had been admonished by Cardinal Bellarmine to abandon Copernicanism! But this was a personal matter and Galileo prayed to heaven that it would stay so. The Decree of March 5 did not mention him, and if all went well this might be interpreted as a sign that no rebuff had been intended as far as he was concerned. Yet Romans could put two and two together: Galileo had been campaigning vigorously for Copernicanism, which had now been officially decried as false and contrary to Scripture. Even Monsignor Querengo joked about it in a letter to Cardinal d'Este,

> Galileo's arguments have vanished into alchemical smoke, for the Holy Office has declared that to maintain this opinion is to dissent manifestly from the infallible dogmas of the Church. We now know that, instead of imagining that we are spinning in outer space, we are at rest at our proper place, and do not have to fly off with the Earth like so many ants crawling around a balloon.

The puff of smoke, the ants, and the balloon are quite ingenious, but Querengo knew better than to speak of the immobility of the Earth as an infallible dogma. The decree that proscribed Copernicus and other works that taught heliocentrism did not involve the infallibility of the Church, the pope or anyone else. It was, in the eyes of those who prepared and approved it, a prudential decision to remove from public circulation works that might lead unwary readers to misunderstand the nature of science and the role of Scripture. The Counter Reformation did not encourage discussion or debates about doctrinal matters. The theological pendulum that the reformers had pushed too far in one direction was now made to swing to the other extreme, but even the most conservative cardinals would not have considered a decree of the Congregation of the Index as offering a definitive statement of the Catholic faith.

So it is understandable that in his letter to Curzio Picchena of 6 March, Galileo should not have alluded in any way to the admonition he had received on 26 February. He could not, however, avoid mentioning the decree of the Congregation of the Index that had come out the day before. He provided, in the mildest terms possible, a summary of its contents, and then went on to say,

As one can see from the very nature of the business, I have no interest whatsoever in it, nor would I have got involved if, as I said, my enemies had not dragged me into it. What I have done can be seen from my writings which I keep in order to be able to silence malicious gossip at any time, for I can show that my behavior in this affair has been such that a saint would not have handled it either with greater reverence or with greater zeal towards the Holy Church. My enemies have perhaps not done as much, since they have not refrained from every machination, calumny and diabolic suggestion, as their Most Serene Highnesses and also Your Lordship will hear at length in due course.

Galileo had toyed with the idea of going to Naples. This was now out of the question, and there was always the convenient reason that "the weather and the roads are just awful," as he wrote to Picchena in the same letter. But he did not rush back to Florence. Grand Duke Cosimo, a few days before the decision of the Holy Office, and ignorant of what was going to happen, had written to ask Galileo to await the arrival of his brother, Cardinal Carlo de' Medici, so that he might accompany him when he visited the pope and be present at dinner parties in order to liven up the conversation. Had the grand duke waited a few days before forwarding these instructions, he might have suppressed them altogether after Ambassador Guicciardini had written from Rome to express his fear that Galileo might prove more of an embarrassment than a help.

While awaiting the arrival of Cardinal Carlo de' Medici, Galileo was not idle but pulled strings to arrange an audience with Pope Paul V on 11 March. The next day he proudly reported to Curzio Picchena that he had been allowed to accompany the pope for a stroll for some three-quarters of an hour, during which he complained of "the malice of his persecutors." The pope

answered that he was well aware of my uprightness and sincerity and, when I showed signs of being still somewhat anxious about the future because of the fear of being pursued with implacable hate by my enemies, he cheered me up and said that I could put all care away because I was held in such esteem by himself and the whole Congregation that they would not lightly lend their ears to calumnious reports, and that I could feel safe as long as he was alive. Before I left he assured me several times that he bore me the greatest goodwill and was ready to show his affection and favor towards me at all times.

By return of post, on 20 March 1616, Curzio Picchena graciously but firmly told Galileo that the grand duke wanted him to calm down, cease making an issue of his views, and return to Florence. Battered but undaunted, Galileo equivocated and replied to Picchena that he felt he had to stay to welcome Cardinal Carlo de' Medici as the grand duke had ordered him. Meanwhile rumors were flying all over Italy that he had been summoned to Rome and charged with heresy. On 20 April, Castelli wrote from Pisa to report that it was said that he had secretly abjured his errors before Cardinal Bellarmine. Three days later, his friend Giovanfrancesco Sagredo confirmed that the same gossip had rumbled through Venice.

Only one course was open to Galileo. He had to appeal to Cardinal Bellarmine himself. He was given a friendly reception, and the cardinal even provided him with a certificate that exonerated him completely:

> We, Robert Cardinal Bellarmine, having heard that it is calumniously reported that Signor Galileo Galilei has in our hand abjured and has also been punished with salutary penance, and being requested to state the truth as to this, declare that the said Galileo has not abjured, either in our hand, or the hand of any other person here in Rome, or anywhere else, so far as we know, any opinion or doctrine held by him. Neither has any salutary penance been imposed on him; but that only the declaration made by the Holy Father and published by the Sacred Congregation of the Index was notified to him, which says that the doctrine attributed to Copernicus, that the Earth moves around the Sun and that the Sun is stationary in the center of the world and does not

move from east to west, is contrary to the Holy Scriptures, and therefore cannot be defended or held. In witness whereof we have written and subscribed the present document with our own hand this twenty-sixth day of May 1616.

With this certificate in his pocket, Galileo felt that he could continue to publicly consider heliocentrism as a convenient, albeit arbitrary, mathematical tool and, in the secret of his heart, hope that the decree might one day be revoked.

A NEW STRATEGY

Galileo's resilience is admirable even if it was not always accompanied by tact and diplomacy. Within a couple of days of receiving the devastating admonition of 26 February 1616, he had taken steps to avoid the opening of a new front in the war between Scripture and Copernicanism. Our source is a letter that he wrote on 28 February to Carlo Muti, the nephew of Cardinal Tiberio Muti, in whose house Galileo had debated the nature of the moon with someone who claimed that if it resembled the Earth because it had mountains, then it should also have living creatures like those we find on Earth. The argument may appear innocuous, but it opened a Pandora's box: If human beings are found on the moon how can they descend from Adam? And if they do not, what about original sin and the significance of the Incarnation of Jesus Christ? It is in order to avoid having these questions raised that Galileo promptly put down his reply on paper. There can be no organic life on the moon because there is no water there. This he inferred from the absence of clouds, but even if it were granted that water occurs on the moon, Galileo points out that this could not be used as an argument that there is life there. The reason is that the variation in temperature is too great, since a lunar day or a lunar night lasts fifteen of our terrestrial days or nights. This means that the surface of the moon is scorched for 360 hours and subjected to incredibly low temperatures during the next 360 hours. Galileo did not have to say

more to feel confident that he had scalded or frozen a potentially dangerous implication of lunar mountains.

A MEDICI ENTERS ROME

Cardinal Carlo de' Medici had planned to reach Rome by Easter, which
fell on 2 April that year, but he arrived more than two weeks later. This
may have had something to do with the preparations for his arrival. The
entry of a Medici cardinal was the occasion of a lavish display, and
Romans, who were fond of such spectacles, were treated to a show that
was impressive, even by their exacting standards.

Galileo had been right not to miss this event, as he wrote to Curzio
Picchena on 23 April but there is no mention of his having been invited
to dine with the cardinal, and he changes subject abruptly to give the
secretary of state an account of his secret dealings with representatives of
the Spanish government. He had offered to sell them his tables of the
periods of Jupiter's satellites, which were, he claimed, accurate enough to
be used to determine longitude at sea. Work on these periods was to keep
Galileo busy for several years, but he never managed to convince the
Spaniards that his scheme was practical enough to be used by seamen.

Ambassador Guicciardini was anxious to see Galileo leave and asked
Annibale Primi, the administrator of the Villa Medici, to prepare the
accounts. When he saw them he almost went through the roof, as we can
gather from his indignant letter to Curzio Picchena of 13 May:

> Strange and scandalous were the goings on in the Garden [the Villa
> Medici] during Galileo's long sojourn in the company and under the
> administration of Annibale Primi, who has been fired by the Cardinal
> [Carlo de' Medici] . . . Annibale says that he had huge expenses. In any
> case, anyone can see that they led a riotous life.

The ambassador ardently hoped that the heat would chase Galileo
out of Rome and put an end to what he called, lapsing into vulgarity, "his

determination to castrate the friars" who opposed him. The message could not have been clearer and the Tuscan court recalled Galileo in a letter dated 23 May. But Galileo could still count on powerful friends, and, before leaving Rome on early in June, he was able to secure glowing testimonials from Cardinal Alessandro Orsini and Cardinal Francesco Maria del Monte.

ROMAN POSTSCRIPT

Galileo had just left Rome when Matteo Caccini, the brother of the Tommaso Caccini who had started all the trouble, wrote to another brother, Alessandro, in Pisa, to tell him that Tommaso was still in Rome and that his *reputation* had been *enhanced* by recent events. Matteo provided his own version of Tommaso's meeting with Galileo in February in which Galileo is said to have been unable to answer objections and to have lost his temper. The decree of the Congregation of the Index is described as directed against Galileo's system, which is *completely* opposed to Scripture, and Galileo himself is said to have formally recanted before the congregation. The Caccini family cannot be described as passionately interested in truth, but not all adversaries of heliocentrism were as petty or mean-spirited. At one of the staged evening disputes, Galileo had debated with Francesco Ingoli, a close collaborator of Cardinal Bonifazio Caetani. Afterwards, the two of them agreed to write down their respective positions. But no sooner had Ingoli done his half, than the Decree of 1616 obtruded, and Galileo was left without the means of writing his rejoinder. As we shall see, this will cast a pall over his relations with Ingoli, who will become a prominent figure in Rome.

CHAPTER FOUR

Roman Sunshine

FOURTH TRIP 23 APRIL–16 JUNE 1624

Galileo was in poor health after his return to Florence in June 1616, and he blamed the city air. He began looking for a house outside the city, and in April 1617 he was able to rent the Villa Bellosguardo on the south side of the Arno, a lovely location from which he enjoyed an unobstructed view of the heavens above and a beautiful panorama of Florence at his feet. Galileo had three children from his common-law wife, the Venetian Marina Gamba, and he placed his two daughters in the neighboring convent of San Matteo in Arcetri, which he could reach in three-quarters of an hour on foot or by mule, when he was well enough to make the trip. His eldest daughter, Virginia, who had taken the name of Sister Maria Celeste, was an intelligent and warm-hearted woman who became a great comfort to her father. The younger sister, Livia, Sister Arcangela in religion, broke down under the strain of convent life and became chronically depressed. His son, Vincenzio, was legitimated by the grand duke and educated at the University of Pisa.

NEW ACTORS ON THE STAGE

Since Galileo's return in 1616, things had changed in Florence and in Rome. In Tuscany, Grand Duke Cosimo, whose health had always been frail, had died on 28 February 1621 at the age of 30. His son and successor, Ferdinando II, was only ten, and his grandmother, the Grand Duchess Christina, and mother, the Archduchess Maria Maddalena, were named regents. When Ferdinando turned 13 in July 1623, he was gradually introduced to his granducal responsibilities but would only take power in his own name in 1628 at the age of 18. In Rome, both Pope Paul V, who had told Galileo that he was safe during his lifetime, and Cardinal Bellarmine had died in 1621, the same year as Cosimo II. The commissioner of the office, Seghizzi, had been appointed bishop of Lodi and had left Rome for his diocese. This meant that, by 1623, the three persons who had the best knowledge of Galileo's dealings with the Curia in 1616 were gone from the Vatican.

A new pope, Alessandro Ludovisi from Bologna, had succeeded Paul V on 9 February 1621, and had taken the name Gregory XV. He promoted two of Galileo's friends to influential positions: Giovanni Ciampoli, now 31 years old, was named secretary for Latin correspondence and, shortly thereafter, secretary for the correspondence with princes, a post that could be compared with that of a private secretary in the British system. Virginio Cesarini, at 28, was made secret chamberlain of the pope, a position of trust where the qualification of "secret" does not refer to the way the appointment was made but to the confidential nature of the assignments it entailed. Ciampoli and Cesarini were members of the Lyncean Academy, and both were fans of Galileo, as we can see from a passage in Ciampoli's letter to Galileo of 15 January 1622: "There is never a shortage of kings and great rulers, but someone like yourself is not to be found, not only in a whole province, but in a whole century." The prose may be inflated, but Ciampoli's feelings were genuine and on 27 May 1623, after an audience with the pope, he was happy to report that he had spent more than half an hour in praising Galileo to His Holiness. And referring to the events of 1616, he added: "If you had had here in those days the friends that you now have, it would perhaps not have been necessary to find ways of recalling, at least as pleasant fictions, those admirable ideas with which you have enlightened our age." Ciampoli will consistently try to create a favorable climate of reception for Galileo's ideas, and he will urge him to act each time he believed opportunity knocked. As we shall see, his timing was not always as good as his determination to serve his friend.

Gregory XV died on 8 July 1623. He had been elected by acclamation, but things did not go so smoothly for his successor. The cardinals were locked in the Vatican, where they voted twice a day, morning and afternoon. No one was allowed to vote for himself, and they were supposed to disguise their handwriting to maintain the secrecy of the election process. A two-thirds majority was required, and each time this number was not reached the scrutineers burned the slips of paper in a special stove with wet straw, which sent up black smoke above the Sigtine Chapel. The Roman summer was not only hot but infested with malaria, and six of the elderly cardinals died before the decisive vote on 6 August when 50 of the 55 ballots were cast for Maffeo Barberini. The cardinal chose Urban VIII as the name under which he wanted to be known, and this time the ballots were burnt with dry straw, to send up white smoke and release the pent-up enthusiasm of the crowd assembled in St. Peter's Square.

URBAN VIII

The news was received with even greater jubilation in the pope's native Florence. Galileo was overjoyed as he reread the pleasant exchanges of letters that he had had with Cardinal Barberini, who, as early as 1611, had called him a virtuous and pious man of great value whose longevity could only improve the lives of others. In 1620 the cardinal had sent him a Latin poem entitled *Adulatio Perniciosa (Dangerous Adulation)* in which he referred to Galileo's discovery of celestial novelties and used the sunspots as a metaphor for dark fears in the hearts of the mighty. The letter of transmittal was signed "as your brother," a gesture of unusual warmth that Galileo knew how to appreciate. He also understood that proper deference was expected of him and he ended his own letters to the cardinal with the suitable, "I am your humble servant, reverently kissing your hem and praying God that the greatest felicity shall be yours." Maffeo Barberini had a nephew, Francesco, of whom he was particularly fond, and when Galileo helped him obtain his doctorate at the University of Pisa the cardinal wrote from Rome on 24 June 1623 to express his appreciation, and even added a postscript in his own handwriting:

> I am much in your debt for your continuing goodwill towards myself and the members of my family, and I look forward to the opportunity of reciprocating. I assure you that you will find me more than ready to be of service in consideration of your great merit and the gratitude that I owe you.

Less than two months later Maffeo Barberini became Urban VIII and, on 2 October 1623, Francesco, then only 27, was created cardinal and became his right hand. Francesco was to remain loyal to Galileo, and it is noteworthy that ten years later when Galileo was sentenced, he did not sign his condemnation with the other cardinal inquisitors.

Galileo would have liked to go to Rome, but he came down with a fever in August 1623 and had to be taken to the home of his late sister, where he was nursed by his widowed brother-in-law and his nephew. In any case, Pope Urban VIII was not granting audiences. At 55, he normally cut a youthful, almost military figure, but like several other cardinals he came out of the conclave exhausted and took several weeks to recuperate. Nonetheless he found time to promote Galileo's friends at the Curia: Virginio Cesarini became Lord Chamberlain, and Giovanni Ciampoli Secret Chamberlain.

Sister Maria Celeste assumed that her father had written a congratulatory letter to the pope, and since he allowed her to read his correspondence, she asked for a copy. Galileo's reply tells us more about social conventions than a whole book of etiquette: One just did not write directly to persons who had reached such an exalted rank! The proper channel was a relative, and Galileo proffered congratulations through Francesco Barberini as soon as he was well enough to write. The pope's nephew replied on 23 September, the very day he received Galileo's letter, to say that the pope's sentiments toward him remained unchanged and that he, Francesco, looked forward to doing something for Galileo. The Barberini pontificate was raising hopes everywhere, and Galileo's fellow Lynceans were not the last to see their chance: on September 30 1623 they welcomed Francesco Barberini as a member of their academy. The timing could not have been better; Francesco was created cardinal three days later.

THE CHALLENGE OF THE COMETS

In the autumn of 1618, three comets had appeared in rapid succession. The last was of unusual size and brilliance, remaining visible from November until January of the following year. It was greeted (like any celestial novelty, be it a quasar or an orbiting station) with considerable interest, and Galileo was urged by his friends to swell the mounting tide of astronomical and astrological pamphlets that were flooding the market. Unfortunately, Galileo was bedridden with rheumatic pains at the time, and he was unable to make any observations. Yet he was free to speculate, and his admirers wanted not so much an accurate description of the size, position, and motion of the comet as an authoritative pronouncement—an oracular verdict on its nature. His literary friends, siding with the *moderns* against the *ancients* in the current debate on poetry, were only too willing to embrace Galileo's *modern view*, whatever it might be. Out of the scores of pamphlets that were circulating, Galileo fixed on a lecture delivered by Father Orazio Grassi, the professor of mathematics at the Roman College, and published anonymously in 1619 in order not to involve the Society of Jesus in a public controversy.

Grassi interpreted the new comet the way Tycho Brahe had accounted for the comet of 1577, and concluded that it was located between the Sun and the Moon. His tone was serene and he said nothing that was deliberately offensive to Galileo, whose name was not mentioned. It is puzzling why Galileo should have singled out this unassuming address for special attention and criticism. He was, of course, fond of polemics, and it is possible that his friend Giovanni Battista Rinuccini pricked his pride when he informed him that the Jesuits were publishing something on the comet that might discredit Copernicanism. "The Jesuits," wrote Rinuccini, "discuss the comet in a public lecture now in press, and they firmly believe that it is in the heavens. Some outside the Jesuit Order say that this is the greatest argument against Copernicus' system and that it knocks it down altogether."

The gist of the argument is that the motion of comets is so swift that their orbits would have to be much bigger than the size that the Copernican universe allowed and, even worse, would probably have to follow paths that are not circular but elongated. Since Newton, we know that the trajectory of comets is not perfectly circular, but Galileo's physics did not allow him to entertain the notion that planets could move in anything but a circle. He tried to salvage the dimensions of the Copernican universe by postulating that comets are just atmospheric phenomena caused by sunlight bouncing off high-altitude vapors. In other words, he thought they were not unlike rainbows or auroras borealis.

Galileo briefed one of his young disciples, Mario Guiducci, who had recently been elected consul of the Florentine Academy and was anxious to create a favorable impression by choosing a fashionable topic for his inaugural lectures. He delivered a series of three talks that were published, under his name, as the *Discourse on the Comets*. The manuscript, examined by Antonio Favaro, the editor of the National Edition of Galileo's *Works*, is largely in Galileo's own handwriting, and the sections drafted (or perhaps merely copied) by Guiducci show signs of revision and correction by the master.

As Guiducci was a lawyer and enjoyed no scientific reputation, it was clear to Grassi that Galileo was the real author, and he prepared a rejoinder, *The Astronomical and Philosophical Balance,* which he published under the pen name of Lothario Sarsi, purportedly a student of his. However, he let his identity be known to friends, and he even sent Galileo a complimentary copy of the book. Galileo was far from pleased to see his ideas hung on a philosophical steelyard and found weightless. He replied in kind and claimed that Grassi was no more than a lightweight in a work he entitled *The Assayer (Il Saggiatore* in Italian) to indicate that Grassi's balance was being supplanted by a much more delicate instrument, one that was used to determine the amount of pure gold in a lump of ore. *The Assayer* took the form of a letter to Virginio Cesarini, the nephew of Prince Federico Cesi, who paid for its publication. It was completed in October 1622 but delayed by numerous suggestions that the Lynceans continued to offer. When Cardinal Barberini was elected pope, Cesi saw that it was time to move, and he promptly commissioned a new frontispiece with the coat of arms of the Barberini family (three bees) and added a dedication to the pope, who was hailed as the patron of the Lyncean Academy.

In an age that has demythologized the heroes of the scientific revolution, admirers of Galileo can at least rest assured that his prose will remain one of the finest achievements of Italian baroque. *The Assayer* is a masterpiece of style. It was wildly acclaimed not so much by scientists as by poets and writers. It is a model of devastating irony, and it is here that we find the brilliant passage on nature written in the language of geometry:

> Perhaps Sarsi thinks that philosophy is a book of fiction created by one man, like the *Iliad* or the *Orlando Furioso,* books in which the least important thing is whether what is written in them is true. Sig. Sarsi, this is not the way matters stand. Philosophy is written in that great book which ever lies before our eyes—I mean the universe—but we cannot understand it if we do not first learn the language and grasp the symbols

in which it is written. This book is written in mathematical language, and the symbols are triangles, circles, and other geometrical figures, without whose help it is humanly impossible to comprehend a single word of it, and without which one wanders in vain though a dark labyrinth.

A SCIENTIFIC PARABLE

It was the pope's custom to be read to at mealtimes and as soon as *The Assayer* was published at the end of October 1623 Giovanni Ciampoli read a number of choice passages aloud. The one we have just quoted was almost certainly one of them. The pope was so pleased that he took the book to peruse it at leisure. He particularly enjoyed the more literary passages and those that were closest to his own understanding of the nature and limits of human knowledge. Ciampoli, who knew his tastes, probably also read him the parable about the song of the cicada, which illustrates the innumerable ways God operates in nature. "Once upon a time," wrote Galileo,

in a very lonely place, there lived a man endowed by nature with unusual curiosity and a very penetrating mind, who raised different kinds of birds for a pastime. He much enjoyed their song, and he observed with great admiration the happy contrivance by which they could transform at will the very air they breathed into a variety of sweet songs.

One night this man chanced to hear a delicate song close to his house, and being unable to imagine that it could be anything else than some small bird, he set out to capture it. He went out onto the road and found a shepherd boy who was blowing into a hollow stick while moving his fingers on the wood, thus drawing from it a variety of notes similar to those of a bird, though by quite a different method. Puzzled, and led on by his natural curiosity, he gave the boy a calf in exchange for his recorder. Pondering this incident, he realized that if he had not chanced to meet the boy he would never have learned that there are two different ways of forming musical notes and sweet songs, and so he decided to travel in the hope of coming across something new.

As the man roved, he discovered that sounds could be produced by the beating of the wings of bees or mosquitoes, by sawing with a bow string stretched over a hollowed piece of wood, by rubbing one's fingertips around the rim of a goblet, or by pushing a heavy door on metal hinges. After a while, as he was beginning to feel that he knew all the ways of producing sounds, he was suddenly confronted with something that baffled him even more than before:

> For having captured in his hands a cicada, he failed to diminish its strident noise either by closing its mouth or stopping its wings, yet he could not see it move the scales, which covered its body, or any other part. At last he lifted up the armor of its chest and there he saw some thin hard ligaments beneath, and thinking that the sound might come from their vibration, he decided to break them in order to silence it. But nothing happened until his needle drove too deep, and transfixing the creature he took away its life with its voice, so that he was still unable to determine whether the song had originated in those ligaments. This experience reduced him to diffidence, so that when asked how sounds were created he used to answer candidly that, although he knew some of the ways, he was certain that many more existed that were unknown and unimaginable.

This passage shows Galileo at his best as a storyteller, but it is important mainly for the lesson that it embodies and to which Urban VIII fully subscribed. As earnestly as we may seek to understand nature, we must never forget that it can produce in an infinite number of ways what we have discovered to be possible by one particular method. In his creative labors, God is not hampered by our limited logic or our imperfect means of experimentation.

The pope was pleased that the grand duke's chief philosopher and mathematician (as Galileo described himself on the frontispiece of *The Assayer*) should be in complete agreement with his own philosophy of science. Little did he suspect that Galileo had no intention of restricting himself to such a tentative approach and was determined, given a chance, to proclaim the physical truth of Copernicanism. Galileo was equally misinformed about the pope's intentions because Ciampoli, in the letter of 4 November 1623, intimated that he could now attempt much more:

> Here is greatly desired something new from your talent, and should you decide to print those ideas, which until now have remained in your mind, I am sure that they would be received most gratefully by the Pope, who does not cease to admire your eminence in all matters and to keep intact the affection that he has had for you in the past.

Of course, Ciampoli was ascribing his own sentiments to Urban VIII, but Galileo had no way of knowing this and he took for hard cash what was only a promissory note.

THE ROMAN RESPONSE

When the first copy of *The Assayer* was displayed in the Bookshop of the Sun in Rome it was immediately snatched up by Orazio Grassi, who walked off in a huff. He announced that though Galileo had consumed three years in writing it, he would remove its sting in three months. This was an allusion to a sarcasm of Galileo, who had said that Grassi's *Balance* might more appropriately have borne the title *Scorpio* since he claimed that the comet had originated in that zodiacal sign and was full of stings. Although Grassi complained of Galileo's biting language, he said that he would not reply in kind and let it be known that he would be happy to make peace with Galileo should he come to Rome. He could not help mentioning that his rival enjoyed the great advantage of having someone to pay for the publication of his works, and he could have added that the Jesuits had been enjoined to exercise restraint and avoid polemics. Unfortunately, Grassi's charitable dispositions evaporated when he saw a letter from Florence in which it was stated that the Jesuits would never be able to counter the arguments in *The Assayer*. If the Jesuits could answer a hundred heretics a year, Grassi declared, they knew well enough how to deal with one Catholic. He drafted a rejoinder to *The Assayer*, but as he was busy as rector of the Jesuit College in Siena between 1624 and 1626, it only appeared late that year. He may have desired to avoid insult, but he made Galileo furious by referring to his book, accidentally or on purpose, not by its proper title of *Il Saggiatore (The Assayer)* but *Il Assaggiatore (The Wine Taster)*, which seemed to imply that Galileo had been drinking when he wrote his book. It was no secret that Galileo knew and loved his wine.

It is regrettable that Galileo's success as a satirical writer was purchased at the price of alienating the Jesuits, who had treated him so handsomely in 1611 and who could have helped him later. His old foe, the Dominican Tommaso Caccini, continued to slander him, and in December 1623, Benedetto Castelli wrote to say that he had learned that Caccini was saying that had it not been for the protection of the grand duke Galileo would have at once been put on trial by the Roman Inquisition. Things were not helped by the arrival in Rome at about this time of Tommaso Campanella's *Defense of Galileo*. It had actually been written in 1616 at the height of the Copernican controversy, and there was consternation when it was printed by a Protestant publishing house. Murmurings against Galileo were revived, but his friends still outnumbered his foes at the end of 1623. The Florentine Giovanni Battista Rinuccini, who was appointed lieutenant to the cardinal who administered Rome, assured Galileo that the pope was glad to hear about what he was doing. His brother, Tommaso Rinuccini, who also held an influential post, added on 20 October that Urban VIII had said that he would be delighted if Galileo's health would allow him to return to Rome.

The Rinuccinis had acted with some prodding from Galileo, who had asked them to let him know about the lay of the land. On 9 October 1623 he had also broached the subject with Prince Cesi:

I have great need of Your Excellency's advice (in whom more than anyone I trust) about carrying out my desire, or perhaps my duty, to come to kiss the feet of His Holiness. But I would like to do it at the right moment and I shall wait until you tell me so. I am turning over in my mind things of some importance for the learned world, and if they are not carried out in this marvellous combination of circumstances, there can be no hope in the future, at least as far as I can see, of ever finding such an opportunity.

Cesi replied unambiguously on 21 October:

Your coming here is necessary and will give much pleasure to His Holiness. When he asked me when you were coming, I answered that an hour delay seemed to you like a thousand years. I added what I could about your devotion to him, and told him that you would soon bring him your book [*The Assayer*]. He admires you, and is more than ever fond of you.

Cesi suggested that Galileo leave for Rome the very next month and stop in Acquasparta, the country seat where he usually resided, to confer on the way. He gave him to understand that this would entail no more than a small detour by Perugia, where he could find a horse to ride to Acquasparta. Galileo gladly accepted, and on 29 October his daughter, Sister Maria Celeste, mentioned her father's trip as imminent and, on the next day, Galileo wrote to Cesi as though he was about to leave.

But history repeated itself and Galileo postponed his departure. On 21 November Sister Maria Celeste expressed concern for her father's health with the sudden onset of cold weather. Her fears were justified, for Galileo was once more bedridden. His Roman friends commiserated and tried to cheer him up. Tommaso Rinuccini wrote on 2 December to say that it was a good thing Galileo did not undertake the journey because the roads were cut by floods. Galileo hoped the skies would soon clear up, and he asked Sister Maria Celeste whether he could do something for her convent when he was in Rome. He knew that the nuns often lacked money to buy food and blankets, and he hoped that the pope might grant them a piece of property to generate enough income to meet their modest needs, as had been done for other monasteries. On 10 December Sister Maria Celeste replied that they were accustomed to material scarcity. What troubled them was something far more important, and this was the lack of spiritual guidance. The current chaplain was uneducated, worldly, and had no experience of monastic life. It would be a great blessing, she confided to her father, if he could be replaced by a priest from a religious order who understood their calling and was dependable.

When the weather improved at the beginning of 1624 Galileo asked the Grand Duchess Christina to give him a letter of recommendation from her son, Cardinal Carlo de' Medici, who was the resident Florentine cardinal in Rome. The letter, dated 14 January 1624, assumes that Galileo will soon be on his way. But bad weather and physical discomfort once again set in. On 20 February 1624, Galileo wrote to Cesi that he had been detained by heavy snow but that he hoped to set off within two or three days. This stretched into a week, at the end of which Galileo got a new letter of recommendation from the grand duke Ferdinando. It was destined for the ambassador Francesco Niccolini, and it makes it clear that Galileo was not travelling in an official capacity:

> Our Mathematician, Galilei, is going to Rome on private business, and we have given him this letter in order that you may help him, as you judge wise and possible. We hope that, as a distinguished servant of our House, he will continue to receive great honors. He must already be well known to the Pope and his principal ministers and, hence, will have little need of your assistance.

The official who drafted this letter was not merely exercising the caution expected of someone who knew that Copernicus had been placed on the Index of Prohibited Books. He was acting under the instructions of the Grand Duchess Christina, who had already made clear in her letter to Cardinal Carlo de' Medici that Galileo was not to be hosted, as in 1611 and 1616, in one of the Medici palaces in Rome. The eminent professor wanted to go to Rome; he could do so with their blessing but not at their expense.

It was well over a month before Galileo finally took to the road on 1 or 2 April 1624. The horse-drawn litter was supposed to have taken him all the way to Acquasparta, but when they arrived in Perugia, some 40 kilometers from their destination, the coach driver found someone who wanted to go to Rome, and he unceremoniously dropped Galileo for a better fare. Galileo spent the night in Perugia, and on the next day, which was Maundy Thursday, he found Prince Cesi's coachman, who was about to leave for Todi with another passenger. As the coachman refused to return to fetch him without explicit orders from the prince, Galileo gave him a letter in which he said that he was not up to riding a horse all the way to Acquasparta and that he would like Cesi to have him fetched. What a pity, Galileo wrote to Cesi, that I will not be able to be with you on Easter!

It does not seem that Galileo made it to Acquasparta by Easter, although the coachman was despatched back to Perugia by the prince on Good Friday. When the two friends met on Easter Monday, 8 April, they had not seen each other for eight years, and they spent the next two weeks in earnest conversation. Their meeting was clouded by the news of the death of Virginio Cesarini, who passed away in Rome on 11 April. This was a blow for both of them but especially for Galileo, who lost not only an admirer but also a close associate of the pope and almost certainly a future cardinal. The kind of help that Cesarini had been able to give Galileo can be seen in the way he had arranged for *The Assayer* to be read by a young Dominican professor of theology, Niccolò Riccardi, who not only gave the *imprimatur*, as the license to print was called, but added what reads like a publicity blurb. Instead of the usual statement that the work was not contrary to religion, he wrote that it contained

> so many fine considerations pertaining to natural philosophy that I
> believe our age is to be celebrated by future ages not only as the heir of

works of past philosophers but as the discoverer of many secrets of nature that they were unable to reveal, thanks to the deep and sound reflections of this author in whose age I count myself fortunate to be born—when the gold of truth is no longer weighed in bulk and with a steelyard, but is assayed with so delicate a balance.

In 1623 Riccardi was still an occasional "consultant" or expert at the Holy Office, but he did not lack visibility. His enormous girth, his weighty eloquence, and his phenomenal memory had earned him the nickname "Father Monster" from King Philip III of Spain. He quickly rose to prominence at the Vatican, and he became master of the sacred palace in 1629, a post that included the responsibility of licensing books to be printed.

PRINCELY CONVERSATIONS

The letter announcing Cesarini's death was probably delivered by the German physician Johann Winther, who arrived in Acquasparta on Sunday, 14 April, and was told upon dismounting that the prince would see him later because he was in conference with Galileo. Winther was served a meal, assigned a beautiful room with a pleasant view, and then called by the prince, whom he found chatting by the fireside with Galileo. What did they discuss late into the night? Prince Cesi was at the time trying to arrange for the publication of a manuscript that he had found in Naples several years earlier. This was the *Medical Thesaurus of New Spain*, a summary of the observations of Mexican natural history made by the sixteenth-century Spanish physician Francisco Hernandez. Cesi was deeply interested in botany and he kept a sizeable herb garden. In all likelihood, he spent some time informing Galileo about his activities as a "simpler," the term for a collector of medicinal herbs in the seventeenth century. He may also have spoken of his desire to publish the constitution of the Lyncean Academy and the microscopical observations that his collaborators had carried out on bees, the symbol of the Barberini family. What he probably did not mention was that his finances were in desperate straits. His father had brought the family to the brink of ruin, and in 1622 they had had to sell their famous garden of antiquities to the Ludovisi, the family then in possession of the papacy. A constant succession of suits threatened to make Cesi bankrupt, and he had to court the new pope to salvage his estate. The help that he could extend to Galileo must be seen in this light. He had no intention of adding to his woes by supporting risky ideas, and it was important that the Lynceans be on good terms with the authorities. Cesi had protected scientists; they might now prove useful in protecting him.

Which brings us to Galileo's hopes for Copernicanism. He must have reminded Cesi about his friendly correspondence with Urban VIII when he was still a cardinal and spoken of his high hopes of persuading him to allow a free discussion of heliocentrism. It is equally certain that he did not breathe a word of the admonition he had received from Cardinal Bellarmine in 1616. The Roman agendas of Cesi and Galileo were not quite the same, and they did not see into each other's cards. Cesi was interested in the promotion of learning and the freedom of research that is necessary for scientific progress, but he was also a man with growing debts who found it useful to use the renown of his academy as a way of securing goodwill. However much Cesi enjoyed the company of prominent figures, he neither wished, nor could, challenge the status quo.

READING THE SIGNS OF THE TIMES

Galileo left Acquasparta on Sunday morning, 21 April and arrived in the Eternal City late at night on the following day. As on his previous journeys, the excitement gave him a sudden burst of energy, and on the morning following his arrival he called on Urban VIII, with whom he spent an hour in the company of Cardinal Antonio Barberini, the brother of the pope, who had arranged the interview. On the next day, Wednesday, he was received for the same amount of time by the Pope's nephew, Cardinal Francesco Barberini. He also paid a visit to Cardinal Carlo de'

Medici to present the letters from Grand Duke Ferdinando and Archduchess Christina. "The rest of the time," he wrote on 27 April to the secretary of state, Curzio Picchena, "I spend on various visits that, in the end, make me realize that I am old, and that to be a courtier one has to be young with the physical strength and the hope of preferment that render it possible to endure this kind of labor."

He must have written in the same vein to Federico Cesi, who replied on 30 April: "The court, my dear sir, is a source of infinite trouble and, beyond the official visits, there are innumerable calls of courtesy to be made . . . I recommend that you take your time and think above all of your health." Cesi's letter does not bear an address but we know from a letter the Lyncean Johann Faber wrote to Cesi on 11 May that Galileo lived close to the Church of Santa Maria Maddalena, roughly 50 meters from the Pantheon. Galileo was not staying with the Florentine ambassador as in 1611 or in the Villa Medici as in 1616. He may have been the guest of Mario Guiducci, who is the person with whom he will mainly correspond after his return to Florence.

In his letter to Cesi, Johann Faber, who was a physician, makes much of the fact that Galileo had given his patient and patron, Cardinal Frederick Eutel von Zollern, a microscope for the duke of Bavaria. Von Zollern had worked in the Curia under Clement VIII and had been created cardinal by Paul V in 1621. He had recently been appointed bishop of Olmütz in Bohemia and was about to leave for his diocese. Galileo showed von Zollern and Faber how to use the microscope, and together they studied a fly. Astonished and delighted, Faber called Galileo "another Creator" because he rendered visible things whose very existence had been unknown until then. This praise and an offer of help did not impress Galileo, who did not tell him anything about his business, as Faber later remarked. Now past 60, Galileo was growing more cautious about the persons who should be informed of the progress of his Copernican campaign. His own letter to Federico Cesi, written four days after Faber's, is studiously circumspect. He says that he could forge ahead "on some of the issues that we discussed together" if he had enough time and patience, but he does not spell out what these issues are. Three days earlier he had been invited by Cardinal Scipione Cobelluzzi to dine with several prominent intellectuals. They had had a long conversation "but without tackling specifically any of our main propositions." Again these propositions are not spelled out, and the next paragraph of the letter is equally short on details:

> I spoke at length with Cardinal Zollern on two occasions. Without being an expert in our field, he grasps the point at stake and knows what is to be done in this case. He told me that he wants to raise the matter with His Holiness before his departure in some eight or ten days from now. I shall gladly hear what he finds out, but there are so many issues that are considered infinitely more important than those I mentioned, and these absorb all the time available so that our questions are neglected.

The larger issue that dominated the papal states was the problem of maintaining an uneasy neutrality between the two major contenders of the Thirty Years' War: Catholic France and its Protestant allies on the one hand, and the House of Habsburg in Spain and Germany on the other. Urban VIII felt that the papacy's independence was constantly threatened by the presence of Spanish power both north and south of the papal states. The energy and diplomacy needed to ward off the menace of becoming an imperial puppet left him little time for astronomical speculation.

It is clear from this letter that as late as 15 May Galileo had not spoken to the pope about Copernicanism, and that he doubted whether Cardinal Zollern would succeed in doing so. Cesi and Galileo may have talked well into the night when they were together in Acquasparta in April, but they do not seem to have come up with any concrete strategy of persuasion. Galileo was feeling the strain, and on 23 May he told Johann Faber that he intended to leave Rome in six days time. "I hope," Faber remarked to Cesi, "that Cardinal Zollern will be able to get something from the Pope concerning the Copernican system." The cat was out of the bag: Nothing had really been achieved and the last hope was Cardinal Zollern, who was willing to speak to Urban VIII personally.

A week later, Galileo was still in Rome and Zollern had not yet seen Urban VIII. On 1 June Faber reported to Cesi that he attended a meeting at Cardinal Zollern's lodgings with Galileo; Father Niccolò Riccardi, the Dominican who had licensed *The Assayer;* and a German named Gaspar Schopp, a Lutheran who had converted to Catholicism. "We found that Father Monster [Riccardi] was very much on our side," wrote Faber, "but he does not recommend that we re-open at this time a debate that has cooled down." The best would be for Galileo to make his point in writing, but in such a way that his enemies could not attack him. The fact that Cardinal Zollern had not, thus far, seen the pope may explain why Galileo had not left for Florence as he had planned. Zollern did manage to see Urban VIII just before his departure for Germany on 7 June, but we must not interpret this as the result of a specific request to discuss the ban on Copernicanism. It was customary for Cardinals who were about to leave Rome to pay a courtesy call on the sovereign pontiff, and during the interview Zollern brought up the topic. The pope, as Zollern informed Galileo, told him that the Church had not condemned nor was about to condemn Copernicanism as heretical but that the theory was rash and that, furthermore, astronomical theories were of such a kind that they could never be shown to be necessarily true.

Galileo also offered in his letter an ironical, and somewhat patronising, account of the discussion he had had with Niccolò Riccardi, the "Father Monster," and Gaspar Schopp. "They might not be as versed in astronomy as one might wish," he wrote,

> but they are nonetheless firmly of the opinion that this is not a matter
> of Faith and that Scripture should not be brought in. As far as truth or
> falsehood is concerned, Father Monster is neither for Ptolemy nor for
> Copernicus, but rests content with his own convenient way of having
> the heavenly bodies moved, without the slightest difficulty, by angels.

Whether Father Monster really believed that angels have such kinetic power is unclear, but there can be no doubt that he was sceptical about the possibility of finding the physical cause of planetary motion. Like Urban VIII, he was happy to let astronomers play around with any model they liked because he was convinced that they could never provide a genuine insight into the workings of nature, even if they rushed where angels fear to tread.

Galileo was anxious to get home to "purge" himself as he confided to Cesi in the same letter, and he planned to leave on the following Sunday, 16 June, in company of his Florentine friends, Michelangelo Buonaroti and Bishop Francesco Nori. Galileo particularly wanted Cesi to know that he had been granted six audiences by the Pope from whom he had received "great honors and favors." He could indeed be pleased with himself as far as his more practical and mundane tasks were concerned. He had the promise of a pension for his son, Vincenzio, and for his daughter, Sister Maria Celeste, the assurance that her convent would be provided with a better chaplain. On his departure the pope presented him with a painting (which Galileo describes as fine but of which he does not indicate the subject matter), two medals, one of gold, the other of silver, and several *Agnus Dei*, as were called the cakes of wax stamped with the figure of a lamb bearing a cross or a flag. There is no indication that the motion of the Earth had been so much as broached. All Galileo really had was what Cardinal Zollern had told him. Encouraging news, no doubt, but still secondhand. The pope had been reported as saying that the Church had not condemned Copernicanism as heretical. But every theologian worth his salt knew that the *De Revolutionibus Orbium Caelestium* had been placed on the list of proscribed books for being "rash" rather than perverse.

Urban VIII believed that the sun-centered universe was an unproven idea without any prospect of proof for the future since astronomical systems are by their very nature mere conjectures. We can devise mathematical games about the cosmos, but we can never know what the building blocks really are. It is silly to make a fuss about what will never be open to confirmation. The pope's position was neither new nor outlandish, and it could be found in Andreas Osiander's preface to Copernicus's *De Revolutionibus*: Astronomical hypotheses are calculating devices; they have nothing to do with questions of truth or falsity. A better way of computing positions is not a theory that can become more credible as evidence increases. As we know from his personal theologian, Agostino Oregio, Urban VIII added a theological justification to his philosophical instrumentalism. It is a commonplace but no less important for that: God is omnipotent and can make in a variety of ways what we know to be possible in one way only, for what is beyond our senses is beyond our ken. We look up to heaven to pray; the rest is mere speculation. Galileo had heard this from Urban VIII, then Cardinal Maffeo Barberini, and there was no reason to believe that the pope had changed his mind.

Galileo made a last visit to Cardinal Francesco Barberini, who gave him letters of greeting for the Grand Duke Ferdinand II and the Archduchess Maria Maddalena. Galileo also left Rome with an ornate Latin letter of Urban VIII to the grand duke, in which Galileo is called "my beloved son who has entered the aetherial spaces, cast light on unknown stars, and plunged into the inner recesses of the planets." The text goes on in this way for several lines and, lest we attach too much importance to its glowing prose, it must be added that it was neither written nor signed by the pope but by the secretary for official correspondence, none other than Ciampoli.

BACK TO COPERNICANISM

Galileo returned to Florence with the feeling that his long-delayed book on the system of the world could be now attempted, but his mind was not completely at ease, and he immediately wrote to Guiducci to ask what had become of his adversaries. On 21 June, Guiducci replied that the Jesuit camp was astir.

> I hear from all sides rumors of the war with which Grassi is threatening
> us to the point that I am tempted to believe that his reply is ready. On

the other hand, I cannot see where he can attack since Count Virginio Malvezzi is almost certain that he cannot gain a foothold on your position concerning the nature of heat, tastes, smells, and so on. The count says that you wrote about that to start a new controversy for which you must be armed to the teeth.

This is the first mention of the problem of the so-called secondary qualities (color, smell, and so on) in the polemic with the Jesuits and, as we shall see, it will prove a sensitive issue.

What Galileo needed was a trial run and he chose as his foil a short anti-Copernican work that Ingoli had written in 1616 and that Galileo had considered unwise to answer after discussion about the motion of the Earth had been censored. Meanwhile, Ingoli had been appointed secretary of the Congregation for the Propagation of the Faith, and Galileo was eager to spread his own Copernican belief. Ingoli's work had been circulated in Italy and abroad, and the Protestant Johann Kepler had even submitted it to a critical review. It was time for a Catholic to take Ingoli down a peg or two, and Galileo made it his summer assignment for 1624. He avoided saying that he had not answered Ingoli earlier because of the condemnation of Copernicus's book in 1616 and implied instead that he had not done so because it would have been a waste of time. "However," he continued,

> I have now discovered that I was completely wrong in assuming this. Having recently gone to Rome to pay my respects to His Holiness Pope Urban VIII, to whom I am bound by old acquaintance and the many favors I have received, I found it is firmly and generally believed that I have been silent because I was convinced by your demonstrations. . . . Thus I find myself forced to answer your work, though, as you see, very late and against my will.

Galileo stressed that, as a good son of the Church, he wanted Protestants to know that Catholics were not all ignoramuses like Ingoli.

They knew the arguments in favor of Copernicus, and if they did not subscribe to them this was because they placed their faith above scientific reasoning. "I hear," declares Galileo,

> that the most influential of the heretics accept Copernicus' opinion, and I want to show that we Catholics continue to be certain of the old truth taught by the sacred authors, not for lack of scientific understanding, or for having failed to consider the numerous arguments, experiments, observations and demonstrations that they have, but rather because of our reverence for the writings of the Fathers, and our zeal for religion.

Protestants should not be misled into thinking that Catholics' attachment to Scripture and the Fathers is the product of ignorance of astronomy and natural philosophy. Galileo rams it in that it is the result of deep faith. This was a dangerous game to play. Placing one's faith in sacred authors above the conjectures of natural philosophers is one thing; insinuating that the arguments deployed by churchmen like Ingoli are worthless is another. Galileo earnestly believed that Christianity is based on revealed truths, and he was convinced that these truths concern faith and morals exclusively and have nothing to do with astronomical hypotheses. He was compelled to conceal this conviction after 1616. What he needed after the election of Urban VIII was elbow room, and paying lip service to the official ruling of the Church seemed a reasonable price. From this position, less secure than Galileo assumed, he once more resumed his defence of Copernicus:

> For, Signor Ingoli, if your philosophical sincerity and my old regard for you will allow me to say so, you should in all honesty have known that Nicolaus Copernicus spent more years on these very difficult problems than you spent days on them. You should have been more careful and not allowed yourself to be lightly persuaded that you could knock down such a man, especially with the sort of weapons you use, which are

among the most common and trite objections advanced in this subject, and when you add something new it is no more effective than the rest.

Having unburdened himself in this way, Galileo let down his guard and risked the following emphatic declaration of his own position: "If any place in the world is to be called its center, this is the center of celestial revolutions, and anyone who is competent in this subject knows that it is the Sun rather than the Earth that is found there." The reason Galileo could get away with this statement is that all astronomical models had a purely "hypothetical" status in the eyes of people like Urban VIII. There was no real epistemological dissonance between Scripture and astronomy simply because astronomy made no truth claims.

Galileo proceeded to outline his arguments for heliocentrism, many of which he later developed in his *Dialogue* of 1632, such as the discussion of why a stone dropped from the mast of a ship falls at the foot of the mast whether the ship is stationary or in motion, or why a cannon ball fired on a revolving Earth has the same range whether it is aimed to the east or to the west.

Galileo completed his 50-page *Reply to Ingoli* by the end of September 1624 and sent it off to his Roman friends. Guiducci was full of praise, and Ciampoli read a few passages to the pope, who was reported to have remarked on the aptness of the observations and the experiments. Ingoli soon heard about the reply and asked to see it. After some hesitation, Galileo agreed and Guiducci prepared a clean copy with deletions and emendations suggested by Ciampoli. Meanwhile Prince Cesi had had time to read the reply, and he strongly advised against showing it to Ingoli or anyone else. On 18 April 1625 Mario Guiducci wrote to Galileo to explain what he thought were Cesi's reasons. Several months earlier *The Assayer* had been denounced to the Holy Office, and Guiducci assumed that this was because Galileo spoke favorably of the Copernican theory. But since the discovery, in 1981, of an anonymous denunciation in the archives of the Holy Office by the historian Pietro Redondi, we know that Galileo was accused of something very different and much more serious, namely endangering the Catholic doctrine of the Eucharist. By endorsing the atomic theory of matter he had rendered himself suspect of denying the concept of *transubstantiation*.

THE DOCTRINE OF THE EUCHARIST

To understand the background to this charge, we have to recall that Catholic thought was dominated since 1564 (the year of Galileo's birth) by the Decrees of the Council of Trent (1545–1563), which were promulgated that year. The Protestant Reformers had tended to emphasize the spiritual, and downplay the literal, meaning of Christ's words at the Last Supper, "This is my body. This is my blood." The Catholic bishops present at Trent wished to stress that these words meant that Christ was really present. They did not intend to explain away the mystery of the Eucharist but to offer an interpretation of the presence of Christ that was not merely symbolic, and they expressed this conviction by saying that the substance of the bread and wine become the substance of the body and blood of Christ (what they termed *transubstantiation*). What is left of the bread and wine are only their *appearances* such as their color, taste, odor, and so on.

A philosophical school to which Galileo was close believed that matter is made up of invisible particles of matter or atoms. On this view, "primary qualities" such as size, shape, and motion are really in the things themselves, but "secondary qualities," namely colors, tastes, and sounds, are not in the objects but in the organs that respond to the stimulus of the "primary qualities." In this sense, they can be called subjective. In *The Assayer*, Galileo had given an atomistic interpretation of the nature of heat, which he described as caused by matter in motion. This view clashed with the common-sense belief that heat is an intrinsic property of bodies. To refute this naive realism, Galileo devised one of his cleverest thought experiments:

> As soon as I think of a material object or a corporeal substance, I
> immediately feel the need to conceive simultaneously that it is bounded

and has this or that shape, that it is big or small in relation to others, that it is in this or that place at a given time, that it moves or stays still, that it does or does not touch another body, and that it is one, few, or many. I cannot separate it from these conditions by any stretch of my imagination. But my mind feels no compulsion to understand as necessary accompaniments that it should be white or red, bitter or sweet, noisy or silent, of sweet or of foul odor. Indeed, without the senses to guide us, reason or imagination alone would perhaps never arrive at such qualities. For that reason, I think that tastes, odors, colors and so forth are no more than mere names so far as pertains to the subject wherein they seem to reside, and that they only exist in the body that perceives them. Thus, if living creatures were removed, all these qualities would vanish and be annihilated.

When someone tickles you with a feather, the unpleasant sensation you feel is in you. It is not a property of the feather. It is a subjective response to an external stimulus. Likewise, says Galileo, tastes, odors, and colors exist in the organs that are affected by them, not in their causes. The theological problem arises as follows: if color, taste, and other "secondary qualities" are pronounced subjective, might this not imperil the teaching of the Council of Trent on the *objective* distinction between the real *substance* of Christ's body and blood and the equally real *properties* of bread and wine? A sensitive soul, or perhaps a malevolent colleague, wrote to the Holy Office to draw attention to this latent danger in the interpretation of the consecrated host. Fortunately for Galileo, Cardinal Francesco Barberini, who was a member of the Holy Office, offered to investigate the matter. He entrusted the task to his personal theologian, Giovanni di Guevara, who read Galileo's work and saw no reason to pursue the matter. "So things calmed down," writes Guiducci, but Cesi feared it was only the lull before the storm.

Cesi was proved right when Grassi published a reply to *The Assayer* in which he raised the very objections that had been made by the anonymous delator. He argued that in the Eucharist the *substance* of bread and wine is converted into the body and blood of Christ and that what we see are only the remaining accidents, such as whiteness. Now for Galileo these accidents were just names, and Grassi aired the concern that such a view was difficult to reconcile with Catholic teaching. At about that time Cardinal Francesco Barberini was appointed papal legate, or ambassador, to France and left for Paris with Guevara. In their absence, it was doubly wise to avoid stirring the waters. Galileo was not happy, but he saw the point.

THE TENSION MOUNTS

Since the summer of 1626 Galileo had another important contact in Rome in the person of Benedetto Castelli, whom Urban VIII had called from Pisa to act as tutor to his nephew, Taddeo Barberini, and to supervise canals and waterworks in the papal states. Castelli was shortly thereafter appointed professor at the University of Rome and spent the rest of his life in the Eternal City. In Pisa, he had acted as tutor to Galileo's own son, Vincenzio, and Galileo asked him to take care of his nephew, also called Vincenzio, to whom he wanted to transfer the ecclesiastical pension he had obtained from the pope for his own son. The nephew, like his father, Michelangelo Galilei, was said to have musical talent, and Castelli found lodgings and a music teacher for him. Unfortunately, Vincenzio was idle and spendthrift, and he displayed a total disregard for the Church. It was not just that he resented the clerical dress and the set prayers that went with his pension or that he stayed out all night in dubious company. He said openly that he did not see why he should join others in worshipping a piece of painted wall. This insolence alarmed Castelli, especially after Vincenzio's landlord complained that if he meant those words seriously he would soon be denounced to the local ecclesiastical authorities. The last thing Galileo wanted was a nephew branded as a heretic in Rome, and the scapegrace was made to leave as soon as possible. During this troublesome episode, Castelli offered to introduce Galileo to a newly discovered relief: tobacco. His first mention of it elicited a request for further information, and

Castelli waxed eloquent on its therapeutic virtues in a letter of 29 April 1628. As far as we know, Galileo was not convinced, and never took to the weed.

While writing out his reply to Ingoli, Galileo did not neglect to refurbish his best weapon, the argument about the tides, which he had already circulated in manuscript form between 1616 and 1618. Father Niccolò Riccardi had not seen it and requested a copy through Johann Faber on 14 September 1624. In a letter to Cesi of 23 September 1624, Galileo confirmed that he had returned to the tides and that the thrust of the argument was the following: "If the Earth is at rest, the tides cannot occur, but if it moves with the motions described, they necessarily follow with all that is actually observed."

Galileo also worked on perfecting his compound microscope, for which he had had to wait for doubly convex lenses, which were difficult to grind. His letter of 23 September, which accompanied the shipment of such an instrument to Cesi, offers a personal comment on what he had himself seen:

> I have observed many tiny animals with great admiration, among which the flea is quite horrible, the mosquito and the moth very beautiful, and I have seen with great pleasure how flies and other little animals can walk attached to mirrors upside down. You will have the opportunity of observing a large number of such particulars, and I should be grateful if you would let me know about the more curious. In short, the greatness of nature, and the subtle and unspeakable care with which she works is a source of unending contemplation.

In honor of the Barberini family, bees were given pride of place, and Galileo had the pleasure of seeing how well the Lynceans could use his instrument in a broadsheet that they published in 1625.

Galileo was also consulted on the new state carriage that Urban VIII wanted to have built, and he seems to have suggested that it should be suspended from 2 springs at the ends rather than be made to rest on one support only. Cardinal Francesco Barberini, who had been entrusted with the decoration of the vehicle, considered painting a sun at the center of the ceiling and placing the twelve signs of the Zodiac around it. Guiducci remarked that this would be in disagreement with the Ptolemaic system. "Of course," he declares in his letter of 15 October 1624 to Galileo, "I am only joking and I don't mean it." Nonetheless, he could not help adding that if the painting were actually executed he would welcome the opportunity of telling the cardinal that it would be prohibited by the Congregation of the Index, and that Ingoli would denounce him. Guidicci was a lawyer and could allow himself a jest, perhaps the last one in the unfolding of this affair. The high drama was yet to come.

CHAPTER FIVE

Star-Crossed Heavens

FIFTH TRIP • 3 MAY–26 JUNE 1630

Galileo had returned to Florence in the summer of 1624 with the conviction that he was now free to write on the motion of the Earth as long as he avoided stating that it was physically true. Within a couple of months he had finished his *Reply to Ingoli* and could now return to his *Dialogue*. To emphasize what he considered his decisive argument for the motion of the Earth, Galileo planned to call the work *The Discourse on the Tides*. It is only when the pope objected that he changed it to *The Dialogue on the Two Chief World Systems*. The work is the record of a discussion spread over four days, like a play in four acts, among three friends who meet in a palace in Venice.

Galileo, who was now over 60, welcomed the opportunity to bring back to life two of his best friends. The first is Filippo Salviati, his host at the Villa delle Selve near Florence, where he had been frequently a visitor. He is Galileo's spokesman and he makes a brilliant case for Copernicanism. The second is the Venetian patrician Giovanfrancesco Sagredo, in whose palace the meeting is held. He is presented as open-minded and unprejudiced, but he is already half converted to Copernicanism and plays second fiddle to Salviati. The third participant, an Aristotelian professor called Simplicio, is a completely fictional character, but Simplicius was the name of a sixth-century Greek philosopher who was famous for a commentary on Aristotle. In Italian, Simplicio also sounds like *simpleton*, and Galileo may have intended the pun. Simplicio is neither very bright nor very well informed and sometimes plays the buffoon who gets kicked in the pants.

A PHILOSOPHICAL AND LITERARY MASTERPIECE

It was a basic tenet of Aristotelian philosophy that the heavens are immutable and that change and decay only occur on Earth. This rested on the assumption that heavenly bodies naturally move in perfect and unending circles while bodies on Earth naturally go straight up or straight down. The distinction was important because it implied that the physics that is found on Earth is not applicable to the heavens above. This philosophical bias had to be dismantled, and in the first day of the *Dialogue,* Galileo chips away at the distinction in order to show that it is no longer plausible to treat the heavens as completely different from the Earth since the telescope has shown mountains on the Moon. Terrestrial physics can and should be extended to the celestial regions argues Salviati, who is careful not to overstate his argument. Sagredo, the voice of sweet reasonableness, points out that plants, animals, and humans could not live on the moon because there is no water there. Nonetheless Salviati does not rule out that the moon could contain creatures very different from us who would praise the Lord in their own way. This left open an issue that will raise eyebrows among theologians. The appearance of supernovae and comets had shown that the heavens are not inalterable, and if the Ancients had been wrong about celestial bodies, might they not have been equally misled about the Earth when they declared that it could not move through space?

The second day of the *Dialogue* examines the possibility of the daily rotation of the Earth. Would it not be simpler, asks Salviati, to allow the

Earth to rotate from west to east once a day rather than have the whole heavens spin around the Earth at a fantastic speed every 24 hours? The traditional view, chimes in Sagredo, could be compared to climbing a cupola to view the countryside and then expect the landscape to revolve around one's head. Aristotelians, of course, knew that a rotating Earth would be simpler; they just thought it preposterous.

The apparent steadiness of the Earth lulled the mind into a false stability and gave rise to such difficulties as the following: If the Earth was moving, the clouds would be blown away and birds could not fly against the constant gale. Worse still, buildings would be flung off the surface of the Earth because the speed of rotation at the equator would be about 1800 kilometers per hour! Or, on a less dramatic note, a stone dropped from a tower would fall not at its foot but slightly to the west because while it was coming down the tower would have moved to the east. The correct answer to these objections is that Earth imparts its global motion to all terrestrial objects. Hence, the air through which birds fly is carried along with the earth. Likewise a stone that is falling shares in the rotation of the Earth just as much as when it is lying on top of a tower. To grasp why we cannot observe that we are rotating, Salviati suggests the following experiment.

Shut yourself with a friend inside a large windowless cabin on a ship. Flies buzz round the cabin, fish swim in a bowl, and a tap drips water into a basin. While the ship is standing still, the flies move back and forth with the same ease, the fish swim equally well in all directions, and the water drips straight into the bowl. If you throw a ball to your friend you need no more force in one direction than in another. Now let the ship move as fast as you like but in such a way that the motion is uniform and smooth. What will you notice? Nothing. The flies, the fish, the drops of water, and the ball will behave just as they did before because the ship's motion is shared by everything in the cabin. No experiment performed inside a windowless cabin can show whether the ship is moving or not. In the same way, no tests carried out on Earth can decide whether it is spinning or at rest. Falling bodies, arrows, or cannon balls will follow the same path whether the Earth is stationary or rotating on its axis.

The third day of the *Dialogue* deals with the Earth's annual motion around the Sun in the company of Mercury, Venus, Mars, Jupiter, and Saturn. The planets are all on circular racetracks around the Sun, but since we observe them from a moving Earth they appear to move backwards or forwards as we overtake or pass them. When we catch up with Mars, for instance, it seems to slow down and when we race ahead it appears to move in the opposite (westward) direction for a while until it resumes its eastward motion. The immobility of our world is an illusion. We spin. We speed through space. We circle the Sun. We live on a wandering star.

The heliocentric system provided a simpler explanation of the motions of the planet, but, however attractive, simplicity is not the last court of appeal in physics. As we have seen, Galileo was convinced that he had found a decisive *physical* argument for the motion of the Earth in the ebb and flow of the sea, which resulted, according to him, from the combined effect of the daily rotation of the Earth and its annual revolution around the Sun. The fourth and concluding day of the *Dialogue* is devoted to this idea and was inspired by what Galileo had seen in the barges that carried fresh water from the mainland to Venice. When these barges slowed down, the water piled up in front, and when they accelerated, the water rose at the other end. The seabeds, reasoned Galileo, are large basins of water and the diurnal and annual motions of the Earth combine to speed up their oscillation or slow them down every twelve hours. Local features such as the orientation and configuration of the seabeds or the shore were presumed to account for variations from place to place. The idea was ingenious; unfortunately, it was also false.

The *Dialogue* is a great scientific treatise, but it is also a literary masterpiece. Galileo's style is not characterized by the bare factualness of the modern laboratory report or the unflinching rigor of a mathematical deduction. Words for him are more than vehicles of pure thought. They are sensible entities; they possess associations with images, memories, and feelings. Galileo knew how to use them to attract, hold, and absorb attention. He did not present his ideas in the nakedness of abstract thought but clothed them in the colors of feeling, intending not only to inform and teach but also move and entice to action. Indeed, he wished to bring about nothing less than a reversal of the 1616 decision against Copernicanism.

SLOW PROGRESS

During the period 1625–1629, Galileo was frequently interrupted by illness and could do little writing. It is only in the autumn of 1629 that he was able to resume his work. He describes his progress to his friend Elia Diodati in a letter of 29 October 1629:

> A month ago I took up again my *Dialogue* about the tides, put aside for three years on end, and by the grace of God I'm on the right path, so that if I can keep on this winter I hope to complete the work and publish it immediately. Besides the material on the tides, you will find many other problems and a detailed confirmation of the Copernican system with a demonstration of the futility of everything that was objected by Tycho and others.

One of the new ideas was the discovery that the apparent path of the sunspots depends on the rotation of the Earth. The facts are as follows: The sunspots trace a straight line only twice a year at the summer and the winter solstices; for the remaining time, they follow an arc that curves upwards for half the year and downwards for the next half. For those who claimed that the Earth was at rest and the Sun went around it every day, it was hard to explain why the sunspots should change their path according to an annual and not a daily cycle. But if the Earth went around the Sun, and the Sun was inclined to the ecliptic (the Sun's apparent path among the stars during the year), then this is just what would be expected. Here was the "ample confirmation of the Copernican system," but Galileo only gave an incomplete sketch of his argument in the *Dialogue*. In a book published at about the same time, his Jesuit rival, Christopher Scheiner, described the inclination of the Sun's axis and accounted for the observed paths of sunspots much more accurately while retaining the assumption that the Earth is at rest.

ECCLESIASTICAL CENSORSHIP

On 24 December 1629, Galileo sent his season's greetings to Prince Cesi and informed him that the *Dialogue* was ready except for the introduction and a few minor points to be revised. Galileo's eyesight was failing, but he declared himself ready to go to Rome to oversee the printing of the book, which he assumed would be undertaken at the prince's expense. Galileo's willingness to undertake this journey did not stem exclusively from his desire to "avoid inconveniencing other people," as he put it. It was also motivated by the dreadful job that the Lyncean Academy had done in 1624 with his *Assayer,* which they had allowed to appear with over 200 misprints.

It is interesting that Galileo does not raise the matter of ecclesiastical permission to publish. Indeed, he does not seem to worry in the least about it. He had no reason to feel otherwise since the new master of the sacred palace, the person who authorized publication in Rome, was now Father Niccolò Riccardi. This was the very man who had approved *The Assayer* with a gush of admiration in 1623. Nonetheless, Galileo knew that ecclesiastical censorship was exercised not only in the case of sensitive subjects, like the nature of the Eucharist, but for books of all kinds. In 1515, Pope Leo X, a Florentine by birth, had decreed that anyone seeking publication must have his work examined by the local bishop or his representative. Printers who started their presses without permission were threatened with fines, excommunication, and the burning of their books. Following the Council of Trent, new restrictions stipulated that authors as well as printers could be excommunicated. Readers also faced the same sanctions, and booksellers were warned to keep an eye on their stock.

Galileo had submitted all his previous works to the requisite scrutiny in the city where they were printed. Since Prince Cesi intended the

Dialogue to appear in Rome, the work had to be examined there despite the fact that the author lived in Florence. This posed no problem since Galileo planned to deliver the manuscript himself and correct the galleys in Rome.

THE EARTH A STAR!

Galileo's Roman friends rejoiced at the good news of his forthcoming trip, and on 5 January 1630 Ciampoli invited Galileo to stay with him. He conveyed "the most affectionate greetings" of Father Riccardi (the "Monster"), who had been made master of the sacred palace and was now in a position to license books for printing. Benedetto Castelli went as far as to tell Riccardi that what had decided Galileo to resume work on his book was the news of Riccardi's appointment. Riccardi had only been assigned to his new post on 2 June 1629, so Castelli was stretching the truth, but the little white lie worked as intended. Riccardi was flattered and replied that Galileo could always count on him. Castelli took this at face value and wrote to Galileo on 9 February to say that as far as Father Riccardi was concerned, everything would go smoothly.

Unfortunately Riccardi did not operate alone. In the same letter, Castelli describes how a few days earlier he had met the pope's nephew, Cardinal Francesco Barberini, at a scientific meeting. The nature of the tides came up for discussion and Castelli blurted out that Galileo had written a wonderful essay on the topic. But Galileo assumes that the Earth really moves, said someone. To which Castelli replied that Galileo did not go beyond showing that if the Earth moved, then the tides would necessarily follow. The qualifier is important. Before Castelli could leave, Cardinal Francesco Barberini told him privately that if the Earth were really in motion, "it would have to be considered a planet, something that seems too much at variance with theology."

Here was the rub. The master of the sacred palace, Father Riccardi, might believe that Copernicanism had nothing to do with Scripture or religion. It was a clever theory that was useful for astronomical computation but about whose truth nothing could be decided. Pope Urban VIII, his nephew Cardinal Francesco Barberini, and other Church dignitaries did not think it was quite so simple. If the Earth travelled around the Sun, it ceased to be at the center of the world and lost its distinctiveness. Changing its location entailed changing its nature. It was no longer unique but just one of several planets. A number of questions then raised their ugly heads, such as: Are there intelligent beings on other planets? And if so, how are we to understand the meaning of original sin, the incarnation, and the whole of redemption? These issues had been mooted as early as 1611 by professors in Perugia and had been passed on to Galileo by Monsignor Piero Dini. Urban VIII, while still a cardinal, had mentioned them to Ciampoli in 1615, and his nephew now felt the need to remind Castelli, and hence Galileo, that they were still a matter of real concern.

Castelli bluffed his way out of this awkward situation by telling Cardinal Francesco Barberini that Galileo could show that the Earth was not a planet, just as easily as he could prove that the Moon was not the Earth. The cardinal was not overwhelmed by the claim but he contented himself with saying that Galileo "would have to prove all this, but as for the rest it could pass." What Francesco Barberini intended by "the rest" is not clear. Bellarmine, his predecessor at the Holy Office, had stated in his letter to Foscarini of 1616 that only a compelling proof of the Earth's motion would warrant reinterpreting the passages in the Bible that appear to state the opposite. In his *Letter to Christina* Galileo had argued that Scripture does not teach how the heavens go but how to go to Heaven, but since the ban on Copernicanism of 1616 he had been careful not to refer to this correspondence. The events of 1616 could not be wished away, and Riccardi, for all his *bonhomie* and good will, could not behave as though they did not exist. Ever the optimist, their mutual friend Monsignor Ciampoli was convinced that Galileo only had to appear in Rome to triumph over any eventual difficulty. Because he had convinced them, Castelli and Ciampoli were sure that Galileo could convince anyone.

ECCLESIASTICAL PENSIONS

The correspondence between Galileo and Castelli reveals another aspect of Galileo's ties with the Church. We have seen that Galileo had obtained from Urban VIII a title of canon for his son Vincenzio. This sinecure was attached to a church in Brescia in northern Italy and would have guaranteed a small annual income for the rest of Vincenzio's life in exchange for no real work. All that was required was receiving the tonsure, namely having some of the hair clipped from one's head as part of the ritual marking the entrance into the clerical state. Vincenzio objected to this, and Galileo requested that the pension be transferred to his nephew, also called Vincenzio. When this did not work, Galileo took steps to have it passed to his grandson, the little Galileo, as soon as the boy was born in December 1630.

The attribution of the income of a canon to a nonresident person was already an abuse, but requesting it for a baby was carrying things too far even for Castelli, who had been charged with negotiating with the authorities. While Galileo was trying to push the deal through, a second canonry became available in the cathedral at Pisa, and he was able to secure it for himself. The papal brief that conferred the title upon him is dated 12 February 1630 and includes the customary reference to the recipient's "honest life and morals, as well as his other praiseworthy qualities of uprightness and virtue." When it became clear after a year's maneuvering that the Brescia canonry could not be transferred to his grandson, Galileo had it placed in his own name. For his remaining years he was to receive from the two canonries a combined annuity that amounted to one hundred scudi. This may have been only one-tenth of his annual salary, but we must recall that as the grand duke's personal mathematician, he was the highest paid official in Tuscany. One hundred scudi was roughly the annual wage of a qualified worker. Galileo was not required to wear a habit or change his lifestyle, but he did have his hair cut, and he received the ecclesiastical tonsure at the hands of Archbishop Alessandro Strozzi on 5 April 1631. From then on, he was a member of the clergy and was occasionally referred to as such in legal documents.

A PRIVATE VISIT?

On 13 January 1630 Galileo confirmed in a letter to Cesi that he wanted his book to be published in Rome and that he was willing to go there to correct the galleys. On 26 January Cesi acknowledged receipt of Galileo's two letters, apologized for the delay in replying due to his increasing ill health, and assured him that as far as the galleys were concerned, Galileo would merely have to tell them what to do.

At about this time Galileo received a letter from Giovanfrancesco Buonamici, the Tuscan ambassador to Spain, to whom he had written in November 1629 requesting information about the period of the tides on the Spanish coast and elsewhere. What motivated this query was Galileo's belated discovery that in the Mediterranean there are two high tides and two low tides each day, and not only one high tide and one low tide as his own theory demanded. Buonamici made enquiries and confirmed that the flow and ebb of the sea followed a 12- and not a 24-hour cycle. This was devastating news for Galileo's explanation of the tides, which postulated one high tide at noon and one low tide at midnight. But Galileo did not panic and merely concluded that these discrepancies could be explained by the odd shapes and the varying depth of the ocean floor. He was so convinced of the validity of his proof of the Earth's motion that he continued to believe, in the teeth of evidence, that the diurnal period in the ocean followed a 24- and not a 12-hour cycle. His faith in his theory was greater than his trust in what sailors reported.

Meanwhile in Rome, Castelli had seen Father Riccardi again and he felt increasingly confident that all would go well, but Ciampoli was beginning to fear that trouble might be brewing higher up. Castelli thought that Galileo should arrive in Rome in some official capacity, but Ciampoli felt otherwise and recommended that Galileo appear to be travelling "for his own pleasure and in order to see friends and patrons."

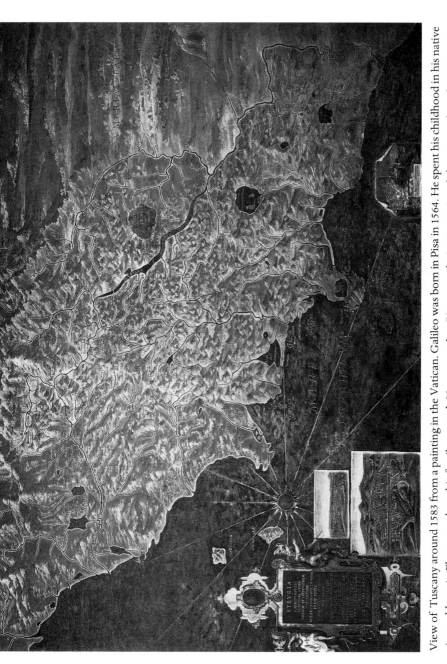

View of Tuscany around 1583 from a painting in the Vatican. Galileo was born in Pisa in 1564. He spent his childhood in his native city and later in Florence where his family moved. He returned to Pisa to study (1581-1585) and then to teach at the University (1589-1592) before being appointed to the University of Padua (1592-1610) where he spent 18 years. He was made Mathematician and Philosopher of the Granduke of Tuscany in 1610, and he returned to Florence where he lived until his death in 1642.

FIORENZA

View of Florence around 1583 from a painting in the Vatican. The Cathedral and the Palazzo della Signoria, the seat of the government of Tuscany, are at the centre. To the left the Dominican church of Santa Maria Novella where the friar Tommaso Caccini preached against Copernicanism on 21 December 1614. To the right, the Franciscan Church of Santa Croce where Galileo is buried.

View of Rome around 1583 from a painting in the Vatican. Galileo did not travel much and he was never outside Italy, but he went to Rome six times in the course of his lifetime. He made his first trip in 1587 to enlist the support of the Jesuit professors of the Roman College (now the Gregorian University) in his quest for a university position. On his second trip in 1611 he was given a triumphant welcome after his telescopic observations of the surface of the Moon and his discovery of four satellites of Jupiter. His third trip in 1615-1616 was less successful: he failed to convince the Roman authorities that Copernicanism was not at variance with what the Bible teaches. On his fourth trip in 1624 he met the new Pope Urban VIII and left with the impression that he could now write about the motion of the Earth. This led to his fifth trip in 1630 to obtain permission to print his *Dialogue on the Two Chief World Systems*. In his sixth and last trip in 1633 he came to face trial.

P CHRISTOPHORVS CLAVIVS

To the left, portrait of the Jesuit Christopher Clavius, and below, painting of the facade of the Roman College, which is now a high school. Galileo make his first trip to Rome in 1587, when he was 23 years old. He met Christopher Clavius who was professor of astronomy at the Roman College and one of the most distinguished mathematicians of his time. Clavius provided Galileo with a letter of recommendation when he applied for a position at the University of Pisa.

he tomb of Pope Gregory XIII in St. Peter's incorporates a marble bas-relief that shows him receiving the
port of the Commission for the Reform of the Calendar that had been at work for several years. Clavius
as one of the main members of this Commission, which was implemented in 1582. The result is still known
the Gregorian Calendar.

Painting in the Vatican showing Sixtus V entering the Basilica of Saint John Lateran, the official cathedral of the diocese of Rome. This was both a religious and a civic event. Pope Sixtus V, the successor of Gregory XIII, reigned for only 5 years (1585-1590) but he transformed the city of Rome. On his first trip to Rome Galileo was able to see how the Pope was making better roads, improving sanitation and building new aqueducts.

Egyptian obelisks had been brought to Rome in Ancient time. Sixtus V erected several of them in the heart of the city and had them surmounted with a cross to indicate the victory of Christianity over paganism. The one above was removed to St. Peter's in 1586, a year before Galileo's first visit to Rome. It bears several Latin inscriptions. One reads, "Christ triumphs, Christ reigns, Christ commands, Christ defends his people from all evil", and another, "Here is the cross of the Lord that dispersed his enemies. The lion of the tribe of Juda is victorious." On the right, the obelisk is being carried to St. Peter's.

The Quirinal, which lies on the highest of the Seven Hills of Rome, was renovated and enlarged by Sixtus V who died there in 1590. The view that extends to St. Peter's on the other side of the Tiber is one of the finest in the city. The Quirinal is now the official residence of the President of the

The "Happy Water" fountain (Acqua Felice in Italian), which was designed by Domenico Fontana, brought water to Rome by means of a restored aqueduct. Water pours out of the mouths of four ancient phorphyry lions One of the most popular public works of Sixtus V, it was inaugurated on 8 September 1589, the feast of the nativity of the Blessed Virgin. The central statue represents Moses striking the rock to draw water, the other two represent Aaron and Gedeon. Below, the coat of arms of Sixtus V.

COSMVS. II:
FERDINANDI ET CHRISTINÆ A LOTHARINGIA F:
MAGNVS DVX ETRVRIÆ QVARTVS

Adriano Haluech Sculp

Portraits of Granduke Cosimo II and his mother the Granduchess Christina of Lorraine. Cosimo, who had been given private lectures by Galileo during the summer months, called him back to Florence in 1610. The Granduchess Christina of Lorraine was responsible for the discussion that gave rise to Galileo's famous *Letter to the Granduchess Christina* in which he argues that the motion of the Earth is not at variance with the Bible.

CHRISTINA A LOTHARINGIA
CAROLI DVCIS LOTHARINGIÆ FILIA
FERDINANDI I. MAGNI DVCIS ETRVRIÆ VXOR

Adriano Haluech Sculp

Views of the facade and the interior of Palazzo Firenze. This was the residence of the Florentine Ambassador the Piazza Firenze near the Piazza Navona. It is now the headquarters of the Dante Alighieri Society. Galileo was a guest here during his second (1611) and his third (1630) trip, as well as during his sixth trip for the period that preceded his trial.

Portrait of Prince Federico Cesi and Facade of the Palazzo Gaddi-Cesi. During his second trip to trip in
Galileo was admitted to the Accademia dei Lincei that Prince Cesi had founded. The publication of Gal
works were financed by Cesi and his death in 1630 dealt a serious blow to Galileo's plans to print his *Dialog
the Two Chief World Systems* in Rome. With Cesi's help Galileo would probably have been able to avoid a
with the Roman authorities. The Palazzo Gaddi-Cesi was the Roman headquarters of the Accademia dei Li
and the inscription records that Galileo was a member.

The Portico of Sixtus V in the Basilica of St. John Lateran bears an inscription that Galileo and his friends were able to read with a telescope from the height of the Janiculum near St. Peter's. The occasion was a dinner party given by Prince Cesi to honour Galileo during his second visit to Rome in 1611.

Views of the interior of the Roman College where the Jesuit professors organized a meeting in honour of Gali
in 1611. His celestial discoveries were praised, and Cardinal Bellarmine was informed that they had be
confirmed by the Jesuits who had begun to use the telescope.

Bust of Pope Paul V by the sculptor Gian Lorenzo Bernini. Paul V granted Galileo an interview during his second visit in 1611, and another on his third visit in 1616 after Copernicus' book on the motion of the Earth had been placed on the Index of Proscribed Books. Galileo respected the ban on Copernicanism but he considered it wrong and hoped that it would soon be lifted.

The Cappella Paolina in the basilica of Santa Maria Maggiore in Rome was built by Paul V under whose under pontificate Copernicus' *On the Revolutions of the Heavenly Spheres* was put on the Index. The chapel was decorated by Ludovico Cardi, known as Cigoli from his native town, who was a friend of Galileo. In the lantern of the chapel, Cigoli painted the Moon at the feet of the Blessed Virgin, not as a smooth round ball but covered with craters as he had been able to observe with Galileo's telescope.

The monuments of Pope Clement VIII (above) and Pope Paul V (below) in the Paoline Chapel were designed by Flaminio Ponzio. The sculptures representing deeds of the two popes were executed by Longhi Silla. It is under the Pontificate of Clement VIII that Giordano Bruno was burnt at the stake in 1600.

Pope Paul V belonged to the family that built the famous Villa Borghese. The Pope was proud of this fact, and when he completed the façade of St. Peter's in 1612 he stressed this in the inscription that runs across the front: PAULUS V BORGHESIUS ROMANUS.

Facade of the Villa Medici, one of several buildings owned by the Granduke of Tuscany in Rome. The Villa is now the seat of the French Academy in Rome. This is where Galileo stayed during his third trip in 1615-1616, and for a few days after his trial during his sixth trip in 1633. Galileo's wrote his "Discourse on the tides" in this beautiful residence in 1616. In this work Galileo argued, erroneously, that the tides result from the combined effect of the daily and the annual revolution of the Earth.

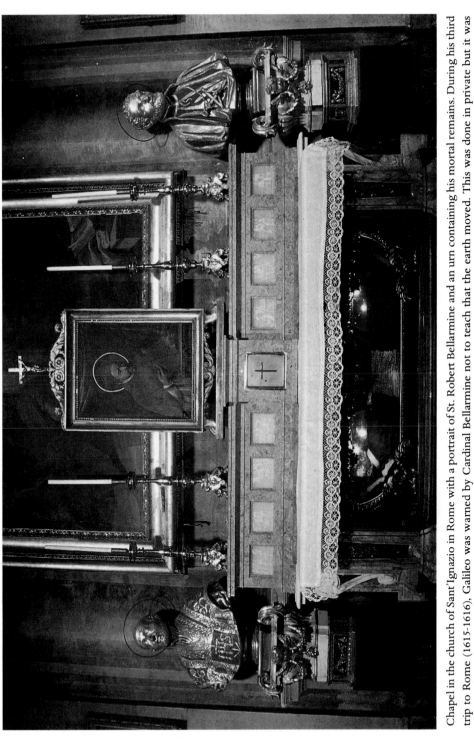

Chapel in the church of Sant'Ignazio in Rome with a portrait of St. Robert Bellarmine and an urn containing his mortal remains. During his third trip to Rome (1615-1616), Galileo was warned by Cardinal Bellarmine not to teach that the earth moved. This was done in private but it was recorded in the minutes kept at the Holy Office. This document was used during the trial in 1633 when Galileo was charged with disobeying orders.

Facade of the Palace of the Propaganda Fide (now the Congregation for the Evangelization of the world) near the Piazza di Spagna. Its first Secretary, Francesco Ingoli, debated Copernicanism with Galileo in 1616 and later put down his objections in writing. Galileo wanted to reply but was deterred by the condemnation of Copernicus' book. After his fourth trip in 1624 when Pope Urban VIII seemed more willing to allow further discussion, Galileo wrote a reply that was not published but was circulated by his friends in Rome.

FRANCISCVS EPISCOPVS OSTIEN. SACRI COL. DE-
CANVS CARD. BARBERINVS SRE·VICECANC.ET SVM·
MISTA FLORENTIN.CREAT.DIE II.OCTOB.MDCXXIII.
Obijt die 10 Decembris. 1679.

G. Valetini Scul·Jo. Jacobus de Rubeis Formis Romæ ad Templum Pacis Cum·Priuil. S. Pontif.

On the left, portrait of Urban VIII who was elected Pope in 1624. He was friendly towards Galileo and grant
him six interviews when he went to Rome for the fourth time in 1624. This made Galileo feel that he could wr
about Copernicanism as long as he did not state outright that the Earth moves around the Sun, and he publish
his *Dialogue on the Two Chief World Systems* in 1632. Urban VIII believed that Galileo had betrayed his trust, a
this influenced the events that led to Galileo's condemnation. On the right, Cardinal Francesco Barberini, t
nephew of Urban VIII and his closest collaborator. A former student at the University of Pisa, he had a genu
admiration for Galileo's works.

On the left, above, the Barberini Palace that was built during the pontificate of Urban VIII and, below, Bernini's celebrated Fontana del Tritone in the neighbouring Piazza Barberini.

The Pantheon is one of the most interesting and best preserved monuments of Roman antiquity. During his fourth trip to Rome in 1624, Galileo lodged nearby and in the immediate vicinity of the church of St. Mary Magdalene.

The Church of Sant'Ignazio that was built at the rear of the Roman College by Orazio Grassi, a Jesuit professor and architect with whom Galileo quarreled over the nature of comets.

TOMMASO CAMPANELLA

The Dominican friar Tommaso Campanella was imprisoned in Naples between 1599 and 1626 when Urban VIII had him freed and and brought him to Rome. Campanella wrote an *Apology for Galileo* in 1616, and he offered to defend Galileo's *Dialogue* when it was denounced in 1632. Galileo was not keen on Campanella's support because he thought it might do him more harm than good.

The Florentine who lived in Rome met in the Church of San Giovanni dei Fiorentini on Sundays and on feastdays. It is here that in August 1632 Fr. Niccolò Riccardi mentioned to a friend of Galileo that the publication *the Dialogue on the Two Chief World Systems* was not being viewed with favour in the Vatican. This was passed on to Galileo and this is how he came to know that real trouble was brewing. Riccardi, a Florentine himself, was in charge of licencing books in Rome and he had authorised publication under pressure from the Tuscan ambassador and Galileo's friends in Rome.

FERDINANDO SECONDO GRAN DVCA DÍ TOSCA NA &c.

Ferdinando II, who succeeded Cosimo II as Granduke of Tuscany, was favourable to Galileo but he told him to go to Rome when he was summoned to appear before the tribunal of the Holy Office in 1633. The Florentine ambassador was instructed to help Galileo, who was treated with unusual clemency for the times and had his condemnation to imprisonment immediately commuted to house arrest.

Facade of the church of Santa Maria sopra Minerva that is built on the site of the temple of Minerva and is the only instance of a Gothic church in Rome. The tribunal of the Inquisition often met in the adjoining convent of the Dominicans.

View of one of the rooms of the ancient Dominican convent of Santa Maria sopra Minerva in the part that is now the library of the Chamber of Deputies. Galileo did not make his abjuration in the church itself but in this room or in one of the two adjacent ones.

The painting by Francesco Allegrini on the ceiling of the "Galileo Room" of the former convent of Santa Maria sopra Minerva celebrates the victory of Simon of Montfort over the Albigensians at the battle of Muret in 1213. Saint Dominic points to the cross as a weapon while the Virgin and child protect the Catholics. The painting was made in the eighteenth century and is posterior to Galileo's trial.

Inner Facade and garden of the Villa Medici. In 1633 Galileo was condemned to prison but the sentence was immediately commuted to house arrest in the beautiful Villa Medici of the Granduke of Tuscany. After a few days, Galileo was allowed to accept the invitation of the archbishop of Sienna where he spent a few months before returning to his home in Arcetri in the suburbs of Florence. It is here that he wrote his scientific masterpiece, the *Two New Sciences*. He died in 1642 at the age of 78 years.

The Grand Duke Ferdinando II, who had turned 18 two years earlier, was now the effective ruler of Tuscany, and his official endorsement would involve the government and complicate matters.

Castelli went on telling Riccardi that Galileo was happy that his book was to be revised by him, and Riccardi kept promising to fix things when he had not seen, let alone read, the manuscript of the *Dialogue*. No one, except the author, knew exactly what the book contained. Neither Cesi nor Ciampoli, nor Castelli, nor Riccardi had held it in his hands. They knew what the main argument was, but they had only a vague notion of how the book was structured or in what way the arguments were marshalled. Riccardi was being asked to buy a pig in a poke, and he was too vain or too kind to declare that he could not give the work a clean bill of health before actually reading it. Galileo's friends were convinced that he had produced a great book, and they were anxious to see it appear. Manipulating Father Riccardi, always so anxious to please, did not seem to them objectionable. Hoodwinking Cardinal Francesco Barberini or, worse still, the pope, however unwittingly, was another matter.

AN ASTROLOGER IN THE WINGS

Like all European courts in the seventeenth century, the Rome of Urban VIII saw the arrival and departure of controversial and sometimes bizarre figures. One of these was the Dominican Tommaso Campanella, who had been among the first to praise Galileo's *Sidereal Message* when it appeared in 1610. Condemned to a life sentence for leading a rebellion against the Spaniards, Campanella was incarcerated in Naples from 1599 until 1626, when Urban VIII had him moved to Rome. It was while he was in prison in Naples that he wrote his *Apology for Galileo,* which was published in Germany without proper ecclesiastical permission in 1622. Campanella was an authority on astrology, and there is some evidence that he was asked by Pope Urban VIII to study his horoscope and suggest ways of avoiding any evil influence that eclipses and comets might exercise, including sickness and disease. This may seem naive to the modern reader, but we must remember that the bacterial theory of disease was unknown in the seventeenth century and that perfectly reasonable people were willing to try any prophylaxis that had not been disproved. Too much caution was better than too little. Campanella was also a prolific and influential writer, and the pope, at least at first, seems to have enjoyed his company. Campanella bragged about one of these conversations, as we know from what Castelli wrote to Galileo on 16 March 1630.

> In the last few days Father Campanella was speaking with His Holiness and he told him that he had had the opportunity to convert some German gentlemen to the Catholic faith towards which they were very favorably inclined. However, when they heard about the prohibition of Copernicus, etc., they were scandalized, and he had been unable to go further. His Holiness answered with these very words: "It was never our intention, and if it had been up to us that decree would not have been issued."

Campanella's admiration for Galileo was not an unmixed blessing. He seized upon the implications of the new astronomy and carried them farther than Galileo himself. For Campanella the telescope had proved conclusively that there are other planets as important as "this star our Earth," and that these could have inhabitants like ourselves or perhaps greater. This kind of speculation was considered flighty in Rome. It was also dangerous: The last thing the Church wanted was an open debate on the nature of hypothetical planetary dwellers. What Urban VIII said to Campanella in 1630 is exactly what he had told Cardinal Zollern in 1624. Copernicanism was not a heresy, to be sure, but it went against the apparent fact that the Earth is at rest at the center of the world, something virtually all biblical scholars took for granted.

THE VISIT IS OFFICIAL

As was becoming customary, Galileo postponed his departure while he tried to obtain an official or semi-official recognition of his trip. Ciampoli had invited him to stay in his home, but Galileo hoped to be lodged in the more prestigious Tuscan embassy at the Palazzo Firenze or in the Villa Medici, where he had been received in style in 1615. As events were to show, it was a good thing that Galileo did not stay with Ciampoli. In April 1630, it began to be rumored that Ciampoli had lost the pope's favor. Although Castelli pooh-poohed the news in a letter to Galileo, the alarm bell had been sounded. Ciampoli had not fallen in disgrace . . . yet. He was to do so at a later date and at the worst possible moment for Galileo.

On 8 April Galileo wrote a long letter to Giovanfrancesco Buonamici in Madrid in which he mentioned that he expected to leave for Rome within eight or ten days in order to return to Florence for the patron feast of Saint John the Baptist on 24 June. But on 18 April, he was still in Florence awaiting a letter of recommendation for the ambassador in Rome. He was helped in this matter by Geri Bocchineri, the brother-in-law of his son, who occupied the influential position of private secretary to Andrea Cioli, the secretary of state. Bocchineri was fond of Galileo and went to some trouble to see that Galileo had the letter for the ambassador on Sunday, 28 April 1630, the date of his departure. Bocchineri also arranged for a granducal litter to fetch Galileo between the eighteenth and the twentieth hour. In the seventeenth century, hours were numbered from sunset, so that this means roughly between 2:00 and 4:00 P.M. in our way of counting. The vehicle was brought to the Convent of San Matteo so that Galileo could bid his two daughters farewell.

Galileo was travelling in an official capacity, but things had been arranged pretty much at the last moment, and the ambassador, Francesco Niccolini, was surprised to see him arrive in Rome, unannounced and unexpected, on the evening of Friday, 3 May. He nonetheless made him welcome and informed Cioli on the next day that he had provided lodging for him "in this palace," by which is meant the official residence, the Palazzo Firenze, and not the villa Medici. In his reply on 11 May, Cioli told Niccolini not to marvel at Galileo's sudden appearance. He also knew nothing about the trip until he was told by the grand duke to give Galileo a letter of endorsement. Fortunately, the ambassador and his wife, Caterina Riccardi, a cousin of the master of the sacred palace, were gracious hosts and they saw to his comfort and welfare.

THE ROME OF URBAN VIII

Galileo does not seem to have kept a close eye on politics, but he could not have failed to notice that things had changed in Rome since 1624, when he had been able to see the new pope, Urban VIII, six times in six weeks. This was no longer possible in the tense political climate of 1630. The Thirty Years' War, which had begun as a clash between German Catholic and Protestant princes had spiralled out of control to involve many other countries including Italy, France, Spain, Portugal, Sweden, Denmark, Poland, Transylvania, and Turkey. By 1630, only a few of the various causes that fuelled the conflict still pertained to genuinely religious issues. Particularly worrisome was the struggle between the Catholic monarchs of France and Spain for control of the Holy Roman empire. As the leader of Christendom, the pope might have been expected to try to reconcile the French Bourbons and the Spanish Habsburg, but whereas he had been papal legate in France and had held the newborn Louis XIII at the baptismal font, he had never been in Spain and he resented its influence in the Italian peninsula. His overt sympathy for King Louis XIII and Cardinal Richelieu irked the Spanish cardinals, who began to denounce his policy. In return Urban VIII grew suspicious of officials who had close ties with Spanish prelates. Unfortunately, Ciampoli was eventually found to be a part of this group.

These worries made the pontiff so restless that he ordered all the birds in his garden killed because they disrupted his sleep with their nocturnal calls. The pope had become enmeshed in the war of the Mantuan Succession, in which French and Spanish interests were again at stake. To cover the high cost of equipping 7,000 infantrymen and 800 cavalry, Urban VIII had to raise taxes in the pontifical states, thereby undermining his popularity. The War of the Mantuan Succession had an even more unfortunate consequence: The Austrian Habsburg troops that crossed the Alps left the plague in their wake in 1629. As we shall see, the disease spread like wildfire.

Discontent with the pope's external policy was fuelled by resentment against the promotions and pensions that he showered on members of his family. Nepotism was a way of insuring that higher officials remained loyal, but it was often used to accumulate wealth at the expense of more worthy causes. Shortly after his election in 1623, Urban VIII had made his brother, Antonio, and a nephew, Francesco, cardinals. In 1628, he added his youngest nephew, also called Antonio, who was barely 19. Meanwhile, he had chosen the middle child among his three nephews, Taddeo, to perpetuate the Barberini name and had married him to the daughter of a titled Roman family.

Urban VIII had always been proud of his gifts as a versifier, and he was only too ready to accept the adulation of courtiers who called him the greatest poet of his age. When he reformed the breviary, the handbook of prayers to be recited each day by persons in holy orders, he did not hesitate to add his own original hymnal compositions in honor of the saints that he canonized. He even undertook a lasting memorial to his name in the basilica of St. Peter by ordering the great architect Gian Lorenzo Bernini to erect a monumental canopy or *baldacchino* over the tomb of the first of the apostles. When Galileo returned to Rome in 1630 the huge bronze *baldacchino* was rising from four marble plinths, each emblazoned on two sides with the Barberini three-bee coat of arms. Four support pillars spiralled upward 29 meters toward the canopy, which was still under construction. The enormous quantity of bronze required for this gigantic structure had been plundered from the Pantheon, which even the barbarians had left intact. The punning gibe, "What the barbarians did not do, the Barberinis did," was soon in the mouth of every Roman. The growing dissatisfaction with the Barberinis found expression in a way that was characteristic of the age: Astrological forecasts prophesying the early demise of the pontiff began to appear. As might be foreseen, Galileo's name was to be associated with these ill-advised horoscopes.

THE OTHER GUEST

While Galileo was being made welcome at the official residence in the Palazzo Firenze, preparations were under way to receive someone else at the Palazzo del Giardino, the Villa Medici where Galileo had himself resided in 1615. The new guest was a 31-year-old painter on his first trip to Rome. His full name was Diego Rodriguez de Silva y Velazquez. Like Galileo, Velazquez was in the employ of a prince, but one of much higher standing, Philip IV, the king of Spain and the most powerful ruler of Europe.

Velazquez had sailed from Barcelona on 10 August 1629 and had stopped in Venice and Ferrara before going to Rome, where he received a warm welcome from Cardinal Francesco Barberini. He was offered an apartment in the Vatican, but when he saw the Villa Medici he fell in love with the place and asked the Spanish ambassador, Count de Mounterrey, to see if he could live there. The count wrote to the grand duke in Florence, who was happy to instruct his Roman ambassador to extend an official invitation to the painter. On 19 May 1630, the Villa Medici was ready for Velazquez, but Ambassador Niccolini voiced unease about Cardinal Francesco Barberini's possible reluctance to relinquish such an attraction. Everything worked smoothly, however, and Velazquez was pleased with his new surroundings, where he made two paintings of the gardens, which now hang in the Prado in Madrid. The scenes they represent are exactly those we can admire today at the Villa Medici. Among the famous works that Velazquez painted in Rome are "Joseph's Bloody Coat Brought to Jacob" and "The Forge of Vulcan," which added to his fame.

Velazquez and Galileo were guests of the Florentine government at the same time, but in different residences. Did they meet? Ambassador Niccolini was a man who enjoyed bringing people together, and Galileo was interested in painting and a friend of some of the best artists of his age. Since their stays overlapped by more than a month, Galileo and Velazquez almost certainly knew of each other's presence, and it is likely that they met at the ambassador's table. Galileo fared better at the Palazzo

Firenze than Velazquez, who fell ill with a "tertiary fever" (perhaps malaria) at the Villa Medici and had to take up residence with the Spanish ambassador after Galileo had returned to Florence.

Velazquez journeyed back to Spain early in 1631. He stopped in Naples to make a portrait of the sister of King Philip IV, Maria, who had just married the king of Hungary, who later became the emperor, Ferdinand III. While in Naples, Velazquez bought some works of another Spanish painter, José Ribera, then at the height of his powers.

PAPAL AUDIENCE

When Galileo arrived in Rome Urban VIII was staying at Castel Gandolfo, some thirty kilometers away, in an old castle that he had restored and turned into his country residence. But no sooner had he returned to Rome around mid-May than he granted Galileo an audience. This was to be their only meeting during the eight weeks Galileo spent in Rome. His Holiness, as we have seen, had to attend to more pressing matters than guesswork about the nature of the rising and the setting of the Sun.

Galileo was probably received by the Pontiff on 18 May, the very day the gossip column known as the *Avvisi* spread the following item of news:

> Galileo, the famous mathematician and astronomer, is here to try to publish a book in which he attacks several opinions held by the Jesuits. He has been understood to say that D. Anna. [Anna Colonna, the wife of Taddeo Barberini, the Pope's nephew] will give birth to a son, that we shall have peace in Italy at the end of June, and that shortly thereafter Taddeo and the Pope will die. This last point is confirmed by the Neapolitan Caracioli, by Father Campanella, and by several articles that discuss the election of a new Pontiff as if the Holy See were already vacant.

Galileo's arrival on 3 May came as a surprise to Ambassador Niccolini, but it was soon no secret that he was in Rome to have his book published. The claim that he attacked the Jesuits was not entirely false since they were reputed to oppose Copernicanism, but the rumor that he had something to do with the news sheets retailing prophecies of the early death of the pope was pure libel. As a professional astronomer, Galileo occasionally cast horoscopes, and a disreputable journalist could seize on that to write a sensational article that rested on no other evidence than the fact that life-threatening forecasts concerning the Barberini had begun to appear. Alas, some of Galileo's friends may have been involved in these dubious exercises in astrological computation.

When Father Riccardi received the *Dialogue* from Galileo's own hands, he passed it on to a fellow Dominican, Father Raffaello Visconti, who was interested in astronomy but whose curiosity extended well beyond into astrology and the occult sciences. He was a personal friend of Orazio Morandi, the abbot of the church of Santa Prassede in Rome, a master of the Hermetic arts and the author of horoscopes. He had even cast one of Galileo, whom he had known since at least 1613. On Sunday, 26 May 1630, roughly a week after meeting the pope, Galileo was invited to dinner by Morandi, in company of Father Visconti and another consultant of the Holy Office. We know nothing of their conversation.

The article in the *Avvisi* denouncing Galileo's dire forecast for the Barberini family attracted attention. Michelangelo Buonarroti, the nephew of the great sculptor by the same name, was in Rome at the time, and Galileo asked him to broach the subject when he met Cardinal Francesco Barberini early in June in order to explain that he was innocent of any astrological foul play. No sooner had Buonarroti mentioned the rumor to the cardinal than the cardinal cut him short to say that he did not believe a word of it and that Galileo had "no better friend than the Pope and himself," as Buonarroti reported to Galileo on 3 June.

PLAYING POLITICS

We do not know what Galileo said to Urban VIII when they met, but the pope did most of the talking during audiences and it was not always easy to get in a word. How much Galileo was allowed to say will remain a mystery, but when he left he was firmly resolved to use all his contacts to get his book published. He had already requested the help of Filippo Niccolini, the brother of Ambassador Francesco Niccolini, and the principal advisor of Prince Giovan Carlo de' Medici, the grand duke's brother. On behalf of the prince, Filippo Niccolini told Visconti that whatever he did to expedite matters would give the grand duke great pleasure. The poor Dominican priest had probably never been the object of so much attention, but, unfortunately, the pressure that was brought to bear came from political and diplomatic figures who knew little about sensitive issues in theology.

The key player remained the pope, and his position had not changed. Galileo knew how Urban VIII felt from the conversation he had had with Cardinal Zollern in 1624. Better still, he had heard it from the pope's own lips probably as early as 1616. What the pontiff had said was recorded by Agostino Oregio, the pope's personal theologian, in a book published in 1629. While still a cardinal, Urban VIII asked a learned friend of his, who had worked out how the planets move on the assumption that the Earth moved, whether some other model was conceivable. If you want to say no, declared the pope, you would have to show that it would imply a contradiction, for God can do anything that is logically possible.

There can be little doubt that the "learned friend" was Galileo, for the pope's argument is echoed at the end of the *Dialogue*. Unfortunately it comes after four days of a passionate defence of Copernicanism and it is placed in the mouth of Simplicio, who did not distinguish himself by his intelligence during that time. Simplicio is made to say to Galileo's spokesman, Salviati, that he considers his ideas ingenious but not conclusive because he bears in mind what he heard "from a most eminent and learned person, before which one must fall silent." He does not doubt that if Salviati were asked whether God, in His infinite power and wisdom, could have produced the tides without setting the Earth in motion, he would reply that He could in a number of ways that we cannot even imagine. "From this," Simplicio says, "I conclude that it would be excessive boldness for anyone to limit and restrict the Divine power and wisdom to some particular fancy of his own."

Having listened impatiently to Simplicio, Salviati burst out,

> What an admirable and angelic doctrine, and well in accord with another one, also Divine, which, while it grants to us the right to argue about the constitution of the universe (perhaps in order that the working of the human mind should not be curtailed or made lazy) adds that we cannot discover the work of His hands. Let us, then, exercise these activities permitted to us and ordained by God, that we may recognize and thereby so much the more admire His greatness, however much less fit we may find ourselves to penetrate the profound depths of His infinite wisdom.

The claim that God can create things in a variety of ways is not ludicrous in itself, but it arrives at an awkward moment after Salviati has shown that reasonable people should embrace the overwhelming evidence in favor of Copernicanism. For someone who had read the *Dialogue* from beginning to end, the passage we have quoted would have an ironical ring, but taken in isolation and without awareness of what comes before, it might pass muster. Galileo was not foolish enough to enjoy a cheap joke at the pope's expense, but he may have been vain enough to think that neither he nor his censors would notice. In this, he was sadly mistaken. When the book finally appeared in print in 1632, someone murmured in the pontiff's ear that he was being ridiculed.

GALILEO'S HIGH HOPES

But all this unpleasantness was in the future. In the spring of 1630 Galileo was convinced that he could carry the day and he applied himself to his correspondence with influential people. In order to ensure the benevolence of the 20-year-old Grand Duke Ferdinando II, Galileo kept him informed of his progress in Rome by writing to Count Orso d'Elci, the grand duke's chamberlain. What Galileo hoped to achieve is known from the chamberlain's reply of 3 June:

> I am happy that you should find that the colleague [Visconti] of the Master of the Sacred Palace realizes that your argument is sound and that he hopes to persuade even the Pope that there is no reason to be unhappy with your proof that the tides are produced by the motion of the Earth.

Galileo was aiming high. In spite of repeated warnings not to offer physical arguments but to stick to astronomical conjectures, he still dreamt of turning Urban VIII round and getting his full endorsement. His letters to his Florentine friends positively encouraged the notion that he had already succeeded in his task. On 3 June 1630 another prominent person, Jacopo Giraldi, wrote to congratulate him on the happy outcome of his business in Rome. Galileo's optimism seemed to be confirmed on Sunday, 16 June, when he received the following communication from Father Visconti:

> The Master [Riccardi] sends his greetings and says that he is pleased with the book and will talk about the frontispiece with the Pope tomorrow. As far as the rest is concerned, once a few small things, such as those that we adjusted together, have been fixed, he will return the book.

The letter is signed, "Your Most affectionate servant and disciple." Galileo had clearly won Visconti over. Together they had revised a few potentially troublesome passages, and Riccardi was satisfied, although he wanted to make a few small changes. All that remained to be discussed with the pope was the frontispiece, an engraving showing Aristotle, Ptolemy, and Copernicus. Just a routine check. Things could hardly have looked better, and when Galileo left Rome on Wednesday, 26 June, he had every reason to feel elated. So did Ambassador Niccolini, who wrote to the secretary of state in Florence that Galileo had achieved all he intended and that "the Pope had been glad to see him and had treated him affectionately. So had Cardinal Barberini, who kept him for dinner. All the Court honored him and treated him with the high consideration that he deserves." The grand duke must have been delighted: Rome seemed not only willing but eager to oblige his personal mathematician.

The political and diplomatic side looked rosy, but what had really been achieved? When Riccardi was handed over the manuscript of the *Dialogue* in April he already knew that the book was an extended plea for Copernicanism. He had asked that this be toned down and that the theory be presented as a mathematical hypothesis for which no physical claim would be made. He entrusted the revision to Father Visconti, who sat down with Galileo and made a few adjustments that probably consisted in deleting claims that the Copernican system was true. Visconti reported that the undesirable material had been excised, and Riccardi, who wanted to please Galileo, the Tuscan ambassador, and the grand duke, expressed his satisfaction. But Riccardi was also concerned with staying on the pope's right side, and he acted with diplomatic cunning. He requested that a "few small things" be revised, and, more importantly, he did not formally allow the book to be printed. He skilfully conveyed the impression that all that had to be discussed with the pope was the minor point of the illustration on the front page. For the time being, he had managed to please both Florence and Rome. Galileo, he surmised, was wise enough to read between the lines and understand what had to be done.

A PATRON DIES AND A FRIEND IS IN TROUBLE

At the beginning of August 1630, Galileo received a blow when he learned that Prince Cesi had died at the age of 45, intestate, and with his finances in a sorry state. The Lyncean Academy was doomed unless Cardinal Francesco Barberini, a fellow Lyncean, came to the rescue. The cardinal did not deem it opportune to do so, and the academy suffered the fate of its founder. This was sad news for all the members of the select club, but it was singularly devastating for Galileo, who had expected Cesi to pay for the publication of the *Dialogue* and iron out the matter of the *imprima-*

tur with the master of the sacred palace. Who would now defray the cost of printing a 500-page book and, worse still, who would be in a position to speak to Riccardi and fix those "few small things"? Cesi may have become less influential in recent years, but he was a great nobleman with relatives in high places, and he had a shrewd grasp of what could and could not be attempted at the Vatican. His death meant that Galileo would have to navigate alone in a sea that was more treacherous than he suspected and where the shoals were no less real for being invisible to the naked eye. A publisher would have to be convinced that the book was marketable, and Galileo would have to attend to the business himself. This could not be done in Rome, and Galileo started casting about for a local Florentine printer.

August brought further bad news. Shortly after Galileo had left Rome for Florence, the Abbot Orazio Morandi was denounced for his astrological forecasts, summoned to the Holy Office, and imprisoned. Galileo requested information from Vincenzio Langieri, a mutual friend, who replied on 17 August that the trial was kept so secret that he had no way of finding out what was going on. All he could say was that it was called "the Big Trial" because so many people were involved. This could hardly have been comforting for Galileo if he remembered that his horoscope was among Morandi's papers.

Ciampoli fared better and on 10 August he wrote a cheery letter to Galileo to say that Urban VIII had confirmed the canonry for which he had applied. He offered to read aloud to the pope the letter of thanks that Galileo would send. This was a nice gesture, but also a way of letting people in Florence know that he still had the ear of the pope.

THE PLAGUE

Galileo had advertised his book outside Italy by writing to friends such as Elia Diodati to tell them that he had found new arguments for the Copernican system and that he planned to publish his book by Easter 1630. When the book did not appear, Diodati became worried and enquired

about Galileo's health—was he still alive? The deadly plague that originated in Germany had spread southward and reached Tuscany in the
summer of 1630. It was to last three years with periods of respite, and it
took an awful toll in human lives: one-third of the population of Venice,
half the population of Milan, and three-quarters that of Mantua. The first
symptom of the contagion was the swelling of the lymph nodes under the
arms or between the thighs. These lumps, called buboes, gave the pesti-
lence the name *bubonic plague*. During its worst visitation, between 1346
and 1349, it killed 25 million people, or one-fourth the population of
Europe. Only a small number of those who contracted the illness recov-
ered. Banished for a time, the plague returned mercilessly. No one knew
why or how. The wildest causes were invoked, from noxious vapors in
the air to the influence of the stars and the planets. The remedies were
just as fanciful: For instance, Galileo's daughter, Maria Celeste, recommended an electuary of dried figs, nuts, rue leaves, salt, and honey to be
taken every morning with a glass of good wine.

The true cause of the contagion, microbes living on black rats, was
only discovered 200 years later. When a sick rat died, its fleas would spread
the disease by leaping onto and biting another rat or a human. Europeans
may have had no inkling of the germ theory of disease, but they had
learned that it was important to avoid contact with those who had
contacted the plague. The Venetian doge in 1348 had ordered that trav-
ellers from contaminated areas be kept in isolation for 40 days, hence
quarantine, from the Italian word for 40. The period of time was not based
on any clinical insight but had been chosen because Christ spent 40 days
in the desert before returning to civilization to begin his ministry.

The plague brought out the best and the worst in people. The 20-
year-old grand duke, Ferdinando II, did not flee to one of his many country
villas but stayed in Florence to dispense comfort and encouragement to
the citizens. Galileo's son, Vincenzio, took to the hills with his pregnant
wife and left his one-year old infant with Galileo in Bellosguardo, where
one of the workers, who had been diagnosed with the plague in October,
had died within a matter of days.

COMMUNICATIONS DISRUPTED

By mid-August the contagion had become serious enough for the Apostolic Nuncio in Florence to write to Rome to warn them. Benedetto Castelli was already informed when he wrote to Galileo on 24 August to urge him to have his book published in Florence as Father Visconti considered appropriate. Commerce between Florence and Rome came to a grinding halt, and letters were held back at the border of Tuscany, sometimes for close to a month. Books were confiscated and frequently destroyed. The least that could happen to them was that their covers would be burned and their pages fumigated.

Galileo managed to speed up his correspondence with Rome by sending his letters to Genoa, which was free from the plague, and having them shipped from there to Rome; the process took about 12 days. When it became clear that he could neither go to Rome nor send the bulky manuscript without risk, he asked Riccardi to be allowed to publish it in Florence. His letter was transmitted by Castelli, who acted as go-between. Riccardi's reply spells out clearly what was expected of Galileo and what had been agreed upon, admittedly before the death of Cesi and the outbreak of the plague complicated matters. "The Master of the Sacred Palace," Castelli wrote to Galileo, on 21 September 1630,

> told me that you had agreed to return to Rome to fix a few small things
> in the preface and the body of the work, but on account of the plague it
> will be enough if you send a copy of the book to Rome so that it can be
> fixed with Monsignor Ciampoli, as need may be. Once this is done, you
> can have it printed in Florence or elsewhere, as you please.

Riccardi was willing to compromise on where the book was published, but he wanted to see a copy before giving his authorization. Castelli realized how important this was, and he allowed himself a word of advice to Galileo: "I consider it absolutely necessary that you send this copy." If we assume that a manuscript page of the *Dialogue* contained about 200 words, then the work ran to roughly 900 pages. Making a copy of such a long work was a tedious and costly affair, and we can understand why Galileo tried to shirk it by putting pressure on Riccardi. He wrote to Caterina Niccolini, the wife of the Roman ambassador, who was the cousin of Father Riccardi, and asked her to intervene. On October 19, she reported that she had been almost completely successful. Riccardi would rest content if Galileo sent the preface and the ending of the book, but he had specified that the book must be revised in Florence by a theologian who was accustomed to this kind of work and belonged to the Dominican friars like himself. He suggested Father Ignazio Del Nente, but he left Galileo free to propose someone else as long as it was a member of his religious order.

Del Nente was a well-known friar who had recently been re-elected prior of the Convent of San Marco for the third time. He was busy at the time with preparations for the canonization of Dominica da Paradiso, the holy woman to whom Florentines prayed for those who had contracted the plague, and the organization of a solemn procession that was to take place on 5 December to transfer the bodily remains of St. Antonino, the protector of the city, from the Convent of San Marco to the cathedral. Galileo feared that Del Nente would not have the leisure to read a scientific work, and he proposed another Dominican, Father Iacinto Stefani, a consultant of the Florentine Inquisition and the former court preacher of Christina of Lorraine. Once again he appealed to the Roman ambassador's wife and entrusted her with the mission of convincing Father Riccardi. On 17 November 1630 she reported that Riccardi had agreed, albeit reluctantly, but that he had once more insisted on seeing the preface and the end of the book before appointing Stefani and giving him "a few instructions."

Castelli, who had also been pressed into service, assured Galileo, on 30 November, that Riccardi had promised him "several times to expedite the licensing of the *Dialogue* and entrust the business to Father Stefani." This was the good news. The bad one was that Father Visconti, the Roman censor who had been favorable toward the *Dialogue*, was "in deep trouble over I do not know what astrological writing." Visconti's difficulties were linked to those of his friend Orazio Morandi, at whose trial an *Astrological Discourse on the Life of Urban VIII*, bearing Visconti's name, had been brought forward. Visconti must have been partly successful in his plea of innocence, since he was only banished from Rome while others received very heavy sentences. Although his career was broken, Visconti was luckier than Morandi, who had died in jail on 7 November 1630, something that Castelli learned only much later. The outcome of Morandi's trial was the Papal Bull *Against Astrologers*, which was promulgated a few months later on 1 April 1631. It renewed the prescriptions of Sixtus V's Bull *Coeli ac Terrae Creator* of 5 January 1586, directed against astrologers who claimed the power of knowing the future and of setting in motion certain secret forces for the good or hurt of the living. Urban VIII commanded that an eye should be kept on such magical arts as were directed against the life of the pope and that of his relatives down to the third degree. Those guilty of such offenses were to be punished not only with excommunication but also with death and confiscation of property. That Galileo's name should have been associated with those of Morandi and Visconti was unfortunate, to say the least.

A TERRIBLE WINTER

The plague continued to be severe throughout the winter of 1630, and public health officials sought to halt the spread of the infection by sending the stricken to hospitals, burning their belongings, and boarding up their homes. Relatives who were trapped inside had to wait 22 days before going out while subsisting on the food that the authorities distributed and that was hoisted up in baskets from the street. The health officers tried to discourage large gatherings, but the clergy organized processions and called on their flock to meet for prayer in the churches. In the clash that ensued, the pope sided with those who wanted larger crowds in the houses of worship. The whole board of health was reprimanded, but they were undeterred and took the difficult decision of imposing a general quarantine that was to have begun on 25 December but was postponed until 22 January 1631 when it became clear that preparations would take longer than expected. Men were allowed out of their home at the beginning of March but women and children were not permitted to leave until 22 April.

During this period, Galileo heard the sad news that his brother, Michelangelo, had died in Munich, and that his widow and children were in a state of penury. Holed up in his villa in Bellosguardo, Galileo turned 67 on 15 February 1631. He was growing old and people were dying all around him. Some 7,000 inhabitants, out of a population of 70,000, had perished in Florence since the outbreak of the plague. Galileo did not want to disappear without seeing his *Dialogue* in print, but he had no news from Riccardi. As soon as he was allowed to leave his forced sequestration, he went down to the Granducal Palace on 6 March 1631 to lodge a complaint about the way things were being dragged out in Rome. He hoped to speak to the grand duke himself but suddenly felt ill and had to return home without doing so.

He decided to put what he had to say in a letter, which he wrote the very next day to Andrea Cioli, the secretary of state. In his long letter Galileo stressed his good will and recalled that he had travelled to Rome to personally hand over his manuscript to the master of the sacred palace, Father Riccardi, who had it examined by Visconti but also read it himself, according to Galileo, before returning it duly signed and authorized. Galileo then went back to Florence intending to send the final version to Prince Cesi, who had agreed to have it published in Rome. Unfortunately, Cesi died before this could be done, and the outbreak of the plague and the disruption of communications up and down the peninsula necessitated publication in Florence. Galileo insisted on the fact that he had secured proper permission for the printer from all the local authorities, from the bishop's vicar to the Florentine inquisitor and the grand duke's official book reviewer. He had even informed (out of courtesy, as it seemed to him) Father Riccardi, only to be told by the wife of the Roman ambassador that he wanted to see the book once again. Galileo then called on the secretary of state to enquire whether the manuscript could safely be sent to Rome. He was warned against trying to do so because even ordinary letters had a hard time getting through, so he merely sent the preface and the ending of the book. This was done so that Father Riccardi might change whatever he saw fit, cutting, rewording, or even describing his ideas as dreams or chimeras. Riccardi agreed that the rest of the work could be revised in Florence by Father Stefani, and this good friar was so moved,

> that he shed tears more than once when he saw with how much humility and reverent submission I defer to the authority of my superiors. He declares, as all those who have read the book, that I should have been begged to publish such as work rather than hindered.

Although satisfied with the preface and the ending, Riccardi never returned them to Galileo. "And my work has been put aside in a corner," laments Galileo, "my life wastes away and I am in continuous bad health." Hence his appeal to the grand duke, "so that while I am still alive I may see the outcome of my long and hard work." But what steps could be taken? Galileo had no hesitation in telling the secretary of state: Find out what Father Riccardi is really up to, and then order the ambassador to have a word with him and tell him in no uncertain terms that the grand duke wants the matter settled promptly, not least to show "what kind of people he has in his employ."

Any unprejudiced person reading this letter could only feel pity for the elderly scientist whose life's work was held up by the incompetence of civil servants. Galileo had made an excellent case for himself, but he had not been entirely candid. For one thing, he had carefully avoided mentioning that the topic was sensitive. There was no reference to the condemnation of Copernicanism in 1616, and not a word was breathed about the injunction he had received from Cardinal Bellarmine not to teach or defend *in any way* that the Earth moves. Furthermore, Galileo's claim that in the spring of 1630 Riccardi personally read the *Dialogue* must be qualified in the light of the report that Riccardi submitted to Urban VIII in 1633. Riccardi states that he could not read the book at the time but that in order to speed things up, he had agreed to see it *page by page* as it came off the press. With this proviso, he granted his *imprimatur* for publication *in Rome*. Neither Galileo nor Riccardi could foresee the death of Cesi, and neither was trying to distort the truth, but both wanted to put their best construction on what had happened. There is no doubt however, that Riccardi had not read the *Dialogue* in 1630 and that his license to print was initially limited to Rome.

POLITICS AT WORK

Galileo's letter to the secretary of state had the effect he desired. It was read to the grand duke who immediately instructed the Roman ambassador to impress upon Riccardi that he wanted the *Dialogue* published without further delay. This seems to have placed Ambassador Niccolini in something of a quandary since he chose not to act himself but instead had his wife speak to her cousin, Father Riccardi. The whole trouble, as Niccolini reported to the secretary of state, on 16 March, was that Riccardi did not want the book examined by Father Stefani but by Father Del Nente. Riccardi was clearly dragging his feet. The secretary of state kept returning to the matter in his correspondence with Niccolini who asked, on 5 April 1631, for another week to win over the master of the sacred palace. The secretary of state granted him six days, after which he wrote to remind him that the orders came expressly from the grand duke. On 13 April Niccolini pleaded again for more time "to find a compromise with the Master of the Sacred Palace if we cannot obtain what we wish." On the next day Riccardi finally accepted the call at the embassy and, after what Niccolini described as a *battle,* he agreed to give the license to print but with a statement to release him of any liability. He promised to put this down in writing so that the ambassador could transmit it to Florence. Niccolini was evidently becoming a little anxious since he insists, in his letter of 19 April to the secretary of state, that he requested a written statement from Riccardi. "To speak the truth," he adds, "these opinions are not welcome here, especially by the authorities." The Florentine government might do as it pleased, but the ambassador did not want to be reprimanded for not sounding the alarm bell.

Easter fell on 20 April that year, and Riccardi used that as a convenient excuse not to produce the statement immediately. He finally got around to writing it on Friday, 25 April and it was forwarded to Florence by diplomatic post two days later. Riccardi points out that, with all the good will in the world, Father Stefani (the reviser whom Galileo had chosen) "did not know the mind of the Holy Father, and could not give an approval that would be sufficient for me to allow the book to be printed without running, for both of us, the risk that some unfriendly persons might find something contrary to the orders that were given." Riccardi insists that he wants nothing more than to please the grand duke, but in such a way "that someone under the protection of so great a Prince may not be threatened in his reputation." This meant, Riccardi spells out, that he could not authorize the publication of a book in Florence outside his jurisdiction. All he could legitimately do was to check whether the instructions of the pope had been followed. If Galileo would send him the preface and the conclusion to the book, he could do just that, and then communicate his approval. If the manuscript could not be mailed because of the restrictions that were introduced on account of the plague, Riccardi was willing to bend even more and write to the Florentine inquisitor to tell him what he had been notified to look for in the book, so that the inquisitor, *acting on his own authority,* might allow it to be published if he found that everything was in order. Riccardi concluded, wistfully, that it would be nice if some entirely different solution could be found, and his signature no longer required.

But the Florentine Government had no better suggestion to offer, and Galileo was showed the letter. He immediately dashed off a note to the secretary of state saying that he was "disgusted." After making him wait for a whole year, the master of the sacred palace was trying to play the same trick on the grand duke. "This is intolerable," declared Galileo, and he suggested calling a conference, to be chaired by the grand duke, with the participation of the secretary of state, the Florentine inquisitor, and other notabilities. The *Dialogue,* in Galileo's eyes, was becoming a matter of national interest. The secretary of state would not go that far, but he wrote to Ambassador Niccolini to tackle Father Riccardi once more and have him write to Clemente Egidi, the Florentine inquisitor, as he had declared himself ready to do.

The pressure was too great for Riccardi and, on 24 May he gave in, but he still tried to have his cake and eat it. He told the Florentine inquisitor that he could "use his own authority." In other words, since the book could not be sent to Rome, it was up to the local inquisitor to do his job. Riccardi was willing to lend a helpful hand by telling him about a few things that the pope had made absolutely clear. First, the title should in no way make mention of the tides. Second, if Scripture was not taken into consideration, Copernicanism could be presented as a theory that accounted for astronomical observations although no claim was made for its physical truth. Third, it was to be made clear that the book was only written to demonstrate that Rome did not condemn Copernicanism without knowing all the arguments in its favor. The preface and the ending, Riccardi added, would be revised in this light and would be returned as soon as this was done. So at the end of May 1631, almost one year after Galileo's trip to Rome, Riccardi had still not found the time or the energy to read what amounted to less than ten pages.

As if all had been settled, Riccardi wound up, "With these precautions, no one in Rome will object to the book, and you will be in a position to please the author and serve his Highness the Grand Duke, who has shown such concern in this matter." Riccardi was trying to have it both ways. Without actually refusing to give the license to publish, he shifted the burden onto the Florentine inquisitor while playing the role of the dutiful servant of both the pope and the grand duke. He held on to the preface and the conclusion of the *Dialogue,* thereby effectively delaying its publication. But Galileo was not to be undone. He had Ambassador Niccolini pester the master of the sacred palace well into the hot Roman summer until Riccardi sent the preface on 19 July and allowed the author to change or embellish the wording, as long he kept the substance. "The same argument must appear in the conclusion," Riccardi added in his letter to the Florentine inquisitor. Clearly he had capitulated before revising the conclusion which contained the views of Urban VIII on the nature and limits of science. These views were dear to the pope, and they should not have been found in the mouth of the dim-witted Simplicio. Had Riccardi read the passage, as he had promised to do, he might have seen and averted the catastrophe.

In informing Galileo of his success, Ambassador Niccolini added, for the first time, a word of sympathy for the much harassed priest. "The Master of the Sacred Palace deserves to he pitied," he writes, "for in these very days when he was being bothered by me, he had a lot of trouble about some other works that appeared a short while ago." We do not know what these other works were, but Father Riccardi had clearly been more generous than his superiors judged suitable.

LET'S PUBLISH . . . AND PERISH

Galileo had not waited for the arrival of the preface to begin printing the *Dialogue*. As early as June, the presses had been set in motion, and some 50 pages (out of a total of about 500) were ready by the time Riccardi bowed to Florentine pressure. The frontispiece needed an illustration, and Galileo and the printer hired Stefano Della Bella, a 21-year-old engraver who was at the beginning of his career. Galileo had him represent three elderly and bearded scholars in fanciful costumes. On the left, with his back turned to us, is the eldest, who is bald and has a long beard. He leans with his left hand on a stick and points to an armillary sphere in the hand of the person next to him. He is identified as "ARISTOTLE," the name written on his sumptuous robe. The scholar in the middle has an oriental headgear and his name, "PTOLEMY," engraved on the fringe of his mantle. The third person, on the right, wears a three-cornered hat and what was considered a nordic garment. This is Nicholas Copernicus, abbreviated as "NIC. COPER" on his clothing. He also points to the armillary sphere with his right hand, but in his left he holds a circular frame with the Sun at the center.

ADVERTISING BEYOND THE ALPS

In spite of his protestations of reverent submission to the will of his "superiors," Galileo never intended to suppress his *physical* proof that the Earth moves. He did not yell this from rooftops in Italy, but he was willing to let it be known beyond the Alps, at least to Diodati, who had been born in Italy but had moved to Geneva and then to Paris on account of the Protestant faith of his family. On 16 August 1631, Galileo wrote to tell him that he had permission to publish his book but not to mention the tides in the title, "Although this is the main argument that I develop in the work. But I have been allowed to outline the Ptolemaic and the Copernican systems and say all that can be said for both of them without coming down on one side."

Galileo thought that it was enough not to formally endorse the arguments for the motion of the Earth that he had marshalled over four days. But this was not what the pope and Riccardi had in mind! They did not expect Galileo to argue for Copernicanism but to vindicate the Roman Curia for condemning it in 1616 by showing that the ecclesiastical authorities (including Urban VIII) knew the arguments for both sides. They wanted him to make clear that the motion of the Earth was a clever theory, useful for computations, but that the evidence for it was weak and controversial, and that the Church had been wise to defend the traditional, literalist interpretation of natural phenomena described in the Bible. This was sound exegesis and, for Urban VIII, it also seemed good natural philosophy. Galileo was in the habit of underestimating the abilities of people who disagreed with him, and Urban VIII suffered from the same human frailty. What is more to the point is that Galileo was instructed not to attempt to prove that Copernicanism was true, and it is hard to believe that he did not recall that he had been warned in 1616 not to teach the system *in any way whatsoever.* But he had outlived Bellarmine. So had Urban VIII.

The autumn of 1631 brought moving of another kind. Galileo's daughter, Maria Celeste, had found a house for rent around the corner from her convent, and Galileo left Bellosguardo to take up residence at Il Gioiello (The Jewel), as it had been dubbed. It was to have been the idyllic place to live out the remainder of his years. As we shall see it was to become, after the trial, his place of confinement.

Foul Weather in Rome

SIXTH TRIP • 13 FEBRUARY–6 JULY 1633

On 21 February 1622, the Florentine printer Giovan Battista Landini heaved a sigh of relief and wrote to a correspondent in Bologna: "Praise be to God, today I finished Galileo's book, which will be presented to the Grand Duke and the Princes tomorrow." One thousand copies had been printed, a large run for the period, and it had taken Landini nine months to complete. As was frequently the case at the time, the title page was a cross between a summary and a publicity blurb, and it ran as follows on so many lines:

DIALOGUE

of

Galileo Galilei, Lyncean

Outstanding Mathematician

of the University of Pisa

And Philosopher and Chief Mathematician

Of the Most Serene

GRAND DUKE OF TUSCANY

Where, in the course of four days, are discussed

The Two

CHIEF SYSTEMS OF THE WORLD,

PTOLEMAIC AND COPERNICAN

Propounding inconclusively the philosophical and natural reasons

As much for one side as for the other.

Florence: Giovan Battista Landini, MDCXXXII

With the permission of the authorities

On Sunday, 22 February 1632, the grand duke was given a copy of the *Dialogue* in a ceremony at his palace in presence of a distinguished French visitor, the Duc de Guise, to whom a copy was also offered. The work opened with a flowery dedication to the grand duke, under whose protection Galileo placed Ptolemy and Copernicus, "in order," he said,

> that they might receive honor and patronage. If these two men have taught me so much that my work may be considered their own, it can also be said to belong to Your Highness, for it was your generosity that gave me leisure to write, and your constant and effective assistance that provided the means by which it finally saw the light of day.

By "effective assistance" Galileo meant the financial help that he had received from the grand duke after the untimely death of Prince Cesi. Galileo stressed in his dedication that Ptolemy and Copernicus were truly great because they were natural philosophers (scientists) who wanted to understand "the work of the omnipotent Craftsman" and not merely clever mathematicians who could calculate the position of the planets. Galileo saw his own work in this light, and it strongly contrasts with what we read in the preface, which follows the dedication and about which Riccardi had made so much fuss. This document, which bears the title *To the Discerning Reader,* is only three pages long, but it is printed in italics and in a typeface that is different from the one used for the rest of the book. It looks and reads like an afterthought:

A few years ago, a salutary edict was promulgated in Rome. It was aimed against the dangerous tendencies of our present age, and imposed a suitable silence upon the Pythagorean opinion that the Earth moves. Some rashly asserted that this Decree was not the outcome of an objective assessment, but the result of bias and incomplete information. Protests were to be heard that consultants, who were completely ignorant about astronomical observations, ought not to have clipped the wings of speculative minds by means of rash prohibitions.

Upon hearing such carping insolence, my zeal could not be contained. Since I was thoroughly informed about that very wise determination, I decided to appear openly upon the theatre of the world as a witness to sober truth. I was at that time in Rome where I was not only received by the most eminent prelates of the Papal Court, but had their applause. Indeed, this Decree was not published without some previous notice of it having been given to me. This is why I propose in this work to show to foreign nations that as much is understood about this topic in Italy, and particularly in Rome, as transalpine diligence can imagine. I shall bring together what was discussed about the Copernican system, in order to make known that the Roman censors were perfectly well informed.

How much of this opening statement is Galileo's and how much is Riccardi's? The reference to a "salutary edict" hardly expresses Galileo's sentiments. He considered the Decree of 1616 distasteful and something of a disaster, and the long and wordy paragraphs that we have just quoted may well have been drafted by Riccardi. The real, ironic Galileo appears in the next paragraph, in which Aristotelian philosophers are ridiculed:

To this end I have taken the Copernican side in the discourse and, proceeding as with a pure mathematical hypothesis, I have tried to show, by every means, that it is more satisfactory than supposing the earth motionless—not, indeed, absolutely, but when compared to the arguments of some professed Peripatetics who do not even deserve that name, for they do not walk about [*Peripatetic* in Greek means "walking about" and was applied to Aristotle, who walked up and down during his lectures]. Rather they are content to worship shadows, and instead of thinking for themselves they rely on a few ill-understood principles that they have memorized.

THE *DIALOGUE* IS DISTRIBUTED

Galileo had a number of copies of the *Dialogue* bound and gilded for personalities in Rome, but Ambassador Niccolini advised him not to send them before the end of May because the quarantine regulations required that books be dismantled, fumigated, and sprinkled with perfume. Galileo was annoyed but undeterred, and he called on another member of the Niccolini family, this time none less than the newly appointed archbishop of Florence, Pietro Niccolini, who was going to Rome at the end of March. It would seem that the archbishop agreed to take some unbound copies but that Galileo decided to wait until he could ship the ones that he had had specially bound at considerable expense. When the quarantine was finally relaxed at the end of May, Galileo gave his friend Filippo Magalotti eight copies to bring to Rome. The first was for Cardinal Francesco Barberini, Magalotti kept the second, and the others were distributed to Father Riccardi; Ambassador Niccolini; Monsignor Giovanni Ciampoli; Father Tommaso Campanella; Monsignor Lodovico Serristori, who was a consultant of the Holy Office; and the Jesuit Leon Santi, a professor at the Roman College. Cardinal Barberini gave his copy to Benedetto Castelli, who read it from cover to cover "with infinite pleasure and amazement," as he told Galileo.

The Jesuit Christopher Scheiner suspected, quite rightly, that Galileo had attacked him in the *Dialogue,* and at the beginning of June he went to a Roman bookshop to enquire about the book. It had not arrived, but someone had seen a copy in Siena and praised it as a masterpiece. On hearing this, Scheiner became extremely agitated and told the bookseller that he would gladly give him ten gold scudi for a copy in order to be able to reply immediately. This was 20 times the list price, and the story quickly went around town. Meanwhile, Galileo had been able to distribute the *Dialogue* elsewhere in Italy, and letters of enthusiastic readers were pouring in from Bologna, Genoa, Padua, Venice, and other centers. On 9 April he had sent a copy to Elia Diodati in Paris, and he intended to ship several more to Lyon in France in order to have them distributed from there.

A COURTIER IN TROUBLE

Getting copies of the *Dialogue* into Roman hands was not Galileo's only concern in May 1632. Disturbing news about his friend Giovanni Ciampoli had reached his ears and he confided his worries to Benedetto Castelli on 17 May: "I am most anxious to learn about our Mecenas [Ciampoli] since a rumor, which was later softened, arrived. Please write immediately." Castelli, who was not familiar with intrigues at the papal court, blandly reassured Galileo on 29 May that Ciampoli was in excellent health, continued in office, and "took these worldly matters light-heartedly." But Castelli was poorly informed, and Ciampoli had been in deep trouble since April.

Urban VIII was a poet in his spare time, and he enjoyed the company of men of letters, several of whom were Galileo's friends. These included Giovanni Ciampoli, whom the pope made secretary of briefs. Ciampoli kept his lyre attuned to papal themes. He wrote verses on the coronation of Urban VIII, the struggle in the Valtellina, the pope's action for peace, the fall of La Rochelle, even the gathering of grapes at Castel Gandolfo. He was also the author of the glowing papal brief that Galileo had taken with him to Florence after his successful visit to the new pontiff in 1624.

Ciampoli put pressure on Riccardi to do what Galileo wished and, as we shall see at the trial, he exceeded his powers. His relations with the pope were at first very intimate, and he became confident that he could read the mind of his master. He also began to long, first with impatience, and later with thinly disguised fretting, for the cardinal's hat that Urban

VIII distributed to men that Ciampoli considered his inferiors. Frustration made him reckless, and he allowed himself to be befriended by the entourage of the Spanish Cardinal Gaspare Borgia, the spokesman of Philip IV and a thorn in Urban's flesh.

At a private consistory that Urban VIII held with the cardinals on 8 March 1632, Cardinal Borgia rose to protest against the pope's failure to support the Catholic King Philip IV against the German Protestants. The pontiff, Cardinal Borgia charged, was unable, or unwilling, to defend the Church. The supporters of Urban VIII were outraged and the cardinals almost came to fisticuffs. The Swiss Guard had to be called in to restore order.

The incident was to prove a turning point in the pontificate of Urban VIII, who decided to purge his entourage of pro-Spanish elements. He was particularly incensed upon hearing of Ciampoli's relations with the Spaniards, and he punished him accordingly. At the time Castelli wrote to Galileo in May, Ciampoli was no longer allowed to see the pope, and in August he was exiled as governor of the small town of Montalto. He was never allowed to return to Rome, and the pope never forgave what he considered to be treacherous behaviour.

The open and violent denunciation of Cardinal Borgia unsettled Urban VIII to the point that he began to see Spanish spies everywhere. He secluded himself more frequently at Castel Gandolfo and, fearing poison, he did not eat food that had not been tasted by an attendant. He suspected that the maneuvers of the Spanish troops that occupied Naples were directed against him. To deepen his fears, in 1631, Francesco della Rovere, the elderly Duke of Urbino, had died and Ferdinando II, who had married Vittoria della Rovere, the granddaughter and only heir of the duke, was expected to inherit his lands. But the pope declared Urbino a vacant fief, moved in his troops, and annexed the Duchy to the Pontifical States. Ferdinando II could do little but protest, and Urban VIII was anxious to show him who was boss in Italy. Ciampoli now imagined that the grand duke of Tuscany might any day sail into the papal ports of Ostia and Civitavecchia, in retribution for the way Urban VIII had snatched

Urbino from the Medici. It is in this unfortunate set of circumstances that Galileo's controversial book appeared.

GIVE ME THE BOOK!

The first sign of trouble came in July 1632 when Urban VIII, who either saw the book or had someone tell him about its content, instructed Father Riccardi to write to the Florentine inquisitor, Clemente Egidi. Riccardi's letter, dated 25 July 1632, shows signs of having been written in some haste,

> Galileo's book has arrived and there are many things that are not acceptable and that the authorities want to see revised. The Sovereign Pontiff has ordered (but only mention my name) that the book is to be withheld. It should not be sent here until you receive what has to be corrected, nor should it be sent elsewhere. Talk about it with the Apostolic Nuncio and, while handling the matter tactfully, see that the order is obeyed.

Equally interesting is the postscript: "Let me know as soon as possible, whether the device with the three fish is the printer's or Galileo's, and write to tell me what it means." Riccardi is referring to the title page of the *Dialogue*, where Aristotle, Ptolemy, and Copernicus are engaged in a conversation on the shore of the sea. At their feet is a device with three dolphins, each gripping the dorsal spine of the one ahead. In Rome someone fancied, with more mischief than wit, that the three dolphins were a veiled reference to the three bees of the Papal arms or to the closed circle of the Barberini cardinals, namely the brother and the two nephews of Urban VIII. This suspicion may have arisen because the three scholars are standing under a canopy where we see five *palle* or balls, the armourial bearings of the Medici, surmounted by the granducal crown. It was also encouraged by the Latin motto, *Grandior ut proles*, just above the dolphins. Translated, it means, "I have grown as my family" and could be construed as a criticism of the favors that the pope showered on his relatives. Fortunately for Galileo, the monogram under the dolphins, "GB" with an "L" underneath, stood for G. B. Landini, the name of the printer, and the device of the three dolphins was a commercial sign. Riccardi was greatly relieved to learn that it appeared on nearly all the works that Landini printed and that it had nothing to do with Galileo. It does say something, however, about the ease with which suspicions could be raised when the reputation of the Barberinis was at stake.

CORRECT, SUSPEND, OR BAN

How matters looked in Rome can be surmised from a letter that Galileo's friend Filippo Magalotti wrote to Mario Guiducci in Florence at the beginning of August 1632. The *Dialogue,* he says, is being examined in order to find out whether it is to be corrected, suspended, or condemned outright. Now the Florentines, who lived in Rome, were in the habit of congregating on feast days in the Church of San Giovanni dei Fiorentini in the via Giulia near the Vatican, and on Monday, 2 August 1632, the feast day of the Knights of St. Stephen, Father Riccardi hastened to the church to see Filippo Magalotti, whom he knew he would find there. He immediately asked for the copies of the *Dialogue* that had been brought from Florence and promised to return them within ten days. Magalotti replied that the copies had been distributed and that the last, his own, was in the hands of Girolamo Deti, the chamberlain of Taddeo Barberini, another nephew of Urban VIII.

The books had arrived in Rome more than two months earlier, and it was clearly too late to recall them. Riccardi saw that there was no point in insisting, and he tried to cover things up by declaring that no harm was intended and that he considered Galileo one of his best friends. Nonetheless, he complained about discrepancies between the published book and the manuscript and lamented "the absence, at the end, of two or three arguments that were formulated by the Holy Father himself, and with which the Pope believed he had convinced Galileo that Copernicanism was wrong." These were missing from the *Dialogue* and Urban VIII wanted action taken. Magalotti saw Riccardi again at the end of the month, and the priest now admitted that the "two or three arguments" to which he had alluded were really only one, namely the argument about divine omnipotence that had been placed in the mouth of Simplicio, who had been played for a fool during the four days of the *Dialogue*.

SLANDERERS AT WORK

In his letter to Guiducci of 7 August 1632, which we quoted above, Magalotti suggested that if the truth were known, the Jesuits had probably been working in underhanded ways to have the book banned. Magalotti based his conjecture on a remark made by Riccardi, "The Jesuits will persecute him bitterly." Some Jesuits, such as Father Orazio Grassi and Father Christopher Scheiner, had legitimate grounds to be annoyed with the cavalier treatment they had received at Galileo's hands, but no surviving document shows that they tried to have his book censured. Riccardi might have meant no more than that the Jesuits would fight Galileo's ideas tooth and nail in their lectures and in their books, but Magalotti inferred that they would attempt to silence him by having his work placed on the Index. This was probably unwarranted, but it is nonetheless the case that things would have gone more smoothly for Galileo if he had kept on good terms with the Jesuits. Galileo came to see them as the cause of his downfall. For instance, before leaving for Rome in January 1633 he will write to his friend Elia Diodati in Paris:

> I hear from reliable sources that the Jesuit Fathers have managed to convince some very important persons that my book is execrable and more harmful to the Holy Church than the writings of Luther and Calvin. Thus I am sure it will be prohibited, despite the fact that to obtain the license I went personally to Rome and delivered it into the hands of the Master of the Sacred Palace.

After his trial, in another letter to Elia Diodati on 25 July 1634, Galileo quotes Father Christopher Grienberger, the professor of mathematics at the Roman College, as having confided to one of Galileo's friends:

> If Galileo had known how to keep on good terms with the Fathers of
> this College, he would live gloriously in this world. None of his misfor-
> tunes would have come to pass and he would have been able to write
> as he wished about anything, even about the motion of the earth.

And Galileo's concludes, "So you see that it is not because of this or that opinion that I have been and continue to be attacked, but because I am not liked by the Jesuits." This feeling of having been slandered rankled with Galileo to his dying day.

THE ENQUIRY CONTINUES

When Riccardi was unable to secure the eight copies of the *Dialogue* that Magalotti had distributed in Rome, he wrote to the Florentine inquisitor on 7 August 1632 to find out how many had been printed and where they had been sent "in order that steps may be taken to get them back." He even allowed himself a personal comment, which is entirely to his credit, "Comfort the author and tell him to keep his spirit up."

On 15 August 1632, Ambassador Niccolini informed the secretary of state in Florence that a commission had been appointed to examine Galileo's book. It was said to be composed of a number of persons who were not well disposed toward him, and Niccolini suggested to Cardinal Francesco Barberini that the commission include "neutral" members. The cardinal replied evasively and would say no more than that he would transmit the request to the pope. The matter was treated in great secrecy, but a friend (almost certainly Riccardi) informed the ambassador that they did not intend to ban the book but only to change a few words.

Shortly thereafter, Ambassador Niccolini received a strongly worded letter from the Florentine secretary of state, who said that he was writing as directed by the grand duke. This was the usual way of conveying that the matter was serious. There can be little doubt that Galileo was behind this letter in which the grand duke expresses his astonishment that a book that was revised and approved two years earlier should now give rise to difficulties. In order to see clearly in the matter, the grand duke requested that the charges be put in writing, as is normal in any judiciary procedure.

As soon as he received this letter at the end of August, Niccolini rushed to the office of Cardinal Francesco Barberini, who received him in a friendly but reserved fashion. He would make no comments beyond saying that the ambassador should have a word with Riccardi, who had obviously been summoned to explain himself. Placed in a tight spot, Riccardi had tried to exculpate himself by saying that Galileo had not followed his instructions and had forced his hand.

FRIENDS AT COURT

Our main source of information about developments in Rome is Filippo Magalotti, who at 73 was still a vigorous man about town. He was also a relative of the Barberinis and as such a person of influence. He enjoyed writing letters, and his correspondence with Mario Guiducci, Galileo's young disciple, is full of local color. On 4 September 1632, Magalotti wrote that he had given Father Riccardi three sheets on which the device of the three dolphins of the Florentine printer Landucci appeared. "Riccardi was overjoyed," he wrote, "and said that this could prove extremely useful to our friend," meaning of course Galileo.

Magalotti also read out to Riccardi part of a letter that he had received from Guiducci in which Galileo was described as eager to conform in every way with what might be decided in Rome. He did not read, however, the passage in which Guiducci added that the book had been sent all over Europe. This would have annoyed the Roman authorities, who assumed that on account of the plague only a few copies had been distributed.

It is an indication of Magalotti's prestige and self-assurance that he took it upon himself to raise the issue of the 1616 ban on Copernicanism. He told Riccardi that he was not far from believing that if the evidence had been carefully weighed the decree might not have been made. To which Riccardi replied that if he had been a member of the Congregation of the Index at that time he would have objected to the book being condemned or banned. In the course of the conversation, Magalotti mentioned that Galileo had written very sensibly about Copernicanism and Scripture in his *Letter to the Grand Duchess Christina*. Riccardi had not seen it and asked for a copy. When Magalotti brought his own, Riccardi started reading the *Letter* on the spot. His first reaction was that Galileo had gone too far, and he wanted to know why the *Letter* had not been published. Magalotti made the obvious reply that the Decree of 1616 precluded any possibility of publication. A few days later, on 4 September 1632, when Riccardi had read the entire *Letter to the Grand Duchess Christina* and was more relaxed, he wanted Magalotti to understand that, as he had told Ambassador Niccolini a few days earlier, "he was only a servant, whose job was to do what the authorities decided." If only Galileo had been more willing to do as told, everything would have worked out, he lamented.

Magalotti's advice to Guiducci and Galileo was the fruit of personal experience and consisted in the recommendation not to act precipitously and to drag things out. Let sleeping dogs lie. At the most, Ambassador Niccolini might speak to Riccardi or even to Cardinal Francesco Barberini, "but never to the Pope," he added, "for reasons that I do not have to enter." Magalotti also wrote to Galileo about the commission that was to examine his *Dialogue*. Although he was not certain as yet who the members were, he thought he could allay Galileo's worst fears:

> Even if the majority of the Commission held that the said opinion is false, I do not believe that they would want to have it declared as such by the supreme authority. This is what I am told by those who are accustomed to work with the Holy Office where matters concerning doctrine are

usually considered . . . In any case, they all agree that unless there is extreme urgency or a declaration of an Ecumenical Council, nothing will be decided either for or against it.

No one at the Holy Office believed that the motion of the Earth had been or was likely to be formally condemned. Such condemnations were usually reserved for doctrinal matters at the heart of Christian belief, for instance, errors concerning the divinity of Christ. An ecumenical council might be necessary for such a radical decision, and it was not expected that the pope would want to go that far. In brief, no formal act of the magisterium of the Church was expected. Furthermore, the experts who worked at the Holy Office knew full well that books placed on the Index might be removed at some later date.

The officials, however, had only a limited knowledge of what Galileo was trying to do, and they seem to have been ignorant of his *Letter to the Grand Duchess Christina*. They had no idea that a new physics and a new astronomy were being born, and they did not anticipate that natural science would raise issues that had not entered the minds of theologians. They could not guess that one day Galileo would be celebrated as the father of modern science and that they would be regarded as petty and narrow-minded. In retrospect, we know that Galilean physics was the wave of the future. They could not.

JESUIT REACTIONS

One of the copies that Magalotti had brought to Rome had gone to a Jesuit professor at the Roman College, and both Father Grienberger and Father Scheiner had seen it by September 1632, when Benedetto Castelli's teaching assistant, Evangelista Torricelli, asked them about it. Grienberger said he liked the book but was not convinced. Scheiner mumbled a few words of praise but added that the argument was difficult to follow because of the large number of digressions, and that he did not want to discuss it because Galileo had behaved so badly toward him.

What role Scheiner played in Galileo's woes is a matter of conjecture. Those who did not like the Jesuits spread the rumor that they had instigated the trial. As happened on other occasions, the Jesuits were credited with less charity than they displayed and more political power than they possessed. This is not to say that Scheiner did not try very hard to prove Galileo wrong or that he did not gloat when Galileo got into trouble. Less than a month after Galileo's condemnation, he completed a book to prove that the Earth was at rest and embarked on a defense of traditional astronomy against Galileo. "To this we are exhorted," he wrote to a friend, "by the Pope, the General of our Order [the Jesuits], his Assistants, and everyone who chooses the right path." While Urban VIII may have expressed the hope that astronomers would teach Galileo a lesson, there is no evidence that he ever spoke to Scheiner. As far as the general of the Jesuits was concerned, he was anxious to discourage his members from becoming involved in public controversy. Scheiner undoubtedly saw himself as redressing a wrong, but the "exhortation" he thought he was answering was probably wishful thinking. From what we know from his writings, he was as keen to blow his own trumpet as was Galileo.

Another Jesuit, Orazio Grassi, is also mentioned as having plotted against Galileo. When replying to Galileo for attacking his work on the comets, Grassi claimed that someone who defended atomism would be hard put to explain how, in the Eucharist, the substance of bread becomes the substance of the body of Christ while the species of color, taste, and so on remain unchanged. Grassi wanted to show that Galileo was a bad philosopher, but there is no evidence that he wanted Galileo's head. Shortly after Galileo's condemnation, in a letter of 22 September 1633 to Girolamo Bardi, who had just been appointed professor of philosophy at the University of Pisa, Grassi declared that he was very sorry about Galileo's trials and that he had always been fonder of his rival than Galileo had been of him. "When I was asked last year in Rome," he continues,

what I thought about his book on the motion of the Earth, I did my best
to placate those were against him and show them the value of the

arguments that he proposed, so that some of them marveled that I should speak so favorably of someone who disliked me and had even offended me. Galileo caused his own ruin by thinking too highly of himself and despising others. You should not be surprised if everybody plots against him.

Girolamo Bardi was a young man of thirty and not a particular friend of Galileo or his circle. Grassi was simply trying to be generous and fair: Galileo had good arguments, but he had antagonised his opponents by treating them the way he handled Simplicio in the *Dialogue*. No wonder he stirred up such animosity.

THE POPE CRACKS DOWN

On 4 September 1632 Ambassador Niccolini had a stormy audience with the pope, who broke out "in an outburst of rage" against Galileo, but even more so against Giovanni Ciampoli, who had told him that everything was fine when he had not even read the book! The pope also took Riccardi to task but was willing to make allowances because the friar had been tricked. Niccolini then tried, as he had been instructed by the grand duke, to obtain that Galileo be notified of the charges against him. The pope answered that the Holy Office was not an ordinary court of law. It studied the case, and if the accused was found guilty he was told to recant. When Niccolini urged his request, Urban replied impatiently: "This kind of information is never given out in advance to anyone. Such is not the procedure. Besides, he knows very well where the difficulties lie if he wants to, since I discussed them with him, and he heard them from myself."

Niccolini now tried another tack: Since the *Dialogue* was officially dedicated to the grand duke of Tuscany by someone who worked for him, might it not be wise to use clemency and hush the matter up? The pope answered that he had banned works dedicated to himself that even had his name on the cover. Furthermore the grand duke, as a Christian prince, should help punish "what causes great prejudice (among the worst ever-conceived) to religion." But a book that has been approved should not be prohibited without at least hearing the author, insisted Niccolini. "This is the best Galileo can hope for," replied the pope, who confirmed that a special Commission of Enquiry had been created "to study every detail, word by word, because this is the most perverse thing that one can have to deal with."

In the highly emotional atmosphere of this papal audience two issues were at stake: one religious, the other political. They were distinct but related. In describing the religious implications of what Galileo wrote, the pope used exceptionally strong language and claimed that they were not only bad but *perverse*. This was said "in an outburst of rage," as Niccolini reported, but since the term was repeated a couple of times, it cannot be dismissed as a mere hyperbole. But why such a fuss over a scientific hypothesis that Urban VIII, when still a cardinal, had been willing to see condemned not as a heresy but as a rash opinion? Urban VIII would even have preferred if the decree banning Copernicanism had not been published. Did someone convince him after 1616 that the motion of the Earth was really pernicious? If so, on what grounds?

From the evidence with which we are already familiar, we can think of three arguments. First, if the Earth moved, a whole set of biblical passages would have to be reinterpreted. This was possible, but it was far from clear that the traditional common-sense interpretation should be replaced by a science that was still in its infancy and had yet to be confirmed. Second, it seemed proper that the Earth should be at the center of the world, given the central place of human beings in God's plans. Furthermore, if the Earth was just one of several bodies around the Sun then the other planets could also have inhabitants, and this raised questions about the meaning of original sin, the Incarnation, and Redemption. Third, if the Earth was not naturally at rest, the physics of Aristotle would be completely wrong. But his philosophy was the conceptual tool that had been used to develop much of Christian theology, for instance, the monumental achievement of Thomas Aquinas.

The notion that the Earth is at the center of the universe was never defined as belonging to the Christian faith, but it was coherent with Christian doctrine. Although the motion of the Earth had no direct bearing on Christian belief as such, the pope and several very good theologians saw it as threatening.

The pope did not discuss these arguments with Ambassador Niccolini. Urban VIII's indignation was directed against the "trickery" of Galileo and Ciampoli and the fact that the conclusion of the *Dialogue* was not at all what he had expected. The religious issue is genuine, but it cannot be dissociated from the more personal crime of lese-majesty. Urban VIII never forgot that he was both a religious leader and a temporal prince. Religious concerns, however distinct, often meshed with the political interests of the Vatican. The pope was anxious to protect the pontifical states, and he kept a close eye on his neighbors. As we have seen, he had snatched the duchy of Urbino from the hands of Grand Duke Ferdinando II of Tuscany in order to enhance his territorial and military power.

The grand duke was only in his early twenties, and the pope wanted him to understand who was the ruler in the Italian peninsula. Ferdinando II had been brought up to respect the sovereign pontiff by his grandmother, the deeply devout Grand Duchess Christina of Lorraine, and his equally pious mother, the Archduchess Maria Maddalena. This is why Urban VIII could speak of the grand duke's duty to repress whatever might prove prejudicial to the faith. Matters were no longer in the hands of some official at the Vatican; the pope himself had taken over, and the grand duke would do well to behave accordingly. Urban VIII also wanted to impress on the Florentine government that he was doing Galileo a great favor by having his book examined by a Commission of Enquiry instead of turning it over immediately, as was the custom, to the Holy Office. In reporting this to the secretary of state, Ambassador Niccolini urged that the matter be handled gingerly. "When his Holiness gets something in his head, that is the end of the matter," he wrote from personal experience, "especially if someone tries to resist, oppose or defy him. Then he takes a hard line and shows no consideration whatsoever."

Ambassador Niccolini's report upset the grand duke to the point that the secretary of state wrote back on 9 September to say that he did not know how things would turn out. Meanwhile the ambassador had called on Father Riccardi, who told him that there was no longer any doubt that the *Dialogue* was an out-and-out defense of Copernicanism. Riccardi had been given the book and he hoped, with his usual optimism, that a few minor changes would be enough. He advised against requesting that Campanella, who had written in praise of Galileo, or Castelli, who was Galileo's former student, be asked to serve on the commission that the pope had appointed. He vouchsafed two important items of news, however. The first was that the Commission of Enquiry consisted of three persons: himself, Agostino Oregio (the pope's theologian and a future cardinal), and the Jesuit Melchior Inchofer, whom Riccardi had personally suggested. At first glance, this seemed to be an excellent choice, because Riccardi had worked with him on the other cases.

The second piece of news was very different. A search in the archives of the Holy Office had turned up the admonition that Galileo had received in 1616 from Cardinal Bellarmine, in the name of the pope and the Holy Office, to abandon the Copernican theory. "This is enough to ruin him completely," declared Riccardi. Why, the grand duke would not have intervened so strongly in favor of Galileo if he had known of this. Riccardi had guessed correctly. The news of the injunction was a bombshell. The grand duke and his advisers were shocked, and the secretary of state hastily wrote to Ambassador Niccolini on 16 September to ask him to thank Riccardi and assure him that they would henceforth be guided by his advice. The pope had accused Galileo of deception. The scales had tipped; far from being the victim of unscrupulous adversaries, Galileo had become the man who acted under a cloak of secrecy. His silence about the injunction of 1616 now looked more than suspicious.

The grand duke was to remain friendly toward Galileo, but he took a more cautious stance in dealing with Rome. In fair return, the pope treated Galileo with a leniency that was rare in the seventeenth century. When he was summoned to Rome in 1633, Galileo was lodged at the

Tuscan embassy and not placed under arrest in the Holy Office, as would normally be done. The few days that he spent inside the Vatican during his trial were not passed in a prison cell but in the comfortable apartment that the notary had vacated for him. He was not served the usual food but meals prepared by the chef at the Tuscan embassy. After his condemnation, he was not incarcerated but placed under house arrest, first at the Villa Medici, then at the palace of Archbishop Piccolomini in Siena, and finally in his own house in Florence.

THE MACHINERY OF JUSTICE

Now that the grand duke knew where he stood, the juridical wheels could begin to turn in earnest. On 18 September 1632, the Florentine Inquisition was informed that the pope wanted both the original manuscript of the *Dialogue* and the official document authorizing its publication in Florence. The return of the plague had rendered communications with Rome difficult, and the Florentine inquisitor sent the manuscript of the *Dialogue* to the pope's brother, Cardinal Antonio Barberini. It arrived with some delay but was in Riccardi's hands by the beginning of November. Meanwhile, the pope had sent one of his personal secretaries to inform Ambassador Niccolini that he had decided, after hearing the report of the Commission of Enquiry, to have the *Dialogue* examined by the Holy Office. The secretary stressed that the pope was being exceptionally generous in imparting this information. The ambassador and the grand duke, as well, were enjoined to secrecy since the matter was now before the Holy Office, and no further information was to be divulged.

On 18 September 1632 the ambassador met with the pope and repeated his plea for leniency toward a man who was the grand duke's official mathematician. Urban VIII replied, according to the ambassador, "that this was why he went out of his way to accommodate him, that Galileo was still his friend, but that these opinions had been condemned some sixteen years ago, and that Galileo had got himself into a fix that he could have done without." After the pope had once more called the whole affair "pernicious," the conversation took what, for the modern reader, is a bizarre turn. The pope said that he was willing to discuss these "troublesome and dangerous" ideas with the ambassador, but that he had to warn him not to mention them even to the grand duke, *under penalty of censure.* When Niccolini begged to be allowed to inform at least the grand duke about the pope's views, Urban VIII refused and said that he should "be glad to have heard them from him in confidence, as a friend, not as an ambassador." It would, of course, be interesting to know what Urban VIII told Niccolini in secrecy. All kinds of conjectures have been put forward, the most recent being that the pope was worried that Galileo's atomic theory might prove subversive if applied to the mystery of the Eucharist. This would have been a serious problem, but it is much more likely that Urban VIII wanted to discuss the injunction of 1616 and his role at the time.

The Commission of Enquiry had met five times before recommending that the *Dialogue* be referred to the Inquisition, and their report was discussed at a meeting of the Holy Office presided by the pope on Thursday, 23 September 1632. Two days later the Florentine inquisitor was instructed to summon Galileo and tell him that he had to be in Rome for the whole month of October. The order was communicated to Galileo in the presence of a notary and two witnesses on 1 October, and Galileo signed a written statement in which he promised to comply.

Now begins the strategy of dragging things out. On 13 October, Galileo wrote a long letter to Cardinal Francesco Barberini in which he pleaded for mercy on the grounds of his advanced age (he was 68 but said he was 70). He claimed that the poor state of his health, the inclemency of the roads, and the bad weather would not allow him to make it halfway to Rome. Instead he offered to respond to objections in writing or to appear before the Florentine inquisitor, the archbishop, or anyone they should chose to appoint. A copy of this letter was read to the grand duke, who was so moved by the plight of the aged scientist that he sent it to Ambassador Niccolini to show to Cardinal Barberini. A glance at the letter was all Niccolini needed to realize that it would do more harm than good, and on 23 October 1632 he wrote to advise Galileo to refrain from sending it. Unfortunately the letter had already gone out, and the best the ambassador could do was make the round of prelates and senior officials to drum up sympathy. On 13 November Niccolini had an audience with the pope, who had seen Galileo's letter and had declared at a meeting of the Holy Office two days earlier that he would brook no further delay. He promised, however, to have a word with his nephew, Cardinal Francesco Barberini, and ask him reduce the period of quarantine that had been reintroduced on the borders of the pontifical states and Tuscany. He was willing to allow Galileo to travel in comfort, but travel he must!

On 20 November Galileo was summoned once again by the Florentine inquisitor and, again before a notary and two witnesses, told to leave within a month. He agreed once more although visibly ill, as the Florentine inquisitor reported to Rome. On December 9, at a meeting of the Holy Office, the pope ordered to write back to Florence that Galileo had to appear in Rome within the prescribed lapse of time. But December found Galileo in bed, and, as the month he had been given was about to elapse, a panel of three prominent doctors was summoned to his bedroom. On 17 December they signed a certificate in which they described their patient as suffering from an intermittent pulse resulting from the general weakness of declining years, frequent dizziness, hypochondriacal melancholy, sluggishness of the stomach, insomnia, pains all over the body, and a serious hernia with rupture of the peritoneum. The slightest change would place him in grave danger of death. In other words, travel would be life threatening.

The certificate was handed over to the Florentine inquisitor, who sent it to the Holy Office, where it was read at the meeting of 30 December 1632. The pope was outraged and declared that if Galileo did not come to Rome of his own free will, he would be arrested and dragged there in irons. The game was clearly up, but Galileo still hoped that he would be able to postpone the trip. Had not Riccardi told him to drag things out? The grand duke and his advisers felt otherwise, and on 11 January 1633 the secretary of state, Andrea Cioli, wrote to Galileo to say that he must leave for Rome. The grand duke wanted him to travel in comfort and would provide a carriage and a "discreet" driver. Galileo would be allowed to lodge at the embassy in Rome but only "on the assumption that he would not stay over a month." This was less reassuring since the Holy Office was notoriously slow in its proceedings.

On 15 January Galileo sent letters to friends in Italy and abroad to inform them that he was being summoned to Rome at the instigation of what he termed his "evil-minded enemies." Earlier, on 28 September 1632, Ascanio Piccolomini, the archbishop of Siena, had written to say that those whom Galileo had vanquished at the scientific level would now attempt to shift the battle to the theological arena. Piccolomini, who had worked at the Holy Office, knew what he was talking about.

A PAINFUL JOURNEY

Galileo left Florence on Thursday, 20 January 1633, and his carriage was halted at Ponte a Centino, near Acquapendente on the border of Tuscany and the papal states. The plague had flared up and rare were those who were spared the full quarantine of 22 days. Galileo was provided with uncomfortable lodgings with only bread, wine, and eggs as food. Nonetheless, when he entered Rome on the first Sunday of Lent, 13 February, he was in surprisingly good health and eager to take up the cudgels. The day after his arrival he rushed out to see Monsignor Alessandro Boccabella, the former assessor of the Holy Office, who was sympathetic to his plight. Upon Boccabella's advice, he immediately proceeded to call on his successor, Pietro Paolo Febei, and the new commissioner of the Holy Office, Vincenzo Maculano, who happened to be out. This flurry of activity did not please the Holy Office, as we shall see. The following day, 15 February, Galileo turned 69 without fanfare. The event is not even mentioned in the correspondence.

On 14 February, Ambassador Niccolini had been to see Cardinal Francesco Barberini to ask that Galileo be allowed to stay at the embassy in Palazzo Firenze "given his age, his reputation and his eagerness to obey."

He was granted his request but on the condition that Galileo neither receive visitors nor pay visits himself. This restriction was repeated by the commissioner of the Holy Office, Vincenzo Maculano, who softened the blow, however, by saying that he was not issuing a command but simply giving friendly advice. Monsignor Lodovico Serristori, a consultant at the Holy Office, who had been given one of the first copies of the *Dialogue* that Magalotti had brought to Rome, called twice in an unofficial capacity, but the ambassador suspected that he had been sent to discover Galileo's line of defense and advise the Holy Office accordingly.

Ambassador Niccolini continued to do what he could. He went to speak to Cardinal Desiderio Scaglia, and Cardinal Guido Bentivoglio who had attended Galileo's lectures as a student at the University of Padua. Both cardinals were members of the Holy Office and the ambassador found them well disposed toward the incriminated scientist. At Galileo's request, the grand duke wrote to them requesting that they facilitate matters for an old and worthy professor, who had made a long and painful trip to show how eager he was to obey the Church authorities.

Ambassador Niccolini saw the pope on Saturday, 26 February 1633, almost two weeks after Galileo's arrival, and he mentioned how touched he was by Galileo's spirit of submission. Urban VIII stressed that he had allowed Galileo to stay at the embassy only because he was a subject of the grand duke. Niccolini showed himself suitably grateful before asking the pope to expedite proceedings in order that Galileo, whose health was poor, might return to Florence. Urban VIII replied that the Holy Office did not proceed with undue haste and that things must take their course. The pope referred to the whole affair as a *ciampolata* (meaning something engineered or inspired by Ciampoli, who had become his *bête noire*) and complained that under cover of speaking hypothetically, Galileo had argued that the Earth went around the Sun. This was in flagrant violation of the injunction he had received from Cardinal Bellarmine in 1616. The pope, as the ambassador reported to the Florentine secretary of state, had now been convinced that there was something seriously wrong with Copernicanism. Things were not going well.

A BET OF FRESH AIR

Galileo, who was accustomed to take exercise and work in his orchard, found confinement painful, and he asked to be allowed to go occasionally to the Villa Medici to take a stroll in the garden. Niccolini made the request, but on 6 March he was still waiting for an answer, and we do not know whether permission was eventually granted. A month after Galileo's arrival, on 13 March 1633, the ambassador had another audience with the pope, who declared that Galileo must go before the tribunal of the Inquisition. "There is no way out," said Urban VIII, "and may God forgive Galileo for meddling in these subjects." He added that they had been friends and had often dined together, but that what was now at stake was a matter of faith. "There is in an argument," the pope declared, "that no one has ever been able to answer, namely that God, who is omnipotent, can do anything. And if he is omnipotent, who can bind him?" Niccolini replied that he had heard Galileo say that he did not claim that the motion of the Earth was proved but that since God could create the world in innumerable ways, he could have made it in this particular way. This upset the pope so much that the ambassador promptly changed the subject and reiterated that Galileo only wished to obey and retract whatever was considered wrong in his writings.

Urban VIII was clearly very fond of "his" argument, and Niccolini was wise to back down. The ambassador understood the pope's sanguine temperament and knew how far he could go. He also understood Galileo's frame of mind, and when he returned to the embassy he judged it wiser not to tell him that he would not escape a trial. In all this sorry affair, pride was to play at least as great a role as doctrine.

THE LONG WAIT

After having been harried to Rome by repeated threats, Galileo was left waiting for weeks to be called for questioning. He became increasingly weary; even Niccolini grew restless. The grand duke had written to

Cardinals Scaglia and Bentivoglio. Lest the other cardinals who were members of the Holy Office take offense at being neglected, the ambassador recommended that they also be sent letters. The grand duke agreed and wrote to each asking for clemency for his elderly servant Galileo. Easter, which fell on 27 March that year, came and went without any news from the Holy Office. Galileo kept himself secluded and consoled himself with the letters from his friends, and especially with those from his daughter Maria Celeste, who wrote to him every Saturday.

Everyone tried to put a brave face on things. From the small town where he had been sent as administrator, Giovanni Ciampoli wrote to Galileo on 5 April to say that he found it strange to have to act as chief magistrate *with the power of life and death* over criminals. The irony was not lost on Galileo, but he must not have found it very funny. Ciampoli claimed to be in good health and find solace in his well-stocked library. He even invited Galileo to visit him as if this were a matter that could easily be arranged. The time for playing games was over, but Ciampoli never seemed to have got the message.

Finally, on Wednesday 6 April, Cardinal Francesco Barberini informed Niccolini's secretary that he wanted to see the ambassador. The next day Niccolini called on him as early as possible and was told, on behalf of the pope, that Galileo would have to go to the Holy Office. Niccolini asked that Galileo be allowed to return to the embassy every evening. Although this was denied, the cardinal promised (always out of consideration for the grand duke) that Galileo would not be placed in a cell but given a comfortable set of rooms that would probably not be locked.

After seeing the pope on Saturday 9 April, Ambassador Niccolini informed Galileo that he would be summoned before the Holy Office. But Galileo, as Niccolini wrote to the Tuscan secretary of state, still thought he could defend his views:

> I begged him, in the interest of a quick resolution, not to bother maintaining them and to agree to what they want him to hold or believe about the earth's motion. He was extremely distressed by this, and since

yesterday I see him so depressed that I fear greatly for his life. I will try to obtain permission for him to keep a servant and to have other conveniences. We all want to cheer him up, and we seek the assistance of friends and those who play a role in these deliberations because he really deserves to be helped. Everyone in the embassy is extremely fond of him and feels the greatest sorrow.

THE TRIAL BEGINS

When Galileo was driven to the Holy Office in the Vatican on the morning of Tuesday, 12 April 1633, he was not being taken to an ordinary courtroom. As Urban VIII had made clear to Ambassador Niccolini, the Tribunal of the Inquisition was a court where defendants were summoned not to justify themselves but to acknowledge their errors and recant. Voluntary confession was not only wise but mandatory. Nonetheless, if being called before the Holy Office was an indication of guilt, the penalty was only decided after an interrogation had taken place.

Galileo had been incriminated on the strength of the report of the three theologians (Agostino Oregio, Melchior Inchofer, and Zacharia Pasqualigo) who had examined the *Dialogue*, in order to ascertain whether the author taught that the Earth moved and the Sun stood still. They unanimously reported that he did and had therefore contravened the injunction given to him in 1616. The unsigned memorandum found in the archives, which we discussed in chapter three, clearly stated that after Cardinal Bellarmine had admonished Galileo and warned him to abandon Copernicanism, Commissioner Seghizzi had ordered him in the name of His Holiness the pope and the Holy Office to abandon the opinion that the Sun is at the center of the universe and that the Earth moves, "nor henceforth to hold, teach or defend it in any way verbally or in writing. Otherwise proceedings would be taken against him by the Holy Office."

According to the document, this had occurred long before Ferdinand had become grand duke, Niccolini ambassador, or Urban VIII pope. Galileo had not only flouted the warning but he had concealed from the grand duke and Father Riccardi that he had been admonished by Cardinal Bellarmine and the commissioner of the Holy Office. Nevertheless the memorandum was unsigned and therefore could not be used as a legal document. Galileo had not forgotten the interview with Bellarmine, of course, but the passage of time had softened the blow. He no longer recollected the exact words, but he did not think that they sealed up all possibility of discussion. After all, when gossipmongers had begun muttering that he had abjured in Cardinal Bellarmine's hands, the cardinal had given him a certificate to the contrary. Galileo had kept this document preciously and had now brought it to Rome. It was his secret weapon, only to be used in case of need.

THE INTERROGATION

We must not picture Galileo as being ushered into the presence of the pope or the ten cardinal inquisitors. He never saw the pope or any of the cardinals during his trial. The interrogation on 12 April 1633 was conducted by just two officials: Commissioner Maculano and his assistant, prosecutor Carlo Sinceri. The pope and the cardinals were probably briefed at their weekly meeting on the next day or they read the minutes, which are preserved with this peculiarity: The questions are in Latin and the replies in Italian. The questions had been prepared beforehand in the official language of the Church, namely in Latin, and they were framed in the third person. For instance, the first one reads: "By what means and how long ago did he come to Rome." In all likelihood the questions were communicated in Italian, the language in which Galileo's answers are recorded.

After Galileo had been shown a copy of his *Dialogue* (referred to as "Exhibit A" in the transcript) and had identified it as his own, the commissioner asked him about his trip to Rome in 1616. He wanted to know what Cardinal Bellarmine had told him, and Galileo, who was ignorant about the memorandum that had been found in his file at the Holy Office, replied as follows:

Cardinal Bellarmine informed me that the opinion of Copernicus could be held hypothetically, as Copernicus himself held it. His Eminence knew that I held it hypothetically, namely in the way Copernicus held it, as you can see from his answer to a letter of Father Paolo Antonio Foscarini, Provincial of the Carmelites. I have a copy where we find these words: "It seems to me that Your Reverence and Galileo wisely limit yourselves to speaking hypothetically and not absolutely." This letter of the Cardinal is dated April 12, 1615. Otherwise, namely taken absolutely, the opinion could be neither held nor defended.

When the commissioner sought to probe further into what Cardinal Bellarmine had said, Galileo thought the moment had come to produce his secret weapon, and he drew out a copy of the certificate, adding that he had the original in Bellarmine's own handwriting. Galileo's triumph was short lived, however, for the commissioner proceeded to ask whether anyone else had been present when they met. Galileo replied that he remembered some Dominicans but that he did not know their names. Did they or anyone else give you an injunction concerning these matters? insisted the commissioner, who had the unsigned memorandum in mind.

Galileo was still in the dark about this document, and since we are not absolutely certain whether or in what form Seghizzi had added his own warning, we cannot know if Galileo recollected it. The commissioner now told him that they knew that he had been given a clear order not to hold, defend, or teach Copernicanism *in any way whatsoever*. Not having seen the memorandum, Galileo could only fall back on what he remembered:

I do not recall that this precept was intimated to me in any other way than by Cardinal Bellarmine. I remember that I was enjoined "not to hold or defend," but there may also have been "nor teach." I do not remember that "in any way" was added, but this may have been the case. I did not give much thought to it or keep it in mind because I was given some months later the certificate of Cardinal Bellarmine of 26 May that

I have presented, and in which it is mentioned that I was ordered not to hold or defend the said opinion. As for the other two particulars of the precept now notified to me, that is "nor teach" and "in any way," I do not remember them, I think because they are not set forth in the certificate on which I relied and kept as a reminder.

The commissioner then came to the crux of the matter and asked whether, "after the aforesaid injunction was issued," Galileo had asked for permission to write the *Dialogue on the Two Chief World Systems*. Galileo answered that he did not consider this necessary because he had not intended to defend but to *refute* Copernicanism. This was false, of course, but he was not interrupted and allowed to give his own account of the steps he had taken to obtain permission to print the book. The Commissioner listened patiently before asking whether he had told Father Riccardi about the injunction that he had received. Galileo had not expected this direct question and his reply, the last at the end of long interrogation, was to determine the evolution of the trial:

I did not happen to discuss that command with the Master of the Sacred Palace when I asked for the imprimatur, for I did not think it necessary to say anything because I had no doubts about it since I neither maintained nor defended in that book the opinion that the Earth moves and the Sun is stationary. Rather I proved the contrary of the Copernican opinion and showed how weak and inconclusive the arguments of Copernicus were.

By claiming that he had argued not *for* but *against* Copernicanism, Galileo had painted himself into a corner from which he would be unable to extricate himself. The Holy Office knew full well that the *Dialogue on the Two Chief World Systems* had been written to demonstrate that the Earth goes around the Sun, something only a silly person, like Simplicio, could fail to see. The tribunal would not take kindly to the suggestion that they were simpletons.

THE EXAMINERS

Galileo's book had been sent out to three experts to determine whether he taught that the Earth moved. They had no trouble in recognizing the thrust of Galileo's argument. The first to submit his report on 17 April 1633, was the distinguished theologian Agostino Oregio, who declared in a brief but unambiguous note that Galileo obviously defended the motion of the Earth. Furthermore, Oregio added that he and Riccardi had already shown this in a report prepared at the request of the pope and submitted to the Cardinal inquisitors.

The second examiner, the Jesuit Melchior Inchofer, and the third, the theologian Zacharia Pasqualigo, reached the same conclusion. Inchofer wrote as though he was personally affronted and even accused Galileo of writing in Italian to persuade "common people in whom errors very easily take root." He felt that "if Galileo had attacked someone in particular who had not argued very skillfully for the Earth's immobility, we might still put a favorable construction on his text, but as he declares war on everybody and regards as dwarfs all those who are not Pythagoreans or Copernicans, it is clear enough what he has in mind."

Galileo was now in deep trouble. There could no longer be any doubt that he had been told not to hold or defend Copernicanism orally or in writing, and that his *Dialogue* was a flagrant violation of this order. By declaring, under oath, that he did not uphold Copernicanism in his book, he left himself open to the suspicion that he was treating the members of the Holy Office as a pack of fools.

A GILDED CAGE

After his interrogation on 12 April, Galileo was assigned to a suite of three rooms in the palace of the Inquisition. He wrote to Florence to say how spacious they were and how graciously he was being treated. His daughter, Maria Celeste, could read between the lines. She knew that her father was in great distress, and she wrote a touching letter to him on 20 April:

The only thing for you to do now is to keep your good spirits, and take care not to jeopardize your health by worrying too much. Direct your thoughts and hopes to God who, like a tender, loving father, never abandons those who confide in Him and appeal to Him for help in time of need. Dearest father, I want to write to you now, to tell you that I share your suffering in the hope of making it lighter for you to bear. I have given no hint of these difficulties to anyone. I keep the unpleasant news for myself and only mention what you say is pleasant and satisfying. Thus we are all awaiting your return, eager to enjoy your delightful conversation once again. And who knows, Sire, if while I sit writing, you may not already find yourself released from your predicament and free of all concerns? Thus may it please the Lord Who must be the One to console you, and in Whose care I leave you.

Meanwhile in Rome Commissioner Maculano was wrestling with the following evidence: Galileo had been given in 1616 an injunction not to hold or defend Copernicanism in any way whatsoever, but he had not told Riccardi about this when he requested a licence to print his book; and although the *Dialogue* unabashedly supported the motion of the Earth, Galileo declared that he had written to show that this theory was wrong.

As the days dragged on, it became clearer to Maculano that things would go very badly for Galileo if he persisted in denying that his book was a defense of Copernicanism. At a meeting of the Holy Office on 28 April, 1633, at which the pope and Cardinal Francesco Barberini were absent, Maculano suggested a course of action that was unusual: He proposed to have a heart-to-heart conversation with Galileo and deal with the matter extrajudicially. Some of the cardinals immediately voiced their doubts about Galileo's willingness to be reasonable, but the commissioner, who was eager to spare Galileo and the Church from more unpleasantness, convinced them to let him try. Here is how he summarized the outcome in a letter he wrote the next day to Cardinal Francesco Barberini, who was at Castel Gandolfo with his uncle, the pope: "Not wishing to lose any time, I went to reason with him yesterday after lunch, and after a lengthy discussion I gained my point by the grace of God, for I made him see that he was wrong and had gone too far." Galileo, the commissioner added, seemed moved and, "as if relieved to have realized his error, he said he was ready to make a judicial confession." He asked, however, for some time to think about the words to use. Having realized that confess he must, Galileo wanted to do so with the least loss of face.

Maculano could be proud of his achievement. The strategy that he had adopted had probably been suggested by Urban VIII, as we can infer from what the commissioner wrote to Cardinal Barberini:

> I hope that His Holiness and your Eminence will be pleased that the case can now be settled without further difficulty. The Tribunal will retain its reputation and be able to deal leniently with the accused who, whatever the outcome, will recognize that a favor has been done to him.

Father Maculano hailed from Florence and knew how things stood between the grand duchy of Tuscany and the papal states. He had been provincial and vicar of his religious order and was later to become archbishop and cardinal. The pope and Cardinal Francesco Barberini appreciated his diplomatic skills, and they instructed him to end the Galileo affair as quickly as possible. When Maculano had proposed to deal extrajudicially with Galileo, several cardinals had been surprised, but when they realized that the pope was pulling the strings they promptly acquiesced. If Galileo confessed his errors, the Holy Office could afford to show mercy and place him under house arrest rather than imprison him in Rome.

THE SECOND HEARING

Once Galileo gave in, the sequel was just a matter of following the routine and showing that due process had been observed. Three days after his interview with Maculano, on Saturday, 30 April 1633, Galileo re-entered the commissioner's office for a second formal hearing. As we know from the recorded transcript, Galileo began by saying that over the last few days he had thought it advisable to reread his *Dialogue,* which he had not looked at for the past three years. He wanted to see whether he had unwittingly given offense. "Not having seen it for so long," he explained,

> I found it almost a new book by another author. I freely confess that it appeared to me in in several places to be written in such a way that a reader, ignorant of my intention, would have reason to believe that the arguments for the wrong side, which I intended to confute, were so expressed that they meant to carry conviction rather than be easily refuted.

Galileo singled out his two prize arguments (the rotation of sunspots and the oscillating motion of the tides) as having been presented too energetically when they were no proofs at all. He supposed, he said, that he had succumbed to the natural complacency that everyone feels for his own ideas and had tried to show himself more skillful than others in devising, even in favor of false propositions, clever arguments. "My error, I confess, has been one of vainglorious ambition, pure ignorance and inadvertence."

Galileo then signed his declaration and, as the procedure required, was sworn to secrecy before being dismissed. Now comes something surprising. As the record reveals, Galileo returned a few moments later to declare his readiness to show his good faith by adding one or two days to his *Dialogue* in order to refute the arguments in favor of Copernicanism "in the most effectual way that God Almighty will be pleased to show me." He begged the tribunal to help him put his good resolution in practice. This was Galileo's last card, and he played it in the hope of saving his book from outright condemnation.

The commissioner offered no comment. Galileo duly signed his second deposition, and this time retired for good. As the pope had already agreed, he was allowed to leave the Holy Office, where he had spent two nerve-racking weeks, and to return to the Tuscan embassy. On 3 May

1633, Ambassador Niccolini wrote to the Florentine secretary of state to say that Galileo was already feeling better and that he hoped that the trial was nearing its end. He was wrong. It was to drag on for almost two more months. The machinery of justice had been set in motion and the wheels could not be stopped.

THE THIRD HEARING

On 10 May, Galileo returned to the Holy Office, where the commissioner officially informed him that he had eight days to present his defense. Galileo already had been told that this was part of the procedure, and he immediately handed over a written statement in which he expressed the hope that his "most eminent and most prudent judges" would recognize that he had neither willfully nor knowingly disobeyed any orders given him but had fallen victim to vanity and the desire to appear clever. He was ready to make amends, and he ended by begging the tribunal "to take into consideration my pitiable state of bodily indisposition, to which, at the age of seventy years, I have been reduced by ten months of constant mental anxiety and the fatigue of a long and toilsome journey at the most inclement season, together with the loss of the greater part of the years of which, from my previous condition of health, I had the prospect." He deemed his decrepitude and disabilities adequate punishment for his mistakes and hoped the Tribunal would protect his honor and reputation from the slanders of his enemies.

Galileo was devastated by his ordeal and returned to the embassy "half dead," as Ambassador Niccolini reported to the Florentine secretary of state. As Galileo waited in suspense, the Tuscan government, increasingly short of cash, confirmed that it would not pay for his expenses beyond the month they had agreed upon. Ambassador Niccolini withheld the information from Galileo and informed the secretary of state that he would cover the expenses himself. The ambassador made this pledge in the full knowledge that the trial could drag on for another six months. The only good news (if it may be called by that name) was that by staying in Rome Galileo avoided a new outbreak of the plague in Florence, where one to four persons died every day.

After the pope's return from Castel Gandolfo, Ambassador Niccolini was granted an audience on 21 May. Urban VIII was in a good mood and said that he expected that Galileo's case could be settled by the following week. Niccolini left with the impression that the *Dialogue* would not be banned outright as long as Galileo published an acknowledgement of his errors and expressed his regrets. The violation of the injunction given to him in 1616, however, would have to be punished in some way or other. For the time being, Niccolini kept up Galileo's morale and did everything to ease the suspense. He even managed to obtain permission for Galileo to be taken out for drives in his carriage provided the shutters were kept half shut. In this way Galileo was able to go to the Villa Medici to stroll in the gardens, and, on one occasion, he went as far as Castel Gandolfo.

Galileo's case was no longer a priority, and more urgent matters were being discussed at the Holy Office. It was only on Thursday, 16 June, when Urban VIII was in the chair, that the Tribunal was seized with the problem of determining the sentence. It was decided that Galileo was to be summoned for one final interrogation to determine what had been his true purpose in writing the *Dialogue,* even using the threat of torture should that prove necessary. The book itself was to be condemned and prohibited, and a prison sentence imposed on Galileo along with some kind of penance in the hope that his public humiliation would serve as a warning for others.

THE LAST INTERVIEW

Galileo was ushered into the office of Commissioner Maculano for the fourth and last time on the morning of Tuesday 21 June. He maintained that he had never held the Copernican theory after its condemnation in 1616 and that he had not advocated it in the *Dialogue,* where he had merely set out the arguments for and against the motion of the Earth.

The commissioner reminded him that, after the enquiry, he was presumed to have held the Copernican theory *at the time* that he wrote the *Dialogue*. He enjoined him to speak the truth, "otherwise it would be necessary to have recourse to the remedies of the law." Galileo answered, "I do not hold this opinion of Copernicus, and I have not held it after being ordered by injunction to abandon it. For the rest, I am here in your hands; do with me what you please." He was then formally commanded to tell the truth, "otherwise one would have recourse to torture," to which he replied, "I am here to obey, but I have not held this opinion after the determination was made, as I said." Galileo signed his declaration and left the room. We can almost hear his judges heaving a sigh of relief.

THE FORMAL ABJURATION

On the next day, Wednesday, 22 June, Galileo was ushered into a room adjoining the church of Santa Maria sopra Minerva, in what is now part of the library of the Italian parliament. This was to be the most unpleasant part of the trial. Galileo was ordered to kneel down while his sentence was read out. "You have rendered yourself," the document declared,

> vehemently suspect of heresy, namely of having held and believed a doctrine which is false and contrary to the Sacred and Divine Scriptures, that the Sun is the centre of the world and does not move from east to west, and that the Earth moves and is not the centre of the world; and that one may hold and defend as probable an opinion after it has been declared and defined contrary to Holy Scripture.

The tribunal was ready to absolve him if he formally abjured his errors, but his book would be proscribed and he would be condemned to imprisonment for an undetermined period of time. As a religious penance they imposed upon him the duty to recite the seven penitential psalms once a week for the next three years. This would have taken him about

20 minutes, but his daughter Maria Celeste relieved him of the burden after securing ecclesiastical permission to take it upon herself.

Of the ten cardinal inquisitors seven were present, the average number at meetings. The most conspicuous absence was that of Francesco Barberini, the pope's nephew, who had always advocated clemency. The second absentee was Cardinal Gaspare Borgia, who had recently inveighed against the pope at a meeting of the cardinals and was probably unwilling to condemn anyone who caused embarrassment to Urban VIII. The third was Cardinal Laudivio Zacchia. No documents explaining these absences have survived, and the three cardinals may simply have been ill or bound by other duties on that day.

After the sentence had been read, Galileo, still on his knees, was made to recite and sign a formal abjuration in which he admitted having violated an injunction not to discuss Copernicanism. "As a result," he continued,

> I have been judged vehemently suspect of heresy, that is, of having held and believed that the Sun is the centre of the universe and immovable, and that the Earth is not the center of the same, and that it does move. Wishing, however, to remove from the minds of your Eminences and all faithful Christians this vehement suspicion reasonably conceived against me, I abjure with a sincere heart and unfeigned faith, I curse and detest the said errors and heresies, and generally all and every error, heresy, and sect contrary to the Holy Catholic Church. And I swear that in the future I will neither say nor assert orally or in writing such things as may bring upon me similar suspicion. If I know any heretic, or one suspected of heresy, I will denounce him to this Holy Office, or to the Inquisitor and Ordinary of the place in which I may be. I also swear and promise to adopt and observe entirely all the penances that have been or may be imposed on me by this Holy Office. And if I contravene any of these said promises, protestations, or oaths (which God forbid!) I submit myself to all the pains and penalties which by the Sacred Canons and other Decrees general and particular are imposed and promulgated

against such offenders. So help me God and the Holy Gospels, which I touch with my own hands. I Galileo Galilei have abjured, sworn, and promised, and hold myself bound as above; and in token of the truth, with my own hand have subscribed the present document of abjuration, and have recited it word for word. In Rome, at the Convent della Minerva, this 22nd day of June 1633.

I, Galileo Galilei, have abjured as above, with my own hand.

In popular accounts it is sometimes said that when Galileo rose from his feet he muttered under his breath, "Eppur si muove" (And yet it moves!). This may have been his inner conviction, but he was wise enough not to express it on that dramatic occasion before his judges. His confession had been part of a deal and the next day, 23 June, his imprisonment was commuted to house arrest in the Villa Medici. Soon thereafter the ambassador requested that Galileo be allowed to leave Rome for Siena, where his friend Ascanio Piccolomini was archbishop. This was granted at a meeting of the Holy Office presided by the pope on 30 June. Three days later Urban VIII decided to allow Galileo to stay with the archbishop rather than in a convent as had been originally planned. Ambassador Niccolini recognized that this was a genuine favor.

BACK IN FLORENCE . . .

Meanwhile in Florence, Geri Bocchineri and Niccolò Aggiunti, who had received no news for some days after the promulgation of the sentence, feared that officials of the Inquisition might be sent to make a search of Galileo's villa. They called on Sister Maria Celeste at her convent and asked for the keys to do what Galileo had told them might be necessary for his safety should certain contingencies arise. Maria Celeste gave them the keys and wrote to her father, with her usual caution: "They feared you were in trouble and seeing how exceedingly anxious they were on your account, it seemed to me right and necessary to prevent any accident that might possibly happen. So I gave them the keys, and permission to do as they thought fit."

What "they thought fit" was probably removing from the house such writings in Galileo's library as might be used further to incriminate him. This may account for the disappearance of those incomplete writings of which mention is made in Galileo's correspondence but of which no trace remains.

NOTIFICATION

The text of Galileo's mortifying sentence was communicated to inquisitors all over Italy and to apostolic nuncios (i.e., papal ambassadors) in the courts of Europe. In Florence it was ordered that it should be read publicly at a meeting to which professors of natural philosophy were to be invited. Anyone who had a copy of the *Dialogue* was to surrender it to the local inquisitors, but just the opposite seems to have happened as people tried to lay hands on the book before it became unavailable. The price of the *Dialogue*, originally half a scudo, rose to four and then to six in the summer of 1633. Fortunio Liceti, the Aristotelian professor of philosophy in Galileo's former university in Padua, complied and brought his copy to the inquisitor. Meanwhile, north of the Alps, everyone clamored for a Latin version. Mathias Bernegger, a professor at the University of Strasbourg, undertook the task of translation, which he completed in 1635. The copies that were sent to Frankfurt and Paris rapidly sold out. Catholics who purchased the *Dialogue,* after Galileo's condemnation knew that a sentence of the Holy Office did not involve the infallibility (the technical term for absence of error) of the Church or the pope, which can only be invoked in special circumstances when an ecumenical council or the pope, acting as the head of the Church, solemnly defines a matter concerning faith or morals. Urban VIII, who was not a modest man, once declared that the pronouncement of one living pope (meaning himself) outweighed all the decrees of one hundred dead ones, but he never considered claiming infallibility in matters concerning natural science.

This was understood by the French philosopher and scientist René Descartes, who thought that the condemnation would eventually be rescinded just as the denial that people could live below the equator, once maintained by some ecclesiastical authorities in the eighth century, was quietly dropped. Nonetheless, the ban on Copernicus was a serious one, and Descartes withheld the publication of his own book in which he described the Earth as moving around the Sun.

HOMECOMING

In Siena, Archbishop Piccolomini did not treat Galileo as a confessed heretic but as a good Catholic and an honored guest. He invited scholars to dine with them and provide Galileo with the opportunity of a lively conversation. Tongues began to wag and someone sent an anonymous letter to the Holy Office in which he claimed that Galileo had disseminated in Siena

> ideas that are not quite Catholic with the support of the Archbishop, his host, who has told several people that Galileo was unjustly sentenced by this Holy Congregation, that he is the first man in the world, that he will live for ever in his writings even if they are prohibited, and that he is followed by all the best modern minds. And since such seeds, sown by a prelate might bear pernicious fruit, I hereby report them.

In December 1633 the Holy Office authorized Galileo to return to his villa in Arcetri, but his movements were restricted. He was free to receive members of his family or friends, but under no circumstances was he to hold meetings or entertain a large number of people. He was not allowed to go down to Florence, but he could visit his daughters in the neighboring convent. Unfortunately, Sister Maria Celeste became ill and died shortly after her father's return on 1 April 1634.

Later that year, Galileo's sister-in-law, Chiara Galilei, came to live with him with her three daughters and her son, but they all perished of the plague shortly after their arrival. Some time after their deaths, finding the solitude of his house at Arcetri insupportable, Galileo invited his nephew Alberto to join him. During the Thirty Years' War this boy had lost the little his mother had had to leave him and was maintaining himself and his younger brother Cosimo on the small amount of money he earned as a violinist and lute player. He stayed with Galileo for a while but eventually returned to Munich, married, and re-entered the service of the elector, so that the old man was again alone. Nevertheless, Galileo managed to complete the manuscript of his greatest scientific work, the *Two New Sciences,* which was given to the Protestant publisher, Louis Elzivier, and appeared in the Netherlands in 1638.

In this new book, Salviati, Sagredo, and Simplicio meet once more to consider, over another period of four days, how bodies move, bend, break, and fall. In the course of their discussion they examine the two fundamental laws of physics that Galileo had discovered. The first is the law of freely falling bodies, which states that all objects (be it an apple dropping from a branch or a boulder falling off a cliff) pick up speed at the same rate regardless of their weight. The second law states that the path traced through space by a missile (be it a stone, an arrow or a bullet) is not just somehow curved but is precisely a parabola.

Galileo feigned surprise that the manuscript of the *Two New Sciences* had found its way to a foreign printing press, but since the book did not mention Copernicanism, the Church decided to let the matter drop. During these years Galileo kept up a correspondence with two friends in France. One was Elia Diodati, who had the *Dialogue* translated and was instrumental in getting the *Two New Sciences* published. The other was the famous aristocrat and scholar Nicolas-Claude Fabri de Peiresc, who had written to Cardinal Francesco Barberini to beseech him, on behalf of the scientific community, to grant Galileo a full pardon. To Diodati, Galileo railed against his enemies; to Peiresc he repeated his conviction that he had committed no crime. "I have two sources of lasting comfort," he wrote,

> first, that in my writings there cannot be found the faintest shadow of
> irreverence towards the Holy Church; and second, the testimony of my

own conscience, which only I and God in Heaven thoroughly know. And He knows that in this cause for which I suffer, though many might have spoken with more learning, none, not even the ancient Fathers, has spoken with more piety or with greater zeal for the Church than I.

DEATH AND POSTERITY

Galileo's eyesight began to deteriorate rapidly in 1637 and blindness was soon added to his miseries. In 1638 he obtained permission to stay in Florence at the house of his son but was still kept under house arrest to the point that he needed a special permission to attend, at Easter, the Church of St. Giorgio a few yards away. In 1639 he was back at Arcetri, where a young scientist, Vincenzio Viviani, came to live with him. Toward the last, Evangelista Torricelli was to join him as amanuensis and companion. Galileo became gravely ill in the autumn of 1641, and after two months of suffering died on the evening of 8 January 1642. His body was brought from Arcetri to the church of Santa Croce in Florence, and preparations were made for a public funeral. The sum of 3,000 scudi was quickly voted by the grand duke to cover the expense of a marble mausoleum. This and other particulars were instantly reported to the Holy Office at Rome. The ambassador of Tuscany received orders to communicate to the grand duke that his intention concerning Galileo's remains would, if carried out, prove most distasteful, and that he must remember that Galileo had during his life caused scandal to all Christendom by his false and damnable doctrine. The ambassador advised that the project both of a public funeral oration and a mausoleum be laid aside, at least for a time.

The grand duke yielded to the pressure from Rome, and Galileo was not buried in the Church of Santa Croce itself but at the end of the corridor leading from the south transept to the sacristy. There, in an obscure corner, on the gospel side of the altar dedicated to Saints Cosmas and Damian, the body rested for nearly a century. The master of the novices, Father Gabriello Pierozzi, placed an epitaph on the wall in 1673, with the tacit consent of the Florentine inquisitor. When Vincenzio Viviani died, in 1703, he conditionally willed his property to his nephew Panzanini and his heirs, charged with the condition of erecting a proper monument to Galileo in Santa Croce as soon as permission could be obtained to do so. Panzanini died in 1733 and the property passed to Giovan Battista Clemente Nelli, who, in 1737, carried out Viviani's pious intention during the pontificate of Clement XII (Lorenzo Corsini), a Florentine. On 12 March 1737, the mortal remains of Galileo were solemnly transferred from the chapel to the main body of the Church and placed in a mausoleum with the approval and in the presence of the ecclesiastical authorities.

REFERENCES

CHAPTER ONE

Antonio Favaro, 1890–1909 (reprint: Florence: Barbèra, 1968) are cited by the title *Opere,* followed by the number of the volume and the page. For instance, *Opere,* XIX, 342 means volume XIX, page 342.

The documents of the trial of Galileo are also found in Sergio Pagano (ed.), *I documenti del processo di Galileo Galilei* (Vatican City: Pontifical Academy of Sciences, 1984), which is quoted as *Documenti,* followed by the page number.

p. 9: *Decrees of the Ecumenical Councils,* edited by Norman P. Tanner S.J., Volume Two: Trent to Vatican. London and Washington: Sheed & Ward and Georgetown University Press, 1990 II, 664.

CHAPTER TWO

p. 22: "Here we have a powerful and elegant argument": final part of *Sidereus Nuncius,* in *Opere,* III, 95.

p. 23: "The Maker of the stars Himself": dedication of *Sidereus Nuncius,* in *Opere,* III 8 56.

p. 25: "Mother of Love": letter from Galileo to Giulano de Medici, January 1611, in *Opere* XI, 12.

p. 27: "And the author runneth": letter from Henry Wotton to the Earl of Salusbury, 13 March 1610, in the *Life and Letters of Sir Henry Wotton* edited by Logon Pearsall Smith, Oxford, 1907, I, pp. 486–48.

p. 29: "Our beloved Mathematician and Philosopher": letter from Grand Duke Cosimo II to Giovanni Niccolini, 27 February 1611, in *Opere,* XI, 60.

p. 29: "In order to put an end, once and for all, to malignant rumours": letter from Galileo to Belisario Vinta, 19 March 1611, in *Opere,* XI, 71.

p. 31: "I arrived in good health on Holy Tuesday": letter from Galileo to Belisario Vinta, 1 April 1611, in *Opere,* XI, 79.

p.31: "Have finally recognised the genuineness of the Medicean planets": letter from Galileo to Belisario Vinta, 1 April 1611, in *Opere*, XI, 79–80.

p.33: "Whom the Grand Duke had appointed professor": quoted in J.A.F. Orbaan, *Documenti sul barocco in Roma*. Rome: Società Romana di Storia Patria, 1920, p. 283.

p.36: "See whether Galileo, professor of philosophy": minute of the Inquisition, 17 May 1611, in *Documenti* 219.

p.39: "I do not have time to write personal letter to all": letter from Galileo to Filippo Salviati, 22 April 1611, in *Opere*, XI, 89.

p.41: "Every day Galileo converts some of the heretics": letter from Piero Dini to Cosimo Sassetti, 7 May 1611, in *Opere*, XI, 102.

p.42: "Loud voices are raised against Galileo": letter from Cosimo Sassetti to Piero Dini, 14 May 1611, in *Opere*, XI, 103.

p.42: "If he had to say something": letter from Galileo to Piero Dini, 21 May 1611, in *Opere*, XI, 107.

p.44: "We can observe at the tips of the Moon's horns": lecture by Odo Maelcote in the Roman College, in *Opere*, III–1, 295.

p.45: "If anyone is allowed to imagine whatever he pleases": letter from Galileo to Gallanzone Gallanzoni, 16 July 1611, in *Opere*, XI, 143.

p.45: "Galileo has, during his stay in Rome": letter from cardinal Francesco Maria del Monte to Cosimo II, grand duke of Tuscany, 31 May 1611, in *Opere*, XI, 119.

p.46: "I am very sorry that you were unable to see me before I left": letter from Cardinal Maffeo Barberini to Galileo, 11 October 1611, in *Opere*, XI, 216.

p.47: "I hear that *Galileo is coming here*": letter from Piero Guicciardini to Curzio Picchena, 5 December 1615, in *Opere*, XII, 206–207. The italicized phrases were originally in cipher.

CHAPTER THREE

p.50: "Already the minds of men assail," *Letters on the Sunspots*, in *Opere* V, 93; "not only false but erroneous", in *Opere* V, 138, critical apparatus.

p.50: "divinely inspired," "contrary to Scripture," *Letters on Sunspots*, in Opere V, 138 critical apparatus.

p.51: "I have been told by a friend of mine": letter from Lodovico Cardi da Cigoli to Galileo, 16 December 1611, in *Opere*, XI, 241–242.

p.52: "The suspicion that I entered into a discussion on philosophical matters": letter from Niccolò Lorini to Galileo, 5 November 1612, in *Opere*, XI, 427.

p. 53: "Here also they do not rest from scheming": letter from Galileo to Federico Cesi, 5 January 1613, in *Opere,* XI, 461.

p. 53: "requires much study": letter from Cardinal Carlo Conti, 7 July 1612, in *Opere* XI, 354; p. 84 "less agreement with Scripture": *ibid.*; p. 84 "that should not be admitted without necessity": *ibid, 355.*

p. 54: "I believe with Kepler": letter from Federico Cesi to Galileo, 21 July 1612, in *Opere,* XI, 366.

p. 55: "Thursday morning I was at table with our Patrons": letter from Benedetto Castelli to Galileo, 14 December 1613, in *Opere,* XI, 605.

p. 56: "When I was overtaken by the porter of Madama Christina": letter from Benedetto Castelli to Galileo, 14 December 1613, in *Opere,* XI, 606.

p. 56: "Began to argue Holy Scripture against me": letter from Benedetto Castelli to Galileo, 14 December 1613, in *Opere,* XI, 606.

p. 57: "Especially when they would always base themselves": letter from Galileo to Benedetto Castelli, 21 December 1613, in *Opere,* V, 282.

p. 57: "Sacred Scripture and nature": letter from Galileo to Benedetto Castelli, 21 December 1613, in *Opere,* V, 282.

p. 58: "Two truths can never contradict each other": letter from Galileo to Benedetto Castelli, 21 December 1613, in *Opere,* V, 283.

p. 58: "As far as the opinion of Copernicus is concerned": letter from Galileo to Giovan Battista Baliani, 12 March 1614, in *Opere,* XII, 34–35.

p. 60: "Concerning the opinion of Copernicus": letter from Federico Cesi to Galileo, 12 January 1615, in *Opere,* XII, 129.

p. 60: "That it is very easy to proscribe a book": letter from Federico Cesi to Galileo, 12 January 1615, in *Opere,* XII, 130.

p. 63: "Very great friend": letter from Galileo to Piero Dini, 16 February 1615, in *Opere,* V, 292.

p. 63: "He took me to his office": letter from Benedetto Castelli to Galileo, 12 March 1615, in *Opere,* XII, 153–154.

p. 64: "Cardinal Barberini, who, as you know from experience": letter from Giovanni Ciampoli to Galileo, 28 February 1615, in *Opere,* XII, 146.

p. 65: "Bellarmine says there is no question": letter from Piero Dini to Galileo, 7 March 1615, in *Opere,* XII, 151.

p. 66: "As a professor of mathematics": letter from Piero Dini to Galileo, 14 March 1615, in *Opere,* XII, 155.

p. 67: "It could not have come out at a better time": letter from Federico Cesi to Galileo, 7 March 1615, in *Opere,* XII, 150.

p. 67: "I confirm once again what I wrote a few days ago": letter from Giovanni Ciampoli to Galileo, 21 March 1615, in *Opere*, XII, 160.

p. 69: "The Archbishop praised the letter": letter from Benedetto Castelli to Galileo, 9 April 1615, in *Opere*, XII, 165.

p. 69: "Are prudent to content themselves": letter from cardinal Robert Bellarmine to Paolo Antonio Foscarini, 12 April 1615, in *Opere*, XII, 171.

p. 69: "The words, *the Sun also rises and the Sun goes down*": letter from cardinal Robert Bellarmine to Paolo Antonio Foscarini, 12 April 1615, in *Opere*, XII, 172.

p. 70: "Admit that we do not understand them": letter from cardinal Robert Bellarmine to Paolo Antonio Foscarini, 12 April 1615, in *Opere*, XII, 172.

p. 71: "As far as I am concerned": letter from Galileo to Piero Dini, May 1615, in *Opere*, XII, 183–184.

p. 73: "Of which we have, or firmly believe we could have": letter from Galileo to Grand Duchess Christina of Lorraine, 1615, in *Opere*, V, 330.

p. 74: "Be reckoned undoubtedly false": letter from Galileo to Grand Duchess Cristina of Lorraine, 1615, in *Opere*, V, 327.

p. 74: "Be welcomed by everybody": letter from Piero Dini to Galileo, 16 May 1615, in *Opere*, XII, 181.

p. 74: "To defend himself against the accusations of his rivals": letter from Grand Duke Cosimo II to Piero Guicciardini, 28 November 1615, in *Opere*, XII, 203.

p. 74: "Full board for himself": letter from Curzio Picchena to Armibale Primi, 28 November 1615, in *Opere* XII, 205.

p. 74: "I do not know whether he has changed": letter from Piero Guicciardini to Curzio Picchena, 5 December 1615, in *Opere*, XII, 207.

p. 76: "Perhaps he is not here on his own volition": letter from Antonio Querengo to Cardinal Alessandro d'Este, 1 January 1616, in *Opere*, XII, 220.

p. 77: "You would be delighted to hear Galileo argue": letter from Antonio Querengo to Cardinal Alessandro d'Este, 20 January 1616, in *Opere*, XII, 226–227.

p. 78: "My business is far more difficult": letter from Galileo to Curzio Picchena, 23 January 1616, in *Opere*, XII, 227–228.

p. 79: "His reputation was growing every day": letter from Gobber to Curzio Picchena, 30 January 1616, in *Opere* XII, 229.

p. 79: "The very person who": letter from Galileo to Curzio Picchena, 6 February 1616, in *Opere*, XII, 231.

p. 79: "And I could go back home any time": letter from Galileo to Curzio Picchena, 6 February 1616, in *Opere*, XII, 230.

p. 80: "Galileo has relied more on his own counsel": letter from Piero Guicciardini to Cosimo II, grand duke of Tuscany, 4 March 1616, in *Opere*, XII, 241–242.

p. 81: "is the center": Propositions sent to the experts of the Holy Office, 19 February 1616, and their qualification: in *Documenti*, 99–100, and *Opere*, XIX, 320–321.

p. 81: "Foolish and absurd in philosophy": censure of the Holy Office, 25 February 1616, in *Documenti*, 99, and *Opere*, XIX, 321.

p. 82: "On the 26th His Excellency Cardinal Bellarmine": Document of the Holy Office, meeting of 25 February 1616, and admonition to Galileo on 26 February 1616: in *Documenti*, 222–223 (document no. 6, was recently discovered and is not in the *Opere*).

p. 83: The "second document" refers to the meeting of the Holy Office on 3 March 1616: in *Documenti*, 223–224, and *Opere*, XIX, 278.

p. 83: "And immediately thereafter": Document of the Holy Office, admonition to Galileo and injunction by Seghizzi, 26 February 1616: in *Documenti*, 101–102, and *Opere*, XIX, 321–322.

p. 84: "it has also come to the knowledge": Decree of the Congregation of the Index, 5 March 1616: in *Documenti*, 102–103, and *Opere*, XV, 322–323.

p. 85: "In the time of Paul V": from the journal of Giovanfrancesco Buonamici, 2 May 1633: in *Opere*, XV, 111.

p. 86: "This was never our intention": letter from Benedetto Castelli to Galileo, 16 March 1630, in *Opere*, XIV, 87–88.

p. 86: "Zollern left yesterday": letter from Galileo to Federico Cesi, 8 June 1624, in *Opere*, XIII, 182.

p. 87: "in which many useful things": decree of the Holy Office, 1 May 1620, in Pierre-Noël Mayaud, *La condemnation des livres coperniciens et sa révocation*. Rome: Gregorian University, 1997, p. 70.

p. 88: "Galileo's arguments have vanished": letter from Antonio Querengo to Cardinal Alessandro d'Este, 5 March 1616, in *Opere*, XII, 243.

p. 89: "As one can see from the very nature of the business": letter from Galileo a Curzio Picchena, 6 March 1616, in *Opere*, XII, 244.

p. 89: "Answered that he was well aware of my uprightness": letter from Galileo to Curzio Picchena, 12 March 1616, in *Opere*, XII, 248.

p. 90: "We, Robert Cardinal Bellarmine": certificate by cardinal Robert Bellarmine to Galileo, 26 May 1616, in *Documenti*, 134 (copy) and 138 (original), and *Opere*, 342 (copy) and 348 (original).

p. 92: "Strange and scandalous": letter from Piero Guicciardini to Curzio Picchena, 13 May 1616, in *Opere*, XII, 259.

p.93: Letter from Matteo Caccini to his brother Alessandro, 11 June 1616, in *Opere*, XII, 265.

CHAPTER FOUR

p.95: "There is never a shortage of kings": letter from Giovanni Ciampoli to Galileo, 15 January 1622, in *Opere*, XIII, 84.

p.96: "If you had had here in those days the friends that you now have": letter from Giovanni Ciampoli to Galileo, 27 May 1623, in *Opere*, XIII, 117.

p.97: "I am much in your debt": letter from cardinal Maffeo Barberini to Galileo, 24 June 1623, in *Opere*, XIII, 119.

p.99: "The Jesuits discuss the comet": letter from Giovan Battista Rinuccini to Galileo, 2 March 1619, in *Opere*, XII, 443.

p.100: "Perhaps Sarsi thinks that philosophy is a book of fiction": Galileo, *Il Saggiatore*, in *Opere*, VI, 232.

p.101: "In a very lonely place, there lived a man": Galileo, *Il Saggiatore*, in *Opere*, VI, 280.

p.102: "For having captured in his hands a cicada": Galileo, *Il Saggiatore*, in *Opere*, VI, 281.

p.103: "Here is greatly desired something new from your talent": letter from Giovanni Ciampoli to Galileo, 4 November 1623, in *Opere*, XIII, 146–147.

p.105: "I have great need of Your Excellency's advice": letter from Galileo to Federico Cesi, 9 October 1623, in *Opere*, XIII, 135.

p.105: "Your coming here is necessary": letter from Federico Cesi to Galileo, 21 October 1623, XIII, 140.

p.106: "Our Mathematician, Galilei, is going to Rome": letter from Ferdinand II, grand duke of Tuscany, to Francesco Niccolini, 27 February 1624, in *Opere*, XIII, 167.

p.107: "So many fine considerations pertaining to natural philosophy": permission by Riccardi for the publication of *Il Saggiatore*, 2 February 1623, in *Opere*, VI, 200.

p.110: "The rest of the time I spend on various visits": letter from Galileo to Curzio Picchena, 27 April 1624, in *Opere*, XIII, 175.

p.110: "The court, my dear sir, is a source of infinite trouble": letter from Federico Cesi to Galileo, 30 April 1624, in *Opere*, XIII, 177.

p.110: "Another Creator": letter from Giovanni Faber to Federico Cesi, 11 May 1624, in *Opere*, XIII, 177.

p. 111: "I spoke at length with Cardinal Zollern on two occasions": letter from Galileo to Federico Cesi, 15 May 1624, in *Opere*, XIII, 179.

p. 111: "I hope that Cardinal Zollern will be able to get something": letter from Giovanni Faber to Federico Cesi, 24 May 1624, in *Opere*, XIII, 181.

p. 112: "We found that Father Monster": letter from Giovanni Faber to Federico Cesi, 1 June 1624, in *Opere*, XIII, 181.

p. 112: "But they are nonetheless firmly of the opinion": letter from Galileo to Federico Cesi, 8 June 1624, in *Opere*, XIII, 183.

p. 114: "My beloved son": letter from pope Urban VIII to Ferdinand II, grand duke of Tuscany, 8 June 1624, in *Opere*, XIII, 184.

p. 114: "I hear from all sides": letter from Mario Guiducci to Galileo, 21 June 1624, in *Opere*, XIII, 186.

p. 115: "I have now discovered that I was completely wrong": letter from Galileo to Francesco Ingoli, July 1624, in *Opere*, VI, 510.

p. 116: "I hear that the most influential of the heretics accept Copernicus' opinion": letter from Galileo to Francesco Ingoli, July 1624, in *Opere*, VI, 511.

p. 116: "For, Signor Ingoli": letter from Galileo to Francesco Ingoli, July 1624, in *Opere*, VI, 512.

p. 117: "If any place in the world is to be called its centre": letter from Galileo to Francesco Ingoli, July 1624, in *Opere*, VI, 539.

p. 118: "As soon as I think of a material object": Galileo, *Il Saggiatore*, in *Opere*, VI, 347–348.

p. 119: "So things calmed down": letter from Mario Guiducci, 18 April 1625, in *Opere*, XIII, 265.

p. 121: "If the Earth is at rest": letter from Galileo to Federico Cesi, 23 September 1624, in *Opere*, XIII, 209.

p. 121: "I have observed many tiny animals": letter from Galileo to Federico Cesi, 23 September 1624, in *Opere*, XIII, 208–209.

p. 122: "I am only joking": letter from Mario Guiducci to Galileo, 15 October 1624, in *Opere*, XIII, 217.

CHAPTER FIVE

p. 127: "A month ago I took up again my *Dialogue* about the tides": letter from Galileo to Elia Diodati, 29 October 1629, in *Opere*, XIV, 49.

p. 128: "Avoid inconveniencing other people": letter from Galileo to Federico Cesi, 24 December 1629, in *Opere*, XIV, 60.

p. 129: "It would have to be considered a planet": letter from Benedetto Castelli to Galileo, 9 February 1630, in *Opere*, XIV, 78.

p. 131: "Honest life and morals": from papal brief, in *Opere* XIX, 465.

p. 132: "For his own pleasure": letter from Benedetto Castelli to Galileo, 28 February 1630, in *Opere* XIV, 82.

p. 134: "In the last few days Father Campanella was speaking with His Holiness": letter from Banedetto Castelli to Galileo, 16 March 1630, in *Opere*, XIV, 87–88.

p. 135: "In this palace": letter from Francesco Niccolini to Andrea Cioli, 4 May 1630, in *Opere* XIV, 97.

p. 139: "Galileo, the famous mathematician and astronomer, is here": *Avvisi di Roma*, 18 May 1630, in *Opere*, XIV, 103.

p. 140: "No better friend than the Pope and himself": letter from Michelangelo Buonarroti to Galileo, 3 June 1630, in *Opere*, XIV, 111.

p. 141: "From this I conclude": Simplicio to Salviati: Galileo, *Dialoge*, in *Opere*, VII, 488.

p. 142: "What an admirable and angelic doctrine": Galileo, *Dialoge*, in *Opere*, VII, 489.

p. 143: "I am happy that you should find the colleague": letter from Orso d'Elci to Galileo, 3 June 1630, in *Opere*, XIV, 113.

p. 143: "The Master [Riccardi] sends his greetings": letter from Raffaello Visconti to Galileo, 16 June 1630, in *Opere*, XIV, 120.

p. 143: "The Pope had been glad to see him": letter from Francesco Niccolini to Andrea Cioli, 29 June 1639, in *Opere*, XIV, 121.

p. 147: "The Master of the Sacred Palace told me that you had agreed": letter from Benedetto Castelli to Galileo, 21 September 1630, in *Opere*, XIV, 150.

p. 148: "A few instructions": Letter from Caterina Niccolini to Galileo, 17 November 1630, in *Opere*, XIV, 167.

p. 148: Riccardi had promised him "several times to expedite the licensing": letter from Benedetto Castelli to Galileo, 30 November 1630, in *Opere*, XIV, 169.

p. 151: "That he shed tears more than once," and other passages from the letter: letter from Galileo to Andrea Cioli, 7 March 1631, in *Opere*, XIV, 215–218.

p. 152: "To find a compromise": letter from Francesco Niccolini to Andrea Cioli, 13 April 1631, in *Opere* XIV, 248.

p. 153: "These opinions are not welcome here": letter from Francesco Niccolini to Andrea Cioli, 19 April 1631, in *Opere*, XIV, 251.

p. 153: "Did not know the mind of the Holy Father": letter from Niccolò Riccardi to Francesco Niccolini, 25 April 1631, in *Opere*, XIV, 254.

p. 154: "Use his own authority": letter from Niccolò Riccardi to Clemente Egidi, 24 May 1631, in *Documenti*, 108–109, and *Opere*, XIX, 327.

p. 155: "The same argument must appear in the conclusion": letter from Niccolò Riccardi to Clemente Egidi, 19 July 1631, in *Documenti,* 113, and *Opere,* XIX, 330.

p. 155: "The Master of the Sacred Palace deserves to be pitied": letter from Francesco Niccolini to Galileo, 19 July 1631, in *Opere,* XIV, 284.

p. 156: "Although this is the main argument that I develop in the work": letter from Galileo to Elia Diodati, 16 August 1631, in *Opere,* XIV, 289.

CHAPTER SIX

p. 158: "Praise be to God, today I finished Galileo's book": letter from Giovan Battista Landini to Cesare Marsili, 21 February, 1632, in *Opere,* XIV, 331.

p. 158: Title page, in *Opere,* VII, 25

p. 159: "That they might receive honour and patronage": Galileo, *Dialoge,* "Dedication to the Grand Duke Ferdinand II," in *Opere,* VII, 28.

p. 160: "A few years ago, a salutary edict was promulgated in Rome": Galileo, *Dialoge,* "To the Discerning Reader," in *Opere,* VII, 29.

p. 160: "To this end I have taken the Copernican side": Galileo, *Dialoge,* "To the Discerning Reader," in *Opere,* VII, 29–30.

p. 161: "With infinite pleasure and amazement": letter from Benedetto Castelli to Galileo, 29 May 1632, in *Opere* XIV, 357

p. 162: "I am most anxious to learn about our Mecenas": letter from Galileo to Benedetto Castelli, 17 May 1632, in *Opere,* XIV, 352.

p. 162: "Took these worldly matters light-heartedly": letter from Benedetto Castelli to Galileo, 29 May 1632, in *Opere,* XIV, 358.

p. 164: "Galileo's book has arrived": letter from Niccolò Riccardi to Clemente Egidi, 25 July 1632, in *Opere,* XX, 571–572.

p. 165: "The absence, at the end, of two or three arguments": letter from Filippo Magalotti to Mario Guiducci, 7 August 1632, in *Opere,* XIV, 370.

p. 166: "The Jesuits will persecute him bitterly": letter from Filippo Magalotti to Mario Guiducci, 7 August 1632, in *Opere,* XIV, 370.

p. 166: "I hear from reliable sources that the Jesuit Fathers": letter from Galileo to Elia Diodati, 15 January 1633, in *Opere,* XV, 25–26.

p. 167: "If Galileo had known how to keep on good terms with the Fathers of this College": letter from Galileo to Elia Diodati, 25 July 1634, XVI, 117.

p. 167: "In order that steps may be taken to get them back": letter from Niccolò Riccardi to Clemente Egidi, 7 August 1632, in *Opere,* XX, 572.

p. 168: "Riccardi was overjoyed": letter from Filippo Magalotti to Mario Guiducci, 4 September 1632, in *Opere*, XIV, 379.

p. 169: "He was only a servant": letter from Filippo Magalotti to Mario Guiducci, 4 September 1632, in *Opere*, XIV, 381.

p. 169: "But never to the Pope": letter from Filippo Magalotti to Mario Guiducci, 4 September 1632, in *Opere*, XIV, 381.

p. 169: "Even if the majority of the Commission": letter from Filippo Magalotti to Galileo, 4 September 1632, in *Opere*, XIV, 382.

p. 171: "To this we are exhorted by the Pope": letter from Christopher Scheiner to Atanasius Kircher, 16 July 1632, in *Opere*, XV, 184.

p. 171: "When I was asked last year in Rome what I thought about his book on the motion of the Earth": letter from Orazio Grassi to Girolamo Bardi, 22 September 1633, in *Opere*, XV, 273.

p. 172: "In an outburst of rage": letter from Francesco Niccolini to Andrea Cioli, 5 September 1632, in *Opere*, XIV, 383.

p. 172: "This kind of information is never given out": letter from Francesco Niccolini to Andrea Cioli, 5 September 1632, in *Opere*, XIV, 384.

p. 172: "What causes great prejudice": same letter, an *Opere*, XIV, 383.

p. 174: "When his Holiness gets something in his head": letter from Francesco Niccolini to Andrea Cioli, 5 September 1632, in *Opere*, XIV, 385.

p. 175: "This is enough to ruin him completely": letter from Francesco Niccolini to Andrea Cioli, 11 September 1632, in *Opere*, XIV, 389.

p. 176: "That this was why he went out of his way to accommodate him": letter from Francesco Niccolini to Andrea Cioli, 18 September 1632, in *Opere*, XIV, 392.

p. 179: "On the assumption that he would not stay": letter from Andrea Cioli to Galileo, 11 January 1633, in *Opere*, XV, 21.

p. 179: "Evil-minded enemies": letter from Galileo to Carlo de Medici, 15 January 1633, in *Opere* XV, 27.

p. 181: "There is no way out": letter from Francesco Niccolini to Andrea Cioli, 13 March 1633, in *Opere*, XV, 68.

p. 182: "I begged him": letter from Francesco Niccolini to Andrea Cioli, 9 April 1633, in *Opere*, XV, 85.

p. 183: "Nor henceforth to hold, teach or defend it in any way": document of the Holy Office, admonition to Galileo and Seghizzi's injunction, 26 February 1616: in *Documenti*, 101–102, and *Opere*, XIX, 321–322.

p. 184: Galileo's first deposition, 12 April 1633, in *Documenti*, 124, and *Opere*, XIX, 337.

p. 185: "Cardinal Bellarmine informed me": same deposition, in *Documenti*, 126 and *Opere*, XIX, 339.

p. 185: "I do not recall that this precept": same deposition, in *Documenti*, 128, and *Opere* XIX, 340.

p. 186: "I did not happen to discuss": same deposition, in *Documenti*, 130, in *Opere*, XIX, 341.

p. 187: "Common people in whom errors" and "if Galileo had attached": report of Melchor Inchofer, in *Documenti* 144–145 and *Opere*, XIX, 352–353.

p. 188: "The only thing for you to do now": letter from Maria Celeste to Galileo, 20 April 1633, in *Opere*, XV, 98.

p. 188: "Not wishing to lose any time, I went to reason with him yesterday after lunch": letter from Vincenzo Maculano to Cardinal Francesco Barberini, 28 April 1633, in *Opere*, XV, 106–107.

p. 189: "I hope that his Holiness and your Eminence": letter from Vincenzo Maculano, 28 April 1633, in *Opere* XV, 106–107.

p. 190: "Seen it for so long, I found it": Galileo's second deposition, 30 April 1633: in *Documenti*, 130–132, and *Opere*, XIX, 343.

p. 191: "Most eminent and prudent judges": Galileo's third deposition and his defense, 10 May 1633, in *Documenti*, 136–137, and *Opere*, XIX, 347.

p. 191: "Half dead": letter from Francesco Niccolini to Andrea Cioli, 15 May 1633, in *Opere*, XV, 124.

p. 193: "Otherwise it would be necessary to have recourse": Galileo's fourth deposition, 21 June 1633, in *Documenti*, 155, and *Opere*, XIX, 362.

p. 193: "You have rendered yourself vehemently suspect of heresy": Galileo's sentence, in *Opere*, XIX, 405.

p. 194: "I have been judged": Galileo's abjuration, in *Opere*, XIX, 406–407.

p. 195: "They feared you were in trouble": letter from Maria Celeste to Galileo, 13 July 1633, in *Opere*, XV, 179.

p. 197: "Ideas that are not quite Catholic": anonymous undated denounciation (listed after a document dated 7 September 1633), in *Opere*, XIX, 393.

p. 198: "I have two sources of lasting comfort": letter from Galileo to Niccolò Fabri di Peiresc, 21 February 1635, in *Opere*, XVI, 215.

PHOTO CREDITS

1. View of Tuscany: Galleria delle Carte Geografiche, Bottega di Girolamo Muziano e Cesare Nebbia, 1580/83 (photo Musei Vaticani)
2. View of Florence: Galleria delle Carte Geografiche, Bottega di Girolamo Muziano e Cesare Nebbia, 1580/83 (photo Musei Vaticani)
3. View of Rome: Galleria delle Carte Geografiche, Bottega di Girolamo Muziano e Cesare Nebbia, 1580/83 (photo Musei Vaticani)
4. Christopher Clavius: Library of the Gregorian University in Rome, unknown author, 17th century (photo Carlo De Santis, with autorization of the Gregorian University)
5. Façade of the Roman College, attributed to Giuseppe Valeriano (photo Emanuele Vagni, Archivio Roma Sacra)
6. Tomb of pope Gregory XIII, by Camillo Rusconi, 1723 (photo Carlo de Santis, Archivio Roma Sacra)
7. Sixtus V going to the Lateran, Salone Sistino, Bottega di Giovanni Guerra e Cesare Nebbia, 1588 (photo Musei Vaticani)
8. Transport of the Vatican obelisk, II Sala Sistina, Bottega di Giovanni Guerra e Cesare Nebbia, 1588 (photo Musei Vaticani)
9. Square and palace of the Quirinale (photo Paolo Soriani, Archivio Roma Sacra)
10. Fountain of the Acqua Felice, Palazzo alle Terme di Villa Montalto, Bottega di Giovanni Guerra e Cesare Nebbia, 1589 (photo Soprintendenza per i Beni Artistici e Storici di Roma)
11. Coat of arms of pope Sixtus V, side façade of the Apostolic Palace of the Lateran, unknown author (photo Paolo Soriani, Archivio Roma Sacra)
12. Cosimo II de' Medici, by Adrian Haelweg, 17th century (photo Istituto Nazionale per la Grafica, courtesy of the Ministero per i Beni e le Attività Culturali)
13. Christina de Lorena, by Adrian Haelweg, 17th century (photo Gabinetto Nazionale della Grafica, courtesy of the Ministero per i Beni e le Attività Culturali)

14. Façade of the palace of Florence, by Bartolomeo Ammannati, 1516-1530 (photo Carlo de Santis, Archivio Roma Sacra)

15. Courtyard of the palace of Florence, by Bartolomeo Ammannati, 1516-1530 (photo Emanuele Vagni, Archivio Roma Sacra)

16. Federico Cesi, by Pietro Fachetti, 1610-1612 (photo Accademia Nazionale dei Lincei, Roma)

17. Façade of the palace Gaddi-Cesi (photo Emanuele Vagni, Archivio Roma Sacra)

18. Loggia Sistina in Saint John the Lateran, by Domenico Fontana, 1585 (foto Paolo Soriani, Archivio Roma Sacra)

19. Courtyard of the Roman College (from below), attributed to Giuseppe Valeriano, 1584 (photo Paolo Soriani, Archivio Roma Sacra)

20. Courtyard of the Roman College (from above), attributed to Giuseppe Valeriano, 1584 (photo Paolo Soriani, Archivio Roma Sacra)

21. Bust of Paul V, by Gian Lorenzo Bernini, Galleria Borghese (photo Paolo Soriani, Archivio Roma Sacra)

22. Paolina Chapel, Flaminio Ponzio, beginning of the 17th century (photo Paolo Soriani, Archivio Roma Sacra)

23. Tomb of Clement VIII in the Paolina Chapel, Flaminio Ponzio, 1606 (photo Paolo Soriani, Archivio Roma Sacra)

24. Tomb of Paul V in the Paolina Chapel, Flaminio Ponzio, 1606 (photo Paolo Soriani, Archivio Roma Sacra)

25. Villa Borghese, by Flaminio Ponzio and Giovanni Vasanzio, 1608-1613 (photo Paolo Soriani, Archivio Roma Sacra)

26. Façade of the Villa Medici, attributed to Bartolomeo Ammannati, end of the 16th century (photo Carlo De Santis, Archivio Roma Sacra)

27. Chapel of Saint Joachim in the church of Saint Ignatius, with a portrait and relics of Saint Robert Bellarmine, Roman school of the 17th century (photo Emanuele Vagni, Archivio Roma Sacra, courtesy of the Fondo Edifici di Culto)

28. Palace of Propaganda Fide, façade by Gian Lorenzo Bernini, 1644 (photo Emanuele Vagni, Archivio Roma Sacra)

29. Urban VIII, by Gian Lorenzo Bernini, towards 1632, Galleria Nazionale d'Arte Antica, Roma (photo Soprintendenza per i Beni Artistici e Storici di Roma)

30. Francesco Barberini, by Guillaume Vallet, 1679 (photo Istituto Nazionale per la Grafica, courtesy of the Ministero per i Beni e le Attività Culturali)

31. Palace Barberini, façade by Gian Lorenzo Bernini, 1623 (photo Paolo Soriani, Archivio Roma Sacra)

32. Fountain of the Tritone, by Gian Lorenzo Bernini, 1642-1643 (photo Paolo Soriani, Archivio Roma Sacra)

33. Pantheon, façade of the centuries 1st B.C. – 2nd A.C. (photo Paolo Soriani, Archivio Roma Sacra)

34. Façade of the church of Saint Ignatius, Orazio Grassi, middle of the 17th century (photo Emanuele Vagni, Archivio Roma Sacra, courtesy Fondo Edifici di Culto)

35. Tommaso Campanella, by Piotti-Pirola, 17th century (photo Istituto Nazionale per la Grafica, courtesy of the Ministero per i Beni e le Attività Culturali)

36. Façade of the church of Saint John of the Florentines, by Alessandro Galilei, 1734 (photo Paolo Soriani, Archivio Roma Sacra)

37. Ferdinand II, by Abraham Bloemaert, 17th century (photo Istituto Nazionale per la Grafica, courtesy of the Ministero per i Beni e le Attività Culturali)

38. Façade of the church of Santa Maria sopra Minerva, unknown author, middle of the 15th century (photo Paolo Soriani, Archivio Roma Sacra)

39. Room of Galileo, now in the Library of the Congress of Italy (photo Carlo De Santis, Archivio Roma Sacra)

40. The battle of Muret, attributed to Francesco Allegrini, in the ceiling of the Room of Galileo, second half of the 17th century (photo Carlo De Santis, Archivio Roma Sacra)

41. Inner façade and garden of the Villa Medici, attributed to Bartolomeo Ammannati, end of the 16th century (photo Vasari)

SELECTED BIBLIOGRAPHY

Biagioli, Mario. *Galileo Courtier: The Practice of Science in the Culture of Absolutism* (Chicago: University of Chicago Press, 1993).

Blackwell, Richard J. *Galileo, Bellarmine, and the Bible* (Notre Dame, IN: University of Notre Dame Press, 1991).

Drake, Stillman. *Galileo. A Very Short Introduction* (Oxford: Oxford University Press, 2001).

Fantoli, Annibale. *Galileo for Copernicanism and for the Church,* 2d. ed. (Notre Dame, IN: The University of Notre Dame Press, 1996).

Finocchiaro, Maurice A., ed. *The Galileo Affair. A Documentary History* (Berkeley: University of California Press, 1989).

Langford, Jerome J. *Galileo, Science and the Church* (South Bend: St. Augustine's Press, 1998).

Lindberg, David C. and Ronald S. Numbers, eds., *God and Nature* (Berkeley: University of California Press, 1986).

Machamer, Peter, ed. *The Cambridge Companion to Galileo* (Cambridge: Cambridge University Press, 1998).

McMullin, Ernan, ed. *Galileo: Man of Science* (New York: Basic Books, 1967).

Redondi, Pietro. *Galileo Heretic* (Princeton: Princeton University Press, 1989).

Renn, Juergen, ed. *Galileo in Context* (Cambridge: Cambridge University Press, 2002).

Reston, James. *Galileo: A Life* (London: Cassell, 1994).

Sharratt, Michael. *Galileo, Decisive Innovator* (Cambridge: Cambridge University Press, 1999).

Shea, William R. *Galileo's Intellectual Revolution* (New York: Science History Publications, 1977).

Sobel, Dava. *Galileo's Daughter. A Historical Memoir of Science, Faith, and Love* (New York: Walker, 1999).

Westfall, Richard S. *Essays on the Trial of Galileo* (Notre Dame, IN: Vatican Observatory Publications, 1989).

INDEX

H